1991

HITCHCOCK'S RERELEASED FILMS

Contemporary Film and Television Series

A complete listing of the books in this series can be found at the back of this volume.

General Editor

Patricia Erens
Rosary College

Advisory Editors

Peter Lehman
University of Arizona

Lucy Fischer
University of Pittsburgh

Gorham Kindem
University of North Carolina
at Chapel Hill

John Fell
San Francisco State
University

HITCHCOCK'S RERELEASED FILMS

From *Rope* to *Vertigo*

Edited by Walter Raubicheck and Walter Srebnick
With a Foreword by Andrew Sarris

 Wayne State University Press   Detroit

We gratefully acknowledge
Richard Gill
and
Walter A. Raubicheck

95 94 93 92 91   5 4 3 2 1

Library of Congress Cataloging-in-Publication Data

Hitchcock's rereleased films : from Rope to Vertigo / edited by Walter
    Raubicheck and Walter Srebnick ; with a foreword by Andrew Sarris.
            p.   cm. — (Contemporary film and television series)
        Includes bibliographical references and index.
        ISBN 0-8143-2325-1 (alk. paper). — ISBN 0-8143-2326-X
    (pbk. : alk. paper)
        1. Hitchcock, Alfred, 1899- —Criticism and interpretation.
    I. Raubicheck, Walter, 1950- . II. Srebnick, Walter.
    III. Series.
    PN1998.3.H58H58 1991
    791.43′028′092 — dc20   90-49240
                                                                      CIP

The book was designed by Mary Primeau.

James Stewart in *Vertigo*. (Cover photo courtesy of Photofest, New York.)

CONTENTS

5

CONTENTS

CONTRIBUTORS

Thomas M. Bauso teaches English and film at Saint Mary's College in Raleigh, North Carolina, where he also chairs the Division of Language and Literature. He has published articles on De Sica, Truffaut, Tourneur, and Hitchcock as well as reviews of contemporary movies.

John Belton teaches film studies in the English Department of Rutgers University, New Brunswick, and has written several books on film. He is currently writing a history of American widescreen cinema.

Lesley Brill teaches film and Renaissance English literature at Wayne State University in Detroit, where he also chairs the English Department. He is the author of *The Hitchcock Romance* (Princeton, 1988) and of articles on film, photography, and literature.

Ann Cvetkovich teaches in the English Department of the University of Texas at Austin. She has published articles on film in *Afterimage* and on Victorian fiction in *Novel* and is currently working on a book on the Victorian novel.

Robert G. Goulet teaches English and film at Stonehill College in Massachusetts. He has published articles on the films of Capra, Sirk, and Leisen.

Ina Rae Hark teaches in the English Department of the University of South Carolina. Her previous publications on film have appeared in journals such as *The Journal of Popular Film, Literature/Film Quarterly,* and *Cinema Journal.*

7

Thomas Hemmeter teaches in the English Department of Mary Washington College in Virginia. He has published articles on Hitchcock in *Mise-en-Scène*, Scorsese in *Literature/Film Quarterly,* and on film adaptations of Hemingway in *A Moving Picture Feast.*

Thomas M. Leitch teaches English and directs the film study program at the University of Delaware in Newark. He is the author of the forthcoming study *The Hitchcock Game* (University of Georgia Press).

Anthony J. Mazzella teaches and chairs the English Department at William Patterson College in New Jersey. He has published articles on Henry James and on adaptations of literature to film and the other arts.

Andrew Sarris, a film critic for *The Village Voice* for many years, now writes for *The New York Observer.* He teaches film at Columbia University and is the author of *The American Cinema: Directors and Directions, 1929–1968* and other books on film.

William G. Simon teaches film at New York University, where he is Chair of the Department of Cinema Studies. He is guest editor of the special issue on Welles in *Persistence of Vision* (no. 7), and he recently coordinated a conference on Welles at New York University.

Robert Stam teaches film at New York University. He is the author of four books on film, including *Subversive Pleasures: Bakhtin, Cultural Criticism and Film* (Johns Hopkins University Press, 1989).

Samuel Taylor is the author of the screenplay of *Vertigo* and many other screenplays, including Hitchcock's *Topaz* (1969). He is also the author of numerous plays, including *Sabrina Fair* and *Avanti!*, both of which were adapted for the screen.

Doug Tomlinson teaches film at Montclair State College in New Jersey. He is the author of numerous articles on film and the forthcoming book *Actors on Acting for the Screen: Roles and Collaborations* (Garland Press).

Katie Trumpener teaches in the German Department of the University of Chicago. She has published articles on German film and cultural life in *Iris, Public Culture,* and *Telos.*

Ann West teaches in the English Department of San Francisco City College. She has written on Welles in *Enclitic* and elsewhere on Ford and Hitchcock.

Robin Wood teaches film at York University in Toronto. In addition to *Hollywood from Vietnam to Reagan,* he is the author of numerous books on major film directors, including the recently published, enlarged *Hitchcock's Films Revisited* (Columbia, 1989).

FOREWORD

If Alfred Hitchcock (1899–1980) were alive today, he might respond to the torrents of scholarly speculation about his works with the remark that he once addressed to one of his beautiful female stars when she began sobbing on the set: "It's only a movie, Ingrid." Even such a shrewd and perceptive admirer as François Truffaut was unable to peer behind Master Alfred's phlegmatic and pragmatic mask. Nor has Hitchcock bequeathed to posterity any enlightening correspondence or any but the most perfunctory interviews. Hence, the movies are the message, and to the extent that one can presume that they have flowed out of the director's unconscious, they can sustain interpretations far more intricate than the director's ostensibly modest intentions.

Back in the sixties I had violent arguments with skeptics who scoffed at my likening of Hitchcock to Kafka and Dostoevsky. My point was then and is now that Hitchcock plus cinema equals Kafka and Dostoevsky, just as Buster Keaton plus cinema equals Samuel Beckett. According to these admittedly arguable equations, Hitchcock and Keaton, more than any other great filmmakers, required the magic of the motion picture medium for their magic to flower. If the cinema had never been invented, Hitchcock would have probably been a minor graphic artist, and Keaton a knockabout vaudevillian. Fortunately, the cinema *was* invented, and Hitchcock and Keaton were among its most innovative sorcerers.

My own secondary role in alerting American readers to the transcendent glories of Hitchcock has been further demeaned by recent

11

film theorists as a primitive contribution to the critical canon. It seems that as I am too much of an academic for the journalists, I am too much of a journalist for the academics. Furthermore, I have not dared venture into the brave new world of the structuralists, the semioticians, and the deconstructionists. I don't even know how to pronounce "diegesis," and I have never understood why one must approach Freud only through Lacan. And if this be deemed egregious "eclecticism," so be it.

No matter. Hitchcock's works fashioned over more than half a century remain both intellectually stimulating and aesthetically gratifying. They can withstand any snobbish assault, and nourish any theoretical system. No critic, no scholar, no doctrine or dogma can provide the last word on Hitchcock.

When I wrote up the citation for his honorary degree at Columbia University, I invoked the cinematically sacred names of D. W. Griffith, F. W. Murnau, and Sergei Eisenstein as prior influences. One can "teach" Hitchcock in purely paradigmatic terms as a seamless fusion of the Germanic style with its shifting frame, its moving camera, and its light-and-darkness dialectic, and the Russian style with its dynamic montage which, as film historian Eric Rhode has noted, means that two plus two equals five.

It is (or at least should be) impossible, however, to detach Hitchcock himself from his oeuvre. Anyone can imitate his technique, but no one can reproduce his sensibility, that volatile mixture of cruelty and compassion, humor and horror, impudence and shame. And it is precisely because he had thoroughly mastered his craft that he was able to unleash all the psychic furies of his art.

Among Hitchcock's detractors, Dwight Macdonald provided perhaps the wittiest riposte to all the encomiums heaped on Hitch: "Homer nods, but Hitchcock never." Ah, but yes, Hitchcock nodded on many occasions. He never quite overcame the hamminess of Ivor Novello in *The Lodger* (1926), the stagebound stasis of *Juno and the Paycock* (1930) and *The Skin Game* (1931), the utter humorlessness of *Sabotage* (1937) and *I Confess* (1953), the failed gothic of *Jamaica Inn* (1939), the misplaced facetiousness of *Saboteur* (1942), the blandness of MacDonald Carey as the "straight" suitor in *Shadow of a Doubt* (1943), the misdirected intensity of *Mr. and Mrs. Smith* (1941), the facile Freudianism of *Spellbound* (1945), the misplaced confidence in Tippi Hedren in *The Birds* (1963) and *Marnie* (1964), and so on.

Hitchcock had legendary squabbles with intuitive actors such as Charles Laughton and Montgomery Clift, and overall he was not the most beloved of directors by the casts on two continents. His mise-en-scène was deemed too precise for the largely mythical glories of improvisation. William Everson once complained that Hitchcock directed audiences rather than actors. Yet some of the most brilliant performances in the history of the medium occur in his films simply because their contexts have been so imaginatively constructed.

Romance and redemption figure strongly in Hitchcock's oeuvre, and he was criticized at the time and has been since for observing the conformist conventions of the genre whereby moral equilibrium is restored to a discernibly amoral universe. He has even been accused of cynicism toward his audiences by imposing his supposedly "happy" endings. A closer look, however, will reveal a subtle unease in Hitchcock's world. Indeed, Master Alfred would have undoubtedly bestowed his blessing on all the scholarship devoted to his career, if only to encourage many closer looks at the still undiscovered clues to his innermost feelings.

Andrew Sarris

ACKNOWLEDGMENTS

Many people were crucial in the creation of this anthology. We would like to express our thanks and appreciation to them. Amy Gilman, Mark Hussey, Ruth Johnston, and the late Richard Gill gave us superb editorial advice. Donald Spoto provided us with useful information. Jackie Myers, Terry Renz, and Joost Zimmerman were essential in the preparation of the manuscript.

The conception of this book began at a three-day conference on the rereleased Hitchcock films at Pace University in June 1986. This conference would not have been possible without the support of Sherman Raskin, Chairman of the English Department in Pace, New York, and Dean Joseph Houle of Pace's Dyson College. Our colleagues in the English Department were instrumental in making this conference a success.

John Belton's essay was first published in *Modern Language Notes* 103, no. 5, and is reprinted by permission of the Johns Hopkins University Press. Lesley Brill's essay appeared first as chapter seven in his *The Hitchcock Romance: Love and Irony in Hitchcock's Films*, copyright © 1988 by Princeton University Press, and is adapted with permission of Princeton University Press. An earlier version of Robert Stam's essay appeared as "Hitchcock and Buñuel: Desire and the Law" in *Studies in the Literary Imagination*, no. 16. Robin Wood's essay first appeared as chapter seventeen in his *Hitchcock's Films Revisisted*, copyright © by Columbia University Press, 1989, and it is used by permission of Columbia University Press.

INTRODUCTION

Hitchcock's Rereleased Films and Cinema Studies

Walter Raubicheck and Walter Srebnick

The extent of the academic and popular response to the five films of Alfred Hitchcock rereleased in 1983–84 — *Rope, Rear Window, The Trouble with Harry, The Man Who Knew Too Much* (1956), and *Vertigo* — raises the question of why Hitchcock's films are such crucial texts for serious film criticism and contemporary film theory. The films of Howard Hawks and John Ford, for example, although sometimes accorded greater significance than those of Hitchcock, are rarely accorded the same amount of attention and study, particularly in the more theoretical discussions of the last decade. Hitchcock, in other words, is of equal concern to movie reviewers, who chide recent directors of thrillers for falling short of the "Master's" masterpieces, and to film theorists — for different reasons, of course. And in the academy, as postmodernism replaces modernism and deconstruction supplants the New Criticism, the cinematic richness of *Vertigo* and *Rear Window* is demonstrated by their continued presence on course syllabi even as the titles of the courses change.

These five films are significant individually within Hitchcock's entire body of work and, in the case of *Rear Window* and *Vertigo*, within cinema history in general. The first of them, *Rope* (1948), is an anomaly within Hitchcock's works and within classical Hollywood cinema. Shot in continuous camera takes of five to twelve minutes and limited to a total of only ten editing cuts, *Rope* departs from the tightly edited montage sequences considered Hitchcock's hallmark. If *Rope* is for Hitchcock an experiment in form, *The Trouble with Harry* (1955) is a radical departure in content since it is his only pure comedy and relies more on ironic reversals in character and situation than on suspense. Hitchcock's next film, *The Man Who Knew Too Much* (1956), is his only remake of an earlier film, one from 1934, and gives us an opportunity to compare changes within his work in technique and narrative structure as well as in ideology. Finally, *Rear Window* (1954) and *Vertigo* (1958) are arguably the masterpieces of Hitchcock's American period. Even before their rerelease they had inspired an enormous critical literature both in Europe and the United States while they were still unavailable for "legal" viewing. For exponents of classical film theory they are works of "pure cinema"—films which reveal the full extent of the medium's narrativizing capability; for contemporary theorists they are central texts in understanding the power of the "look" in classical Hollywood cinema, as well as self-reflexive treatises on the nature of film production and the audience's experience of film itself.

The ten-year period in Hitchcock's work bounded by *Rope* and *Vertigo* contains only one other film of equivalent artistic stature to the rereleased films: *Strangers on a Train* (1951). This period links the first decade of Hitchcock's American filmmaking—beginning with *Rebecca* in 1939, when he was working under the aegis of producer David Selznick—to his last artistic period, which began with *North by Northwest* in 1959 and *Psycho* the following year and ended with his last film, *Family Plot*, in 1976. Using lighting, color, editing, and sound in stylized and realistic ways, Hitchcock's work of this period bears the impact of his collaboration with figures such as cinematographer Robert Burks, film editor George Tomasini, composer Bernard Herrmann, and screenwriters John Michael Hayes and Samuel Taylor. The style Hitchcock developed during the ten-year period of the rereleased films—with its expressionistic use of color and music, its preponderance of subjective point-of-view shots, its alternation of long takes with montage sequences—reinforced his growing concern with the irrational forces beneath the seemingly placid surface of contemporary American life.

Alfred Hitchcock behind the camera. (Photo courtesy of Photofest, New York.)

The five films that are the focus of this volume are among the most important in his long career, and the long period of their inaccessibility was therefore a major loss to theorists of film as well as to the movie-going public. Interestingly, the reason for their removal from the marketplace had nothing to do with artistic merit and everything to do with business. *Rope* was the first of two films Hitchcock made for his own production company, the short-lived Transatlantic Pictures, and he retained his rights to the film. In 1953, Hitchcock signed an agreement with Paramount Pictures which gave him the rights to five future films and ultimately gave Paramount the rights to only one (*To Catch a Thief*). Hitchcock went on to make *Rear Window, The Trouble with Harry, The Man Who Knew Too Much, Vertigo*, and *Psycho* for Paramount between 1953 and 1960, and under the agreement Hitchcock retained the rights to these films. In 1962 he sold the rights to *Psycho* to MCA/Universal for a significant amount of corporate stock. By 1973 the films that were eventually rereleased — all of which were still owned by Hitchcock —

were removed from circulation as the director's lawyers began to negotiate new financial arrangements for their showing in theaters and on television. The process took almost ten years, during which time Hitchcock died and interest in his complete works intensified. Therefore, the rerelease of the five films, beginning in the fall of 1983 with *Rear Window*, was a significant event in film studies and in recent film history.

The essays on the rereleased films in this volume must be seen against the backdrop of fifty years of critical response to Hitchcock's work. Beginning in the 1930s when he was still working in Britain, Hitchcock began to attract attention for both the texture and the substance of his thrillers, particularly their tight and witty editing, brisk narrative pacing, and precise sense of social class. However, many of the same critics who earlier had praised his British films regarded Hitchcock's relocation to the United States and Hollywood in 1939 as the beginning of the decline of his artistry, a falling off from the heights of *The Thirty-Nine Steps* and the disappearance of the humor of *The Lady Vanishes*. They claimed that, beginning with his first American film, *Rebecca* (1939), Hitchcock had sacrificed the substance and wholeness of his art for a glossy, commercialized Hollywood style that was slick and sentimental and which substituted overwrought plots for the inventive rhythms of the earlier films.

Recognition for Hitchcock's American films was largely fostered by a group of French critics of the 1950s centered around the journal *Cahiers du Cinema*. Unlike the British and American critics who were disappointed in Hitchcock's American work, these French critics regarded his American films as metaphysical and psychological masterpieces, and his highly touted English period largely as an apprenticeship for them. In 1957 two of the leading figures of this group, Eric Rohmer and Claude Chabrol, wrote the first full-length study of Hitchcock. Taking an ethical and theological approach to Hitchcock's American films, they defined him as a Catholic artist whose great theme is the exchange of guilt between the guilty and innocent figures in his films. They argued that Hitchcock's "innocent" protagonists' proximity to the criminal and the crime forces them to confront their own responsibility and culpability in a fallen world. In some cases this means that wrongly accused characters, even as they attempt to demonstrate that they are victims of mistaken identity, must go through the process of the exchange of guilt.

Rohmer and Chabrol seemed to have a special preference for the four (now rereleased) films produced before 1957, the year their book was published. They regarded *Rope* as the film which inaugurated Hitchcock's artistic independence in America, since it marked the end of his association with David Selznick and his debut as his own producer; more importantly, they saw it as the film which signaled the beginning of a period of artistic maturity and greatness. Even though many critics condemned *Rope* as a failed formal experiment, Rohmer and Chabrol regarded it as a morally complex film which expanded the boundaries of cinematic form and the architectural possibilities of direction. *Rear Window*, which had disappointed many critics who regarded it as a slight, commercial venture limited by a static urban setting, was for them a masterpiece of the transfer theme, showing the pervasiveness of original sin and our mutual complicity in evil even when we passively observe it. Nor did they go along with the prevailing contemporary consensus that *The Trouble with Harry* was a minor, comic digression; rather, they considered it an ironic exploration of Hitchcock's theological themes. They also regarded *The Man Who Knew Too Much* as a variation on *Rear Window*'s theme of universal moral culpability, this time with characters who are forced to take responsibility for their own lives and the fate of people across the world, not just across the courtyard.

Although the theological bent of Rohmer and Chabrol was greeted with some skepticism, the seriousness and precision of their reading of Hitchcock's American films began to change the course of Hitchcock criticism; in addition, the other critics in the *Cahiers* group also helped to advance the cause of the American films, and the rereleased films in particular. Jean Douchet, for example, found in *Rear Window* a subtext about the cinema itself, an idea which helped the development of the postmodernist notion of self-reflexivity. Andre Bazin, the founder and leader of this group, who had the most reservations about Hitchcock's intellectual substance, did a landmark interview with him which helped to solidify Hitchcock's status as an *auteur*: a director who, as the controlling creative consciousness of his films, "authored" them by guiding their conception and production and by giving them the stamp of his stylistic and thematic uniqueness. Indeed, few directors fit the notion of auteurism as effectively as Hitchcock. Beginning with *Rope*, the creative control he exercised over his films and the continuity of his artistic and technical collaborations show a consistency that is extremely rare in Hollywood.

During the 1960s, when auteur theory was at its height, Hitchcock enjoyed a wide expansion of his critical reputation. Part of the reason for his new status in America must be ascribed to the efforts of critic and journalist Andrew Sarris. Additionally, in 1965 Robin Wood published in England *Hitchcock's Films*, which acknowledged some of the basic ideas of the French critics, but secularized and broadened their approach. Using the moral perspective of the British critic F. R. Leavis, Wood developed an influential thesis about the "thematic cohesion" of Hitchcock's films of the 1950s which emphasized their concern with the moral and emotional values underlying human relationships. He placed special emphasis on *Rear Window* and *Vertigo* in his study, calling the latter one of the four or five greatest films ever made. In the following year, 1966, Truffaut published his book-length Hitchcock interview which illuminated many of the technical issues underlying the films and reaffirmed the *Cahiers* position about the artistic and thematic superiority of the American period.

Using the work of *Cahiers* critics, as well as Wood and Truffaut, as a point of departure, critics throughout the United States and Europe entered into what had become a Hitchcock dialogue by the late 1960s and early 1970s. Much of the criticism of Hitchcock that appeared in the United States during this period had close affinities to the thematic, structural, and stylistic concerns of then-current literary criticism, from the New Criticism and its preoccupation with the close examination of the text and the theme of self-actualization, to the growing interest in structuralism and its focus on the underlying patterns of narrative. Some critics moved beyond the issues of guilt and responsibility and began to examine the director's presentation of sexuality, including the obsessive voyeurism of his American films, and his manipulation of his audience. Others even expressed serious caveats about the new status Hitchcock had been accorded.

Raymond Durgnat in *The Strange Case of Alfred Hitchcock* (1974) decided that Hitchcock was essentially an entertaining master of a genre who occasionally, as in *Vertigo*, rose to great films with serious content. Durgnat brought an interesting element into the critical discussion of Hitchcock by treating the cultural milieu that pro-

duced the films, a perspective that has become increasingly important for more recent criticism. Still others insisted upon the "thematic"
complexity in the films that earlier critics had found. Donald Spoto,
for example, in *The Art of Alfred Hitchcock* (1976) argued that the
director's thrillers were really about personal growth, individual responsibility, self-realization, and the need for love.

More recently, William Rothman's *Hitchcock: The Murderous
Gaze* (1982), which begins with *The Lodger* (1926) and ends with
Psycho (1960), uses frame-by-frame analysis to explore the viewer's
link to Hitchcock, the enigmatic author whose control of the camera
implicates us morally and psychically in the actions of the murderers
in each film. Although Rothman's study of five black-and-white Hitchcock films does not discuss any of the rereleased films, his thesis
about viewer participation could easily apply to them as well. Published in the same year as Rothman's study, Elisabeth Weis's *The
Silent Scream: Alfred Hitchcock's Sound Track* is an excellent, book-
length technical study of the director's use of sound to explore the
mental state of characters and to enrich the thematic concerns in his
films. Weis shows how Hitchcock employs the three concurrent elements of the sound track — dialogue, sound effects, music — alternately
to support or counter his visual style. In *Rear Window*, for example,
Weis shows how Hitchcock deliberately effects a dramatic separation of what we see and hear, thus lending another level of meaning
to the narrative.

Although auteurism and thematic textual readings of films no longer
dominate film studies, their impact is still strongly felt and can be
seen in this volume in the essays of Leitch, Mazzella, and Brill. Film
theory of the last decade and a half has moved away from auteurism
toward psychoanalytical readings of film texts. Critical studies of
Hitchcock have been central in this evolution. The rereleased films
have been the special focus of theorists who analyze the forces within
the human psyche, which Hitchcock presents through complex
strategies of narration and visualization. Freud's notion that the
erotic drive is in constant conflict with censoring agents within and
without the mind is central to these recent critical projects. Hitchcock's own interest in psychoanalysis, explicit in *Spellbound* (1945)
and *Marnie* (1964), is also evident in the persistent psychological conflicts that mark the rereleased films. Literary criticism and theory
that is derived from Freudian premises has, therefore, found much

23

to discuss in his films. In particular, the conflict between law and desire, central to Freud's theory of repression, is regarded by psychoanalytic theory as the site of psychic terror in Hitchcock's work.

Freud's theories, then, in conjunction with recent feminist ideas, provide for many theorists the psychological key to Hitchcock. It is interesting that postmodernist film study has coincided with the growth of revisionist readings of Freud himself, notably those of Jacques Lacan, a French psychoanalyst whose interest in semiotics and structural linguistics led him to describe the Freudian stages of psychosexual development in terms of the appropriation and use of language. In Lacan's system the pre-Oedipal phases in Freudian theory correspond to the "realm of the imaginary." This period in the infant's life culminates in what Lacan calls the "mirror stage": the construction of identity through images, a perception which ultimately proves unrealistic and illusory. Early in the imaginary stage, according to Lacan, the child does not have a sense of physical wholeness, but when it sees a reflection of itself in a mirror it begins to identify itself as this reflected body, which has a perfect unity. However, since gaining a unity is achieved through the act of looking, this first step toward self-awareness is marked by both narcissism and the mistaken identification of what is looked at with one's self. The resolution of the Oedipal dilemma itself is defined as entrance into the symbolic realm, the social matrix shaped by the "signifiers" of language: or, as defined in relation to codes of power, the Law of the Father. In this volume these ideas are central to Robert G. Goulet's study of Hitchcock's *Rope*.

Lacan's semiotic psychoanalysis has had great appeal for recent film theorists because of the essential technology of cinema. Most importantly, the screen itself can be regarded as a "mirror" and the process of watching the cinematic image upon it therefore returns us to Lacan's imaginary realm. Christian Metz, a contemporary French film theorist, has done the most influential thinking along these lines. Metz notes that unlike the child during the actual mirror stage, the spectator does not actually see an image of himself or herself on the screen; living in the symbolic order has trained the spectator to realize that he or she exists as a discrete subject—the mirror is no longer needed to achieve this self-recognition. Yet he argues that the spectator watching a film identifies with the power of the camera to "look," or in practice to frame and ultimately project images upon the screen, and in doing so the viewer regresses to the mirror stage, of total pleasure at "seeing" oneself in control of both self and environment. Thus, although film "discourse" participates in the symbolic through dialogue and narrative structure, the signifiers of the visual language of film are imaginary in that they encourage regression to a pre-Oedipal stage of wish fulfillment.

Metz's application of Lacan to film texts has a significant relation to other psychoanalytic approaches to cinema, particularly those of Raymond Bellour, a theorist who has used his study of Freud and Lacan to construct several extraordinarily intricate, shot-by-shot analyses of major sequences in several Hitchcock films. He concludes that an Oedipal "trajectory" marks the narrative patterns of these films: Hitchcock becomes an "enunciator," a manipulator of image and speech in the film, delineating male desire in relation to women, who function in the text only as indices of the progress of the male character's journey toward psychosexual fulfillment.

Bellour's essays, then, clearly have an ideological resonance for feminist theorists who are increasingly concerned with the importance of psychoanalysis in exposing the male power dominance in society and culture. Indeed, many of Bellour's most important essays were published in *Camera Obscura: A Journal of Feminism and Film Theory.* Similarly, Laura Mulvey, whose influential 1975 essay "Visual Pleasure and Narrative Cinema" has been a focal point for much controversy concerning woman in narrative film and woman as a spectator of narrative film, draws on Freud and Lacan for their theoretical premises. Mulvey focuses on the masculine "look" or "gaze" which both defines what a woman is in the film and reveals that the hidden — or "displaced" — purpose of the film is to satisfy male erotic desire. Watching a movie is thus a voyeuristic experience for a male spectator, and films like *Vertigo* and particularly *Rear Window,* which contain an overwhelming number of male point-of-view shots, have lately been seen and read as classic cases of male sexual obsessions. The female spectator, then, can experience only a masochistic pleasure as she identifies with the woman on the screen.

More recent feminist theorists, however, have argued that the female spectator is not merely passive, but has her own equivalent of the male subject's desire. Tania Modleski's *The Woman Who Knew Too Much* (1988) is the most recent book-length study of the director from a feminist perspective. Using the Freudian premise of the essen-

25

tial bisexuality of both male and female, Modleski supports the more recent feminist notion that the female spectator is not limited to masochism, but instead experiences visual pleasure in watching the women on the screen that is uniquely female and her own. Modleski's own position is that the female's bisexuality threatens patriarchy by reminding men of their own bisexual nature and the feminine aspects of themselves, both of which challenge their authority and dominance. She believes the violence toward women in Hitchcock's films results from male hostility toward this threat. In this collection the notion of spectatorship and the feminist analysis of gender and power inform the readings of Hitchcock's rereleased films by Ann Cvetkovich, Ina Rae Hark, Robert Stam, and Robin Wood.

Just as feminist criticism has been strongly influenced by the theories of Jacques Lacan, another postmodern theory that has left its mark on all the humanities is that associated with the philosopher Jacques Derrida: deconstruction. Derrida insists that truth and reason, the highest values of traditional humanism, are infected by relativity to the utmost degree; that in fact all hierarchical distinctions or logical sets of opposition within human discourse are untenable. The critic under Derrida's influence identifies the points in the text at which the apparent logical consistency of the discourse breaks down, thereby demonstrating that all opposing attempts to determine a precise, intended meaning within the text in question are useless and, ultimately, fraudulent. For example, Thomas Hemmeter's discussion of *Rope* in this volume deconstructs the film's ostensible moral basis. Thus, when film theorists use Derrida's ideas, they may do so to reveal the inconsistencies that undercut classical cinema's espousal of bourgeois values or humanist ethics. Additionally, they argue that a film, like all discourse, has no fixed relation to the world outside itself. Katie Trumpener's analysis here of *Vertigo* demonstrates how all facets of the film replicate each other to create an enclosed self-reflexive system.

Interestingly, the most recent critical books on Hitchcock — those by two of our contributors, Lesley Brill and Robin Wood — depart both from postmodernist theory, such as deconstruction, and from the feminist criticism that regards Hitchcock's films as explicitly patriarchal texts. Brill's *The Hitchcock Romance: Love and Irony in Hitchcock's Films* returns to an auteurist, "thematic" approach to Hitchcock and uses the mythic conceptual framework of Northrop

Frye. Far from viewing the director as manipulative and obsessive, Brill regards Hitchcock as essentially life affirming and comic in his allegiance to the narrative pattern of romance. Unlike Brill, Robin Wood in his new study does directly draw upon recent film theory. Complementing the auteurist and moral perspective of the original book, *Hitchcock's Films Revisited* incorporates Marxist, feminist, and psychoanalytic readings. However, in contrast to critics who now treat Hitchcock as an enunciator of patriarchal ideology, Wood sees the films as exposing the psychic and political damage caused by male-dominated social structures and institutions.

The unifying factor in this broad range of approaches and the key to the centrality of Hitchcock's work to current discourse on film is form, in particular, the unique formal qualities of cinema. Hitchcock's typical statements to the effect that he is more interested in how to tell a story than in the story itself are, of course, exaggerations, but exaggerations of a basic truth: Hitchcock is the filmmaker, sui generis. Even those who criticize his reliance on the suspense fiction genre for his sources admit that despite this narrow range of character and situation Hitchcock exploits the medium more rigorously and ingeniously than almost all, if not all, other filmmakers.

Truffaut's tribute to Hitchcock is the essence of the auteurist approach, focusing totally on cinematic form with little concern for theme or moral vision:

> Hitchcock is universally acknowledged to be the world's foremost technician; even his detractors willingly concede him this title. Yet, isn't it obvious that the choice of a scenario, its construction, and all of its contents are ultimately connected to and, in fact, dependent upon that technique? . . . Whatever is *said* instead of being *shown* is lost on the viewer . . . because of his ability to film the thoughts of his characters and make them perceptible without resorting to dialogue, he is, to my way of thinking, a realistic director.[1]

An obvious example of what Truffaut means is the long Albert Hall sequence in the remake of *The Man Who Knew Too Much*, in which Jo McKenna's gradual realization of the impending assassination and her increasing desperation are presented solely through a montage of point-of-view shots that are accompanied by the rising crescendo of the orchestra's music. And in *Vertigo*, when Scottie follows Madeleine up and down the streets of San Francisco and in and out of museums, parks, and shops, Hitchcock's point-of-view editing and tight close-ups delineate without any use of dialogue a psyche falling into an obsession.

The celebration of Hitchcock's formal approach to filmmaking, which began with the auteurist critics in the 1960s and still continues today, makes the continuing preoccupation with his films more comprehensible. Recent advanced film theory is more concerned with film as a mode of discourse than it is with the achievements or the canon of any particular director, and since, arguably, cinema can be analyzed in its purest form in Hitchcock's films, theory finds them the most useful texts for its "speculations." Lacanians in the critical tradition of Raymond Bellour, concerned with the implications of "the look" in classical cinema for psychosexual perspectives on movies and culture, find "the look" most obviously in a Hitchcock film that privileges the visual over the verbal in conveying the nuances of relationships. *Rear Window*, for example, is composed largely of a collage of "looks," as Jefferies gazes at several women across the courtyard and at the erotic displays presented within his apartment by Lisa. Deconstruction, meanwhile, intent on identifying the disruptive signifiers within a film's coded polarities, is supplied by an abundance of Hitchcockian images with which to expose the chinks in the chain of binary structures. And narratologists find no director whose stories are told more exclusively in visual terms and therefore whose films are so clearly models for an intensive analysis of the importance of point of view and editing in narrative cinema. Thus, whatever value judgments are made from whatever theoretical or ideological perspective — whether Hitchcock is condemned or celebrated, condescended to or admired — the films themselves are essential texts for the study of cinema. In this volume the essays of Thomas M. Bauso, John Belton, William G. Simon, and Doug Tomlinson are all concerned with the formal relation of the technology of the cinema to the way we understand narrative film.

In addition to form, another common concern in Hitchcock criticism is the process of social and cultural reflection in his films. Commentators as diverse as the French *Cahiers du Cinema* writers and the more recent exponents of contemporary film theory have found Hitchcock's films to reflect the tensions of their time periods. Hitchcock's rereleased films acknowledge social and cultural issues of the 1950s without becoming "problem" films, such as *On the*

Waterfront (1954) or *Twelve Angry Men* (1957). Unlike a director such as John Ford, whose fifties films such as *The Quiet Man* (1953) and *The Searchers* (1957) largely retreated from reality into a quasi-mythical world of existential heroes, Hitchcock did speak to the concerns of this period in his settings, characters, and narratives.

The period from 1948 to 1958 was a transitional one for American society and Hitchcock incorporated some of the fears and changes of these years within his films. In *Rope* the narrative of David's murder by Brandon and Philip appropriates some of the national issues of World War II and its aftermath. The conflict between the extremity of their act and its theoretical validation in the notion of a superior morality had an immediacy to an American audience that had lived through a war which had demolished the claims of Nazi supremacy. The film's concern with morality and prerogatives of power and privilege also takes on a special significance for a country that found itself cast in the difficult role of political leadership in the world. Similarly, *The Man Who Knew Too Much*, which places a middle-class American family at the center of international intrigues governed by political and cultural issues it does not understand, reflects a concern with America's position in the world and with the increased responsibility and vulnerability this caused by 1956.

Rear Window and *Vertigo* have frequently been discussed together as central texts that mirror 1950s American culture. In its presentation of urban proximity and the temptation to spy on one's neighbors, *Rear Window* recalls the preoccupations of 1950s sociology with the growing impersonalization and atomization of city life, and politically with the spying and accusations of the McCarthy years. *Vertigo* is a visual document of the rootlessness, loss of identity, and alienation of the late 1950s as well as of the standardization of the female image of that time.

This last concern, the representation of women and the related issues of power, sexuality, and gender, has received more attention with regard to these five films than any other. The psychosexual implications of the murder in *Rope*; the presentation of the aggressive sexuality of Lisa and the passive voyeurism of Jeff in *Rear Window*; the flowering of the repressed sexuality in *The Trouble with Harry*; the unmasking of the sexual politics of the American couple and of family life in *The Man Who Knew Too Much*; the obsessive, even sadistic recreation of a woman to fit male-created images and desires in *Vertigo*: all have been central to the way Hitchcock is perceived and interpreted.

When we consider the five rereleased films from this and the other critical perspectives we have discussed, their accidental grouping becomes fortuitous. They lend themselves to the broadest variety of viewpoints for both the beginning student of film studies and the specialist. This anthology brings together this critical diversity and is intended for both audiences. Its goal is not simply to expand the reader's awareness of Alfred Hitchcock and his position in film history, but to present the aesthetic and intellectual pleasure that is film itself.

Notes

1. François Truffaut, *Hitchcock*, rev. ed. (New York: Simon and Schuster, 1984), 16–17.

I
THE WORLD OF THE RERELEASED FILMS

By 1954 Alfred Hitchcock had been directing films for almost thirty years. In the following six years he made a series of films that remain central texts for both critical and theoretical writing about his work, films which have also had enormous popular appeal: *Rear Window* (1954), *To Catch a Thief* (1955), *The Trouble with Harry* (1955), *The Man Who Knew Too Much* (1956), *The Wrong Man* (1957), *Vertigo* (1958), *North by Northwest* (1959), and *Psycho* (1960). Of these eight, four are among the rereleased films that are the subject of this volume. That Hitchcock's films reached their fullest formal and thematic development during this six-year period is widely acknowledged, so that varied readings of the rereleased films, such as those in this book, enable us to establish the social and artistic matrices of that cultural phenomenon, the "Hitchcock movie."

Rope (1948) is somewhat of an anomaly among the rereleased films in that its date locates it in an earlier phase of Hitchcock's work: its postwar concern with the effects of nihilism and its rigid restrictions on camera editing make it a distinguished film, but one whose focus is not on the erotic ambivalences of male-female relationships and which does not use point-of-view editing and the dramatic montage effects that mark the themes and form of the 1954–60 group.

As early as 1935, when *The Thirty-Nine Steps* indicated that Hitchcock's British period (1926–39) had reached its maturity, the director had established a reputation for thrillers with a brilliant camera and editing style and a narrative that integrated into the suspense the erotic interplay of his heroes and heroines. In this film as well as in the original *Man Who Knew Too Much* (1934) and *The Lady Vanishes* (1938), however, Hitchcock did not explore the formation or reformation of the couple much beyond the limits of traditional romantic comedy.

James Stewart and Grace Kelly in *Rear Window*.

Hitchcock's move to Hollywood in 1939 made possible not only new settings and technical advances, but his exploration of darker and more problematic aspects of male-female relationships. *Rebecca* (1939), *Suspicion* (1941), *Shadow of a Doubt* (1943), *Spellbound* (1945), and *Notorious* (1946) all examine the precariousness of personal relationships, especially the individual's struggle with the demands of the larger social order. Indeed, critics have long recognized that Hitchcock's films take his protagonists from a state of separateness and isolation to a point where they are drawn into relationships with other human beings and are more fully integrated into the world in general.

This tendency became even more explicit in the rereleased films. The following essay, Thomas M. Leitch's "Self and World at Paramount," is a discussion of the motif of personal and social integration in the three rereleased films that were written by screenwriter John Michael Hayes: *Rear Window, The Trouble with Harry,* and *The Man Who Knew Too Much.* For Leitch these films share a preoccupation with the relationship of the individual to the demands of the larger social community, a theme he finds throughout Hitchcock's work. In these films individuals struggle to find bases of commonality and commitment through which they give their lives meaning. The protagonists overcome their alienation and isolation and achieve fulfillment once they realize they need not bow to social conventions or stereotypes to form fulfilling relationships.

SELF AND WORLD AT PARAMOUNT

Thomas M. Leitch

Universal's rerelease of five Hitchcock films long unavailable has not only introduced contemporary audiences to individual films like *Rear Window* and *Vertigo*, but has also redefined the shape of Hitchcock's career. In particular, Hitchcock's early years at Paramount, during which he made four films whose screenplays were written by John Michael Hayes, now appear clearly as his most affirmative period.

In the absence of *Rear Window* (1954), *The Trouble with Harry* (1955), and the second version of *The Man Who Knew Too Much* (1956), the early years at Paramount had been represented by *To Catch a Thief* (1955), in which John Robie (Cary Grant), a former cat burglar, is roused from retirement on the Riviera by accusations that he is committing a new series of burglaries that ape his style. The theme of a hero trapped by his reputation is familiar from such earlier Hitchcock films as *The Lodger, The Thirty-Nine Steps*, and *Notorious*. Given its attractive stars, its leading tone of light comedy, its location photography on the Riviera, and its decorative visual style,[1] the film might be described as adopting a take-it-or-leave-it attitude toward material Hitchcock had treated more urgently in his forties films. But it might more positively, and more accurately, be described as a game whose thematic material is only a pretext for enjoyment. The primary game which gives the story its shape is the playfully competitive romance between Robie and Francie Stevens (Grace Kelly). Within this framework other games abound, most of them logically inconsequential. Robie spends the first twenty minutes of the film, for example, trying to escape from the police, but in the next shot after his capture he is enjoying a drink outside his villa; the police have chased him only to let him go, as in a game of fox and hounds. Similarly, Robie's determination to masquerade as Conrad Burns from Oregon serves no purpose except to heighten his own and the audience's pleasure. Even the game between Robie and Francie, though played for higher stakes, is less important for its cognitive content than for the experience it provides the players, and in this case the audience: Francie is determined to make Robie deflower and finally marry her; Robie is determined to maintain his independence by avoiding romantic commitments.

To Catch a Thief is widely and aptly considered a decorative trifle, its comedy agreeable but shallow. But the other films Hayes wrote for Hitchcock at Paramount, though equally witty and amusing, develop similar thematic material with a penetration and concentration that allows us to see *To Catch a Thief* as marking one stage in a genuinely affirmative period, not simply as a temporary escape from Hitchcock's customary pessimism. Most of Hitchcock's films have at their heart a conflict between an ideal of personal identity and the demands of the social world. In the series of films beginning with *Rebecca*, identity was treated preeminently as a problem to be resolved,[2] a problem dramatized by the conflict between heroes and villains, or more pointedly between heroes and the police who attempt to impose a social identity on such unwilling figures as Alice White in *Blackmail* and Guy Haines in *Strangers on a Train*. The police in the Hayes films, by contrast, are either comically incompetent, marginal, or helpful to the hero; in any case, they are never certifiers of public identity. This latter function is taken over by the closed community, defined in *To Catch a Thief* by the pair of lovers, in *The Man Who Knew Too Much* by the nuclear family, and, more surprisingly, in *Rear Window* and *The Trouble with Harry* by the neighborhood of sympathetic people. The four Hayes films thus develop a similar conflict between self and world but mark the only time in Hitchcock's career when that conflict can be resolved without either hypocrisy or retreat, because the world is now defined as a place which, although it may oppose particular desires of the individual, offers a stable context, indeed the only such context, within which to define one's identity. Like *To Catch a Thief*, the other three films all dramatize the relation between self and world through the development of a sexual relationship whose principals, particularly the men, fear the very consummation they desire and which therefore focuses on the maneuvering of heroes and heroines as they learn to trust each other. The ultimate success of each relationship marks an affirmation deeper than that of Hitchcock's British comedies because it acknowledges more fully the fears that such relationships must overcome.

Many of Hitchcock's films revolve around attempts to vindicate innocent heroes. But each of the Hayes films begins with characters who are obviously guilty of something, guilty precisely (as it turns out) by virtue of their individuality, their determination to define themselves as autonomous individuals in opposition to the social order, and later shows them integrating themselves into a society that defines them more fully and compassionately than their individuality can. In Hitchcock's chase films, the function of society is precisely to fix individual guilt. But in the Hayes films, for the only time in Hitchcock's career, society offers, if not forgiveness or escape from individual guilt, the possibility of transcending guilt and thereby reaching a level of self-discovery unavailable to the isolated individual.

The need for this kind of self-transcendence is clearest in the case of L. B. Jefferies (James Stewart), the housebound hero of *Rear Window*, who begins by spying on his neighbors to pass the time as he is recovering from a broken leg and ends by uncovering a murder. Encouraged by Hitchcock, critics have united in pronouncing Jefferies a voyeur whose idleness, immobility, visual stimulation, and keen imagination link him to the film's audience. Since virtually all the camera setups are from inside Jeff's apartment, we are restricted almost exclusively to his point of view as he pieces together the clues that will convict Lars Thorwald (Raymond Burr) of killing his wife. Despite this identification, however, the film is far from taking Jeff on his own terms as a man who just happens to be watching his neighbors. Both Jeff's girl friend Lisa Fremont (Grace Kelly) and his nurse Stella (Thelma Ritter) chide him for snooping, and the way the camera isolates Lisa and then Jeff in their conversations makes it clear from the beginning that Jeff is more interested in watching his neighbors than in pursuing his romance with Lisa.

It is not that the neighbors are more interesting than Lisa; one of their principal attractions, in fact, is that they offer Jeff a safe way of considering his relationship with her. Every set of neighbors Jeff watches—the newlyweds, the ballet dancer Miss Torso, the spinster Miss Lonelyhearts, the composer struggling to finish his song, the sculptress who gives Thorwald unwanted advice about his flowers, the owners of the dog Thorwald eventually strangles, and the bickering Thorwalds themselves—is organized around a love relationship,[3] and every relationship is somehow deviant or deformed. Miss Lonelyhearts and the composer both dedicate themselves to absent or hypothetical lovers; Miss Torso entertains groups of men Jeff considers potential boyfriends and Lisa wolves; the older couple treat their dog as a child; the sculptress expresses neighborly concern by meddling; and the newlyweds are comically at odds almost from the beginning, with the groom repeatedly opening the shade and sitting in the window and his bride repeatedly calling him back to bed. The Thorwalds offer a more pointed analogy to Jeff and Lisa's own situation. Since we cannot tell why Mrs. Thorwald, like Jeff, is confined to her room or why Thorwald has decided to kill her—we only know that she constantly complains about him and that he is carrying on with another woman—there is reason to fear that Lisa and Jeff, who disagree about everything, will end up as the Thorwalds, perhaps because she will become tired of taking care of him or because he will grow restless with her domestic demands. As Jeff gazes around his courtyard, in fact, he is watching a kaleidoscopic prophecy of his future, a catalog of the number of ways love can go wrong.

Jeff is not the first Hitchcock hero to fear emotional intimacy, but he is the first whose fear takes the form of preferring voyeurism to consummation, mediated experience to direct involvement. Holding a wineglass Lisa has filled for him, he watches Miss Lonelyhearts share a toast with her imaginary lover and silently holds his glass up too. He is sharing her emotion, but she does not know that, because he is watching her without revealing himself, experiencing her vulnerability without making himself vulnerable to her. It is appropriate that Jeff, a magazine photographer (that is, a professional watcher), prefer this kind of mediated, nonreciprocal relationship to the intimacy Lisa offers him. We can see how he became interested in her—she is a model, a professional object-to-be-watched, whom he has photographed for a magazine cover—but appreciate as well why their romance is foundering. The film's narrative moves toward breaking down Jeff's voyeuristic sense of independence from Lisa and his neighbors, a sense that is tied by the photographic equipment he uses in his spying to his determination to retain control of the gaze: to define his relationships with others as those he controls by watching his partners without being watched himself. It is precisely this independence, on which he bases his identity, which precludes the openness that would release his true identity.

In order for Jeff and Lisa to earn their happy ending, they both need to prove their compatibility to each other. Lisa, who has disdained the active life Jeff leads, proves herself a worthy mate for him by sneaking into Thorwald's apartment to get the proof his wife is dead: the wedding ring, which she triumphantly displays behind her back to Jeff across the courtyard as the police question her. The ring clearly links the dead Mrs. Thorwald with the woman who wants to be the future Mrs. Jefferies. Jeff, more importantly, proves his concern for Lisa when he ignores his own danger from Thorwald, who has seen Lisa's gesture, and sends Stella down to the police station to bail her out. Before this final episode, however, Jeff must confront the embarrassment of having his friend, the police detective Tom Doyle (Wendell Corey) pair him with Thorwald when he interrupts Jeff's tirade about Thorwald's hidden life with a significant glance at Lisa's negligee and asks, "Do you tell your landlord everything?" Jeff bridles at this remark, but he accepts its import, marking the first time in the film when he acknowledges that he, like Lisa, Thorwald, and the rest of his neighbors, is someone to be looked at.

It might seem even more perverse that Jeff gets interested in Lisa only when she is put on display as an object to be watched in Thorwald's window. But the scene is the opposite of perverted; far from regarding Lisa as merely an object, and therefore, finally, a legitimate object of attention, Jeff is now regarding her with frantic, self-forgetful concern. It is the first time in the film when his looking out his window has carried with it any of the emotional engagement we normally associate with looking, and Lisa is the first person he has watched who knows she is being watched, who returns his look,

and who is therefore an agent, not just an object. Even so, there is
irony aplenty in the scene. Jeff, who has counted all through the film
on being able to watch his neighbors without the threat of involvement, now finds that he cannot share Lisa's danger, try as he may.
He cannot forbid her from remaining in danger; he cannot warn her
Thorwald is about to return; he cannot help her fight Thorwald off.
He can only appoint the police as agents to rescue Lisa from Thorwald's apartment by arresting her for robbery. And when Thorwald
intercepts the signal Lisa is sending with the wedding ring, Jeff becomes vulnerable himself—more vulnerable, more isolated and immobile, than Thorwald has ever been, as the film demonstrates by
slowing and magnifying the sounds of Thorwald's approach to Jeff's
apartment. Jeff tries to save himself by blinding Thorwald with
flashbulbs—not only relying on the tools of his trade, but forcing
Thorwald to assume once more the position as object of his gaze—
but he can delay him only briefly. Ultimately, his rescue depends on
the police, just as his convalescence depends on the loving attention
of Lisa, which he is now finally ready to accept.

Jeff's fall from his apartment makes him, naturally enough, the
object of the gaze of all his neighbors—it is evidently the first time
most of them have become aware of his existence. Moreover, the
film's final sequence ties up the various love knots in the community
constituted by these neighbors in conventional repetitions (the sculptress is working on a new statue, the older couple has a new dog),
romantic pairings (the composer, whose song has saved Miss Lonelyhearts from comitting suicide, plays it for her in his apartment), and
jokes (the bride finds out the groom has lost his job, and Miss Torso's
boyfriend Stanley, returning from the service, turns out to be short,
homely, and more interested in her refrigerator than in her). Like
most of Hitchcock's films, *Rear Window* has an ending (the substitution of an ideal community of lovers for a pathological collection
of deformed lovers) that does not really resolve the problems the
film has posed. But Jeff at least has overcome his crippling sense
of voyeuristic independence by seeing himself in his neighbors and
his neighbors in himself, and so accepting his necessary ties to his
community. When we last see him, he is finally, for the first time
in the film, ignoring them, peacefully sleeping, while a pan over to
Lisa, dressed in the height of casual fashion, putting down *Beyond
the High Himalayas* and picking up a copy of *Harper's Bazaar*, indi-

41

cates that she has learned how to share Jeff's life without giving up her own.

Rear Window marks a watershed in Hitchcock's career for at least three reasons. It is the first of his films to use voyeurism as an explicit metaphor for the kind of male dominance based on male insecurity.[4] It allows us to see several earlier films as exploring the same relation between patriarchal authority and the fear of insecurity even though they use different metaphors: the police in *The Lodger* and *Blackmail*; the problematic father figure in *The Man Who Knew Too Much* (1934), *Rebecca*, and *Shadow of a Doubt*; and the spies in *Notorious*. Finally, it suggests, for nearly the only time in Hitchcock's work, the possibility of conversion for the hero, who can become less authoritarian and disengaged by facing and overcoming his fears about himself.

A similar pattern emerges in *The Man Who Knew Too Much* (1956), with the most important difference being the relationship between the leads, who are not lovers experimenting with the idea of marriage but a married couple forced to come to terms with their long-standing commitments. Like Bob and Jill Lawrence in Hitchcock's 1934 version of the story, Ben McKenna (James Stewart) and his wife Jo (Doris Day) still play at their relationship even though they have been married for years. Together with their son Hank (Christopher Olsen), they joke about Ben's losses last year in Las Vegas, and Jo sings duets with Hank, dances with him, and tells him, "Oh, you're divine." Their jokes at once mask and display the instability of their marriage. When their son Hank is kidnapped to prevent Ben from passing on the message given to him by the dying agent Louis Bernard (Daniel Gelin), not only the McKennas' son, but their relation to each other, is at stake.

Even before this crisis, Ben and Jo McKenna had disagreed about everything, from whether Bernard was acting suspiciously to who should answer the door. Their disagreements, we soon learn, are rooted in an unresolved conflict: Jo has given up her stage career and moved to Indianapolis to be a doctor's wife, but neither she nor her husband has come to terms with the problems her sacrifice raises. These problems surface as soon as she is recognized by Mr. and Mrs. Drayton (Bernard Miles and Brenda de Banzie) as "*the* Jo Conway," and continue as an undercurrent when Jo asks when they will have another child, whether they are about to have their monthly fight, and why her husband is trying to give her tranquilizers when he has repeatedly complained about her taking too many pills. Neither one seems especially close to Hank, whom they are eager to arrange baby sitting for,[5] or to each other, since they rarely touch each other at all before Hank is kidnapped by the Draytons.

Ben imagines himself chosen for no good reason for the misfortune that befalls him when Bernard makes him his confidant. The screenplay makes it clear, however, that Bernard does not so much bring the McKennas trouble as reveal the trouble already present among them. During a scene in a restaurant in Marrakech, Jo observes Bernard with another woman and acts insulted that he begged off their dinner engagement on the grounds of a business meeting, but Ben attempts to calm her. A minute later, however, she is attempting to calm Ben, who is at the point of confronting Bernard. His final remark—"I don't know what he's doing here, but I'm beginning to dislike what he's doing to our whole night"—prepares us for his reaction toward Hank's kidnapping by denying any personal responsibility for the family's misfortunes and so indicating his vulnerability to any disruptions that reveal the cracks in the family's surface. After Bernard is killed and Ben is summoned to the office of the police inspector for questioning, he unwittingly aggravates Hank's danger by replying to the inspector's request for Bernard's message with a tirade about his unwillingness to comply. Then he self-righteously insists on taking the call that tells him Hank has been kidnapped (if he had only cut his tirade two minutes shorter or delayed taking the call, he would have handed over the message and been off the hook), and finally sends Drayton back to the hotel, from which the Draytons immediately disappear. This kind of egoistic self-reliance, which Ben has obviously been practicing for years at his wife's expense, is what he needs to outgrow in order to make common cause with her.

In one sense, Hank's kidnapping establishes that common cause, just as it did for the Lawrences. But unlike the Lawrences, who work separately with considerable success, the McKennas find it both necessary and difficult to work together. Ben cannot even think of a good way to share the news with Jo except in a professional capacity (compare Jeff's dogged professionalism in *Rear Window*): he refuses to tell her what he knows about Hank until he has given her a sedative ("I'm the doctor. . . . I make my living by knowing when and

43

how to administer medication"). Frantic with anxiety but already dropping off to sleep, Jo rises up from her bed, but he holds her and pushes her back in a parody of the embrace that might have led to that second child. Later that night, as she lies unblinking on the bed and he packs their bags and tells her, "We're going to London," several alienating low-angle shots of him are presented from her point of view. But the scene ends with their first real, albeit anguished, embrace.

Arriving in London (where Jo receives a bouquet labeled "Welcome home"), Ben suddenly finds himself recast from the head of the family to Jo's consort: a crowd of her admirers turns out at the airport to greet them, and one of her friends addresses him as "Mr. Conway." Although the Scotland Yard man Buchanan tells them that "we might find him quite soon indeed if we work together," Ben and Jo cannot even work with each other; Jo accuses Ben of acting "as if you're the only one concerned with this," and they are both close to tears on the phone. The most optimistic note is struck by the surprisingly sympathetic Buchanan, who says, "I have a son myself. I don't know what I'd do" (compare the accusatory Gibson in the 1934 version), as if his temperate attitude could impose greater family unity from outside.

But Buchanan's withdrawal to the far end of the room in which he and Ben are talking also represents a fear which will be more fully developed in the following episode at the taxidermy shop: the fear, following from Ben's own self-ordained isolation, that everyone who might help him is withdrawing or retreating from him. As the dying Bernard had fallen away from him, leaving his hands streaked with makeup, Hitchcock's tight shot reversals communicated Ben's sense of vertigo, of a sudden annihilating alienation from the world, a sensation repeated in the Draytons' desertion. In the taxidermist's shop, after the younger Ambrose Chapell, convinced that Ben is a lunatic, has retreated to the furthest depth of his workroom and asked his father, in an inner room, to call the police, Ben rushes toward him, pleading, before he realizes his mistake. In the following scene, when Ben and Jo discover the conspirators' hiding place, Ben once again makes a futile rush forward, this time toward Hank's voice, only to be struck down.

This scene offers an instructive example of what happens when the McKennas try to work together. Jo, left behind when Ben rushed off to the taxidermy shop, has had the idea that the Ambrose Chapel Bernard mentioned is a place, not a person. So she goes there and calls Ben from a phone booth outside. When he arrives, she wants to call Buchanan, but he demurs, and they go in together. Even though Mrs. Drayton recognizes them, she is unable to make her husband understand their danger until Jo, at Ben's request, gets up to call the police. The McKennas' failure to recover Hank is laid to Ben's inability to stall for time while Jo is calling Buchanan, Jo's slight but painful delay in getting a promise of help, and the responding officers' skepticism about Jo's story. After beginning the scene united in purpose and plan, the McKennas end it widely separated, Jo en route to the Albert Hall, Ben climbing the bell rope to the cupola above in order to escape from the locked and otherwise deserted chapel.

Now at last, however, the moment of complete cooperation is at hand. When Ben follows his wife to the Albert Hall, Jo, who has already realized the assassination attempt will take place there, clutches him, tells him everything he needs to know to find the assassin (the music significantly masking the words of their reunion from the audience), and screams at the moment the shot is to be fired. Ben, in the meantime, having unsuccessfully attempted to enlist the help of the police, is in time to prevent the murderer's escape, although he chases him to his death. At the end of this scene, having finally established their ability to work with each other, the McKennas are able to ask Buchanan for "that help you promised us."[6] In the final scene at the foreign embassy where Hank has been taken, Ben and Jo indeed require all the help the police can give them — without the police cordon surrounding the embassy, their plan would never have worked. But the plan is theirs, or more accurately Ben's plan, depending for the first time on his wife's talents and his acceptance of her own professional identity: while she distracts the guests at the embassy by singing, he will search for Hank. Their brief conversation on the way to the embassy indicates the nature of their new cooperation. Ben tells Jo: "So if they ask you, we're all set." Jo replies: "What if they don't ask me?" Ben: "Have you ever been to a party where they didn't ask you?" On their arrival at the embassy, when the statesman whose life Jo had saved begins to ask, "I wonder if you would —," Ben, intemperate as ever, interrupts: "I'm sure my wife would be delighted to sing for you, Your Excellency." Clearly

45

the McKennas' renewed intimacy, like that of Jeff and Lisa in *Rear Window*, does not simply constitute an abdication of individual personality. But it is not until the very end of the scene, when Ben, threatened by Drayton's pistol, tells Hank, "Do as he says," that Ben finally shows himself able to control his own ideas and emotions even for a moment—a moment that gives him just enough time to catch Drayton off guard and push him down the stairs. The film's final shot, which places Ben, Jo, and Hank together for the first time in the context of a supportive community—Jo's friends, who have come to represent her public and the public in general—is its most exultant affirmation of the link between individual identity, the family unit, and the larger community.

How inclusive this community might be, and how radical are the incongruities that might give it birth, is the theme of *The Trouble with Harry*. *The Trouble with Harry*, whose principals spend the entire film alternately burying and exhuming the corpse of a man found dead in the Vermont woods in order to assuage their guilt and conceal their possible involvement in his mysterious death, is a one-joke film. The joke turns on the extremely unsentimental, matter-of-fact attitude that everyone adopts toward the dead Harry Worp. Captain Wiles (Edmund Gwenn), who thinks he has shot him accidentally, chides him for coming so far from home to die. The absent-minded Dr. Greenbow (Parker Fennelly), his nose in a book, trips over the corpse, mutters an apology, and walks off in a new direction. A local tramp steals his shoes, and Sam Marlowe (John Forsythe) sketches his portrait. When Arnie Rogers (Jerry Mathers), having discovered the body in the film's opening scene, returns with his mother Jennifer (Shirley MacLaine), and she tells him that the man is taking "a deep, wonderful sleep," and adds, "Come on, let's go home and get some lemonade," her response seems at once consistent and outrageous. The outrage is based on the audience's reverence toward the fact of human death, especially on the necessity of ritual observances, such as funerals, to distinguish people from animals. Treated as a nuisance, an obstacle, or a source of shoes or images, Harry seems comically less than human.

But this apparent diminishing or misplacing of Harry's humanity is gradually shown to be operating in the service of a deeper, communal idea of humanity, for Harry's death, unlike his life, has the power to unite the people around him into a community. At the beginning of the film, Hitchcock's standoffish New Englanders have little to do with each other, and especially with the apparent outsiders among them: Jennifer, who has lived in the village for only a few years, and Sam, a painter who has come for the summer. Miss Gravely (Mildred Natwick) and Captain Wiles have never been inside each other's homes or learned each other's first names. The gathering place for the village has been the general store, run by Mrs. Wiggs (Mildred Dunnock), and its representative authority figure has been her son Calvin (Royal Dano), the deputy sheriff who forbids hunting on posted land "because I posted it." Calvin's rules allow the community to operate by stifling personal expression (e.g., hunting, the great pleasure of Captain Wiles's life) in the name of meaningless formalities. As the unobserved pieties toward the late Harry Worp come to seem more and more meaningless, Calvin gradually reveals himself as the true outsider. Although he has lived in the village all his life, his narrow concern with the law blinds him to everyone else's activities (the film ends just as he is finally about to discover the body that has been arranged for him to find), and his fondness for tinkering with noisy old cars introduces the one discordant note into the film's generally bucolic sound track — a note far more discordant than that of Captain Wiles's harmless three rifle shots.

The other outsider to the community is Harry himself, who has forced himself on Jennifer, his sister-in-law, and followed her in order to take her back with him. Finally, dazed after Jennifer hits him with a bottle, he insults and attacks Miss Gravely. Like Calvin, Harry represents the letter of the law estranged from its spirit. It is therefore fitting that his death be treated with a complete disregard for the letter of the law (everyone is willing to cover up for whomever may have killed him) in observance of its spirit. This spirit, a sense of compassion and concern for others, allows Harry's death to assume its proper importance, as a natural event entirely proper to the community.

The propriety of Harry's death is secured by the final revelation of how he died: he suffered a sudden seizure in the woods. But the film has intimated much earlier that Harry's death was not the outrage it seemed. The setting of the story at the height of the New England autumn emphasizes death as part of a natural cycle, a cycle that is echoed by the time frame of the story (it begins early one morning and ends early the following morning) and the low-angle shot

47

of Arnie standing over Harry's body, its feet to the camera, as if he were growing out of the man we later learn is his uncle. Unlike Calvin Wiggs, who treats death as an outrage, an extraordinary event whose implications are inevitably suspicious, the other principals are drawn together by their growing ability to accept Harry's death as a natural event in the life of the community. Since Harry never shared the deeper humanity of the communal life of these survivors, their concern for each other — Sam's for Captain Wiles, Captain Wiles's for Miss Gravely, Miss Gravely's and Sam's for Jennifer — is doubly natural.

If the film's story emphasizes the importance of the community in releasing the energy and confirming the morality of its individuals, Hitchcock's visuals are equally important in establishing the community as the natural or unmarked unit of humanity, so that the isolated individual seems exceptional and deviant. The visual composition of *The Trouble with Harry* is completely unlike that of any of Hitchcock's other films. For the only time in his career he avoids close-ups entirely and works in the range from mid-shot to long shot. Individual compositions tend to balance figures against each other or against their surroundings, which thus achieve far more importance than in most Hitchcock films. Since most of the characters remain resolutely poker-faced through most of the film, small changes of expression and gesture become disproportionately significant: when Miss Gravely extends an arm to Captain Wiles over Harry's corpse and thanks him, her gesture has more impact than the firing of a machine gun in a Sylvester Stallone film. It is this comically quiet gesture which confirms the united purpose of Miss Gravely and Captain Wiles and looks forward to their eventual marriage. Hitchcock's preference for two-shots rather than shot-reversal sequences, particularly in the scenes between Jennifer and Sam, tends to present the frame, rather than the individual, as the fundamental human unit. And the gradual progression of the visuals not only from day to night but from exteriors to interiors suggests the gradual building of a social order, whose center is Jennifer's front room, out of the natural experience associated with the plot of land in which Harry is repeatedly interred.

The editing of the film is as unusual as its choice of camera distances. The episodic nature of the opening half hour of *Rear Window*, in which Jeff's neighbors were repeatedly engaged in the same activities on the same parts of the same set, had led Hitchcock to use an unprecedented number of fadeouts to segment the film, and especially to represent the passage of time. The fades slowed down the rhythm of the film and gave its repeated events a vaguely ritualistic quality. *The Trouble with Harry* uses just as many fades, but for a different reason. Hitchcock's plan to shoot the film on location in Vermont was ruined by heavy rains that allowed only a few exterior shots to be made before the trees lost their autumn foliage.[7] In addition to process shots allowing the shooting of outdoor scenes indoors, Hitchcock also used some exterior extreme long shots — of a church, a meadow, and several groups of trees — as introductory shots for each episode. These shots, which are unique in Hitchcock's films, are reminiscent of what Noel Burch has called the "pillow-shots" of Yasujiro Ozu:[8] they break the action into episodes and simultaneously provide a sense of the primacy of the nonhuman environment, so that human action itself is perceived as having an irruptive force. Both the camera setups and the editing of the film, in other words, tend to organize the story around the environment and its interactions with the characters, and so encourage us to take the long view of Harry's death. The emphasis is not on assigning individual guilt — although Calvin Wiggs is treated as a threat, he is never offered seriously as a moral authority — but in recovering from a trauma, and the best response to Harry's death is one which allows the community to grow in sympathy with the natural rhythms the film so carefully establishes.

Sam Marlowe differs from the other heroes of these films in being initially the victim of an isolation he has not chosen; his entrance into the community does not involve a conversion but rather a process of mutual discovery, the realization of the principal characters that the isolation resulting from the imposition of authoritarian figures like Harry and Calvin Wiggs is too high a price to pay for the observation of social conventions. Another way to make the same point is that John Forsythe (who shares star billing, just below the title, with Edmund Gwenn) does not portray the same kind of hero that James Stewart does; his film does not focus so much on his entrance to the community as on the larger community itself, renewed and reaffirmed by its response to Harry's death. By comically satirizing social conventions in the name of a deeper sense of community, Hitchcock seals the most affirmative film of his most affirmative period.

49

Whether working with Hayes and other congenial collaborators—the cinematographer Robert Burks, the editor George Tomasini, and, for the first time on *The Trouble with Harry*, the composer Bernard Herrmann—helped develop this side of Hitchcock or whether the optimism of this period is traceable exclusively to Hayes is open to question. But there is no question that Hayes's refusal to follow Hitchcock to Warners for *The Wrong Man* marks the end of this period. The self that is triumphantly integrated with the world was shortly to vanish from Hitchcock's work, whose focus turned instead to the disintegration of Rose Balestrero in *The Wrong Man*, Scottie Ferguson in *Vertigo*, and Norman Bates in *Psycho*. In these later Paramount films, and in the chilly detachment of his Universal films, Hitchcock turned again, and decisively, from the social optimism of the Hayes films.

Notes

1. It was one of Paramount's first releases in the new VistaVision process, which produced a wide-screen image without sacrificing depth of field. Robert Burks, Hitchcock's cinematographer since *Strangers on a Train*, was awarded an Oscar for his work on the film.
2. Consider the relation between the two Mrs. de Winters in *Rebecca*, the suspicious behavior of Johnnie Aysgarth in *Suspicion* and of Uncle Charlie in *Shadow of a Doubt*, the investigation of the false Dr. Edwards in *Spellbound*, the burden of Alicia's reputation in *Notorious*, and the riddles of criminal guilt in *The Paradine Case, Under Capricorn*, and *Stage Fright*.
3. Robin Wood was the first to draw attention to this pattern in *Hitchcock's Films* (New York: A. S. Barnes, 1965), 64. The analogy is emphasized by the film's music, which is entirely diegetic and consists almost entirely of love songs, including, for example, not only the composer's song-in-progress, "Lisa," but "Amore," "To See You Is to Love You," "Mona Lisa," and—as Thorwald is carrying parts of his wife's body out in his samples case—the Rodgers and Hart waltz "Lover." See Elisabeth Weis, *The Silent Scream* (Rutherford, N.J.: Fairleigh Dickinson University Press, 1982), 113–17.
4. See Robert Stam and Roberta Pearson, "Hitchcock's *Rear Window*: Reflexivity and the Critique of Voyeurism," *Enclitic* 7, no. 1 (1983); repr. in Marshall Deutelbaum and Leland Poague, eds., *A Hitchcock Reader* (Ames: Iowa State University Press, 1986), 203.
5. Jo is clearly close to Hank, as their song and dance in the hotel room indicate. But the undercurrent of sexual rivalry implied by their relationship—Jo's pretended evening out with her son is more successful than her real night out with her husband—prevents their intimacy from seeming as reassuring as it might.

6. Although declining to agree with François Truffaut that the 1956 Albert Hall sequence was better than the 1934 version, Hitchcock emphasized a single difference he evidently considered an improvement: the presence of the husband, presumably in order to make the climactic set piece mark the first time husband and wife had successfully worked together. See Truffaut, *Hitchcock*, rev. ed. (New York: Simon and Schuster, 1984), 93–94.

7. See Donald Spoto, *The Dark Side of Genius* (Boston: Little, Brown, 1983), 355.

8. See Burch, *To the Distant Observer*, rev. and ed. by Annette Michelson (Berkeley: University of California Press, 1979), 160–61. In Hitchcock's case, the shots differ from establishing shots precisely in their failure to indicate just where the ensuing scene takes place.

II
THE FORM OF DESIRE:
REAR WINDOW (1954), *VERTIGO* (1958), AND CINEMATIC REPRESENTATION

Rear Window and *Vertigo* are by common consent Hitchcock's masterpieces of the 1950s. Each is defined by a central pattern of what the French critics of that era referred to as cinematic "architecture," a formal or structural design which controls the narrative and the audience's experience of it. In *Rear Window* it is the confinement of the camera and the setting of the film within the city backyard of the protagonist, L. B. Jefferies.* The spatial limits of Jefferies's cinematic world control his observations and meditations upon his neighbors across the way and, ultimately, his narrativization of what he thinks he sees. Sharing his point of view, we become trapped in this world and narrative with him.

Unlike *Rear Window, Vertigo* superficially seems to open up its cinematic space by using several dramatic locales in San Francisco and along the California coastline. However, the viewer soon notices that the characters, the narrative, the camera movement, and even the audience itself are controlled by the vertiginous spiral that defines this film. Soon we are as trapped and seduced as the victimized Scottie, caught in his fears and obsession.

Both narratives, then, are about traps, victimization, and obsessions: themes which Hitchcock explored throughout his career. Jeff's fixation on Thorwald, trapped and victimized by a nagging invalid wife, has its parallel in Scottie's all-consuming involvement with Madeleine, an involvement which becomes his personal trap, as he falls victim to Gavin Elster's scheme and his own growing obsession

---

*Commentators on *Rear Window* are divided over whether to spell the protagonist's name as "Jeffries" or "Jeff(e)ries." Since the latter spelling appears on James Stewart's leg cast at the opening of the film, we have adopted "Jefferies" throughout this anthology.

James Stewart in *Rear Window.* (Photo courtesy of Photofest, New York.)

with this woman. Whereas in *Rear Window* we share Jefferies's desire to find Thorwald guilty of having murdered the absent Mrs. Thorwald, in *Vertigo* we allow ourselves to become seduced with Scottie and are not only unable to recognize that a crime is being committed, but at the film's end we also want the crime itself, which has now been uncovered for us, to disappear. Each film, then, manipulates us into sharing both the visual and psychic point of view of the protagonist. We become, in the case of *Rear Window*, to para-

phrase Jefferies's girl friend Lisa, cynical "ghouls" who do not want
to face the disappointment that a man may not have murdered his
wife; in the case of *Vertigo*, we suspend judgment and disbelief to
entertain the contrived history and the sham aura of the supernatural
surrounding Madeleine so that we can participate vicariously in Scottie's fantasy and obsession. In both films, then, Hitchcock forces
not only his characters, but his audience, both male and female, to
confront the unsettling reality of their own desires. According to the
feminist theory that emphasizes the process of spectatorship, these
desires are conditioned by the point of view of the masculine protagonist and the male viewer, both of whom are under the control
of the male director/enunciator. So a woman watching the film may
be limited in her "visual pleasure" to the narrow masculine confines
permissible within the patriarchal culture that has dominated Hollywood cinema.

Some postmodern theorists believe that the spectator is also trapped
and victimized in these films in that all apparent "meanings" are
subverted by deliberate ambiguity or an unbroken chain of reflexive
images that ultimately cannot refer to anything outside themselves.
The viewer concerned with explanations of the mystery and/or fantasy in *Rear Window* and *Vertigo* is constantly forced to confront
the artificial quality of filmmaking and film texts and thus the ir-
relevancy of traditional notions of genre and theme. The films thus
become self-reflexive machines that replicate the process of their
own creation: they are ultimately "about themselves."

In the first essay of this section, "Author, Auteur: Reading *Rear
Window* from Woolrich to Hitchcock," Anthony J. Mazzella explores the relation between prose and film narrative by comparing
Rear Window to the Cornell Woolrich short story upon which it is
based. Mazzella shows how Hitchcock introduced female characters,
expanded the story's violence, and enlarged the conception of Jefferies to include his fear of sexual inadequacy. According to Mazzella,
the camera becomes analogous to Woolrich's first-person narrator,
and in exploring the perceptions of Jefferies it takes its cues from
the audience, becoming the agent of our desires and fears, making
us share the responsibility for his voyeurism, his near demise, and
his ultimate survival.

Mazzella's concern with the way a cinematic text was transposed
from a literary one raises issues about the relation of narrative to

the formal apparatus of cinema: camera technique, editing patterns, movie sets, and acting styles through which the director creates meaning. John Belton's "The Space of *Rear Window*" is one of several essays in this collection concerned with formal structure and cinematic technique. Belton approaches *Rear Window* from the perspective of the representation of space within its single set. He makes a distinction between what he calls theatrical and cinematic film space: the former is the product of set design and fixed camera position; the latter of framing, camera movement, and editing. The use of these two forms of space is crucial in the construction of the narrative. *Rear Window*, he argues, plays with the viewer's perception and traditional understanding of each kind of space in relation to narration. Belton studies the psychological dimensions of the different spaces of the film—Jefferies's apartment, the courtyard, the apartments across the way—in terms of the way they shape the narrative. Belton shows how space is ultimately used to create not only the objective elements in the narrative, but also the viewer's subjective perception of it.

Another paper concerned with cinematic form is Doug Tomlinson's " 'They Should Be Treated Like Cattle': Hitchcock and the Question of Performance." Beginning with the director's often-quoted quip that film actors need to be controlled like cattle, Tomlinson shows how the director, far from ignoring the importance of acting, developed in these films a "gestural choreography" specifically for the cinema. He focuses on *Vertigo* as the richest example of the director's "visualization of performance" and demonstrates how the physical gestures in the performances of Kim Novak and James Stewart are tailored to the director's camera and editing strategies, revealing the more complex aspects of character. Hitchcock's tightly controlled concept of character, he shows, created a precise kind of performance system unique to the cinema.

The relationship of the psychological dimension of character to narrational pattern in these films is the focus of William G. Simon's "Hitchcock: The Languages of Madness." Beginning with a discussion of the various narrative modes in *Rear Window*—authorial, analytical, point-of-view—Simon shows how in *Vertigo* the most psychologically complex of these modes, the point-of-view shots from Scottie's perspective, become an "experiential" pattern of narrative which foregrounds the character's subjective experience for

James Stewart and Kim Novak in _Vertigo_. (Photo courtesy of Photofest, New York.)

the audience. This visual presentation of the character's irrational behavior becomes more profound than verbal attempts within the narrative to explain it. Simon regards this emphasis on visualizing the madness within characters as part of the director's insistence on the centrality of the irrational in human life.

For several of our essayists Hitchcock's work exposes the impact of patriarchy on erotic life and gender roles. In his comparative study, "Hitchcock and Buñuel: Authority, Desire, and the Absurd," Robert Stam shows how Buñuel's explicit attacks on authority figures and institutions have affinities with Hitchcock's dark exploration of society's rigid codes and their damaging effects on the psyche. He analyzes the narrative tension in both artists' works as stemming from the guilt of the protagonist as he fluctuates between rational law and irrational desire. Ultimately in Hitchcock's films the conflict results in voyeurism, fetishism and, in the case of *Vertigo*, necrophilia. In his discussion of *Rear Window*, Stam analyzes the Jefferies figure as analogous to the film's spectators: his desire is manifested as scopophilia, "looking" as the primary source of sexual pleasure. For Stam the focus of the rereleased films and other works of the late American period is always on the overwhelming guilt formed by repressed desire. Like Buñuel (but implicitly rather than explicitly), Hitchcock challenges cultural institutions that create repression.

Like Stam, Ann Cvetkovich sees Hitchcock's work in the context of repression and dehumanizing, patriarchal institutions. In her comparison of Hitchcock's *Vertigo* and De Palma's *Body Double*, "Postmodern *Vertigo*: The Sexual Politics of Allusion in De Palma's *Body Double*" Cvetkovich examines the latter director's "quotations" of Hitchcock as a way to critique gender roles in both films' time periods, the 1950s and the 1980s. Cvetkovich is concerned with De Palma's allusions to Hitchcock, not for parasitic purposes, but for commentary on the increasing tendency in our culture to make voyeuristic sexuality and pornography the norm, rather than an aberration. Cvetkovich shows that Hitchcock's work can be utilized for cultural criticism by the contemporary filmmaker with a postmodern inclination to appropriate images and motifs from classic films of earlier periods.

In her essay "The Concept of the Fantastic in *Vertigo*," Ann West draws on recent postmodern theories about the subversion of traditional genres and artistic conventions and defines Hitchcock's use of the fantastic to alter the traditional relationship of artist to audience. Hitchcock exploits ambiguity, refusing to ascribe natural or supernatural explanations to the events he films. Lacking such a resolution, *Vertigo* provides no logical intelligibility to its audience. The spectator, then, shares Scottie's vertigo and his unsuccessful attempt to interpret and make coherent the hallucinatory events that constitute the film. For West the fantastic is not used by Hitchcock to shock or mystify, but instead to make possible limitless interpretations.

Theorists who are influenced by the ideas of Jacques Derrida and who are therefore concerned with the "self-reflexivity" of cinematic texts focus on the tendency of narrative film to reveal its "constructed" quality. Katie Trumpener, in her essay, "Fragments of the Mirror: Self-Reference, Mise-en-Abyme, *Vertigo*," stresses Hitchcock's desire to unsettle his audience by constantly reminding viewers that what they are watching is artifice, not reality. She utilizes the concept of metonymy (naming the part for the whole) to describe visual and narrative repetitions in *Vertigo* that form a "broken mirror" of endless reflexivity and ambiguous meaning. Hitchcock's film is really about its own artistic creation and physical production, about the relationship of the director to his audience. Techniques of self-reference in Hitchcock, according to Trumpener, are not used for self-congratulation, but for audience manipulation.

AUTHOR, AUTEUR

Reading *Rear Window*
from Woolrich to Hitchcock

Anthony J. Mazzella

In the 1973 video interview prepared by Richard Schickel and
aired on PBS, Alfred Hitchcock commented on a link between literature and film: "Literature," Hitchcock said, "can [create an emo-
tion] by the way the language is used or the words are put together.
But sometimes you find that a film is looked at solely for its content
without any regard to the style or manner in which the story is told.
And, after all, that basically is the art of the cinema. One reads a
book and, providing all the story elements [are] there, the characters are there, it's best to lay the book aside." It is instructive,
however, to pick it up again because a comparative analysis makes
possible a better understanding of both works, especially the film
adaptation, since the differences from the original are so readily apparent. The differences, then, underscore the adapter's interests,
approaches, and themes; and for the viewer who is also a reader,
the double journey becomes doubly illuminating.

This methodology as it involves Hitchcock, nearly 80 percent of
whose feature films are based on a literary source, is perhaps best
illustrated by *Rear Window*. The 1954 film stars James Stewart,

Grace Kelly, and Thelma Ritter; the screenplay is by John Michael Hayes; and the source is a 1942 story by Cornell Woolrich originally entitled "It Had to Be Murder." In the February 1986 volume of *Columbia Library Columns,* Francis Nevins calls Hitchcock Woolrich's "cinematic soul-brother," and considers Woolrich "the greatest writer of suspense fiction that ever lived."

A bizarre resting place, even a grotesque one in the case of the film, is common to both works, as is the murder of a wife by a husband, an attempted second murder, and a voyeur as central character. The differences, however, are striking, perhaps none more so than the nearly total absence of women in the Woolrich work. Apart from the murder victim, the mistress, the forerunner of Miss Lonelyhearts, and the newlywed wife, there are no major women characters in the story. There is no Miss Torso, no sculptress, no offscreen soprano practicing the scales, no Lieutenant Tom Doyle's wife on the phone, no baby sitter on the phone, no woman with the dog, no Stella the nurse, and, above all and "starting from the top," no Lisa Carol Fremont. One can perhaps attribute the presence of women in the film to their absence in the story. Certainly, the role women play in the film, especially that of the Grace Kelly character, is to assert their presence in the world dominated by the protagonist.

Jeffries is the central character in both works (or "Jefferies," as it is spelled in the film, evidenced by the spelling in the script itself and the on-screen inscription on the cast on his broken leg: "Here lie the broken bones of L. B. Jefferies"). His last name is pronounced the same in both, he is called "Jeff" in both, and his movements are circumscribed in both—limited as they are to his apartment and to the view it commands from its rear window. In both he observes strange activities in an opposite apartment (in both works belonging to Lars Thorwald and his wife Anna). In both, Jeff[e]ries (I use this hybrid spelling only when referring to the dual version of the Jeff character) communicates his concerns to a friend on the police force, Boyne in the story, Tom Doyle in the film (though initially in the script it was Coyne, a possible pun on the name of the creator of Sherlock Holmes); is greeted with skepticism in both; and has to provide the proof of what he believes has been a murder. The murderer catches on that there is an observer in both, and in both the murderer breaks into Jeff's apartment and tries to kill him—by shooting him in the story and pushing him out the window in the film.

In the story, Thorwald is lithe and agile; he continues to fire, but is shot and falls to his death from a great height on the roof. He is captured in the film and explains what had been buried in the flower bed. When asked if she wants to know what it was, Stella, initially unaware of the gruesome irony, declares, "I don't want any part of it." Then when she becomes aware, she does a double take. Anna Thorwald is cut up in the film, her body scattered in the East River. In the story, she is buried whole in the newly laid concrete floor in the renovated kitchen above the Thorwalds' apartment. Certainly, murder is a violent act, but the murder of Mrs. Thorwald in the film is far more violent than its source in the story.

The presence of Mrs. Thorwald in both is a pointed reminder that major women characters are absent from the story but added to the film. Indeed, there is another, more significant omission/addition connecting the two works. The centerpiece is Jeff[e]ries. And if the Hitchcock-Hayes approach to the process of adaptation is to add to the film what the story lacks, then perhaps women, violence, and Jeff[e]ries are all connected, the two works taken together illuminating these three subjects.

Take Jeff[e]ries, for instance. Since we know a good deal about his profession in the film, it would follow that we would know little or nothing about his profession in the story. This is clearly the case. We know nothing about what he does for a living. Furthermore, we do not know until the end of the story precisely why he is trapped in his apartment. We are told in the second paragraph of this first-person narrative merely that "my movements were strictly limited just around this time. I could get from the window to the bed, and from the bed to the window, and that was all." Only in the story's final paragraph do we learn the full explanation: we are informed that a Doctor Preston arrives, announcing, "Guess we can take that cast off your leg now." Therefore, Jeff[e]ries in both works has his leg in a cast. How this happened is told to us visually in the opening sequence of the film when we are shown his leg in a cast, the smashed camera, and the picture of the racing-car accident. We conclude that he is a professional photographer who paid the price of a broken leg to secure the prized photograph.

In the story, we have no idea of what caused his leg to be put in the cast or of Jefferies's background. His past is almost as much of a secret as the murder of Mrs. Thorwald. The story, then, comes to involve a double discovery—Jeff learning the truth about the murder, and the reader gradually piecing together a picture of Jeff. Jeff's opening words in the story become our assignment in reverse: He says, "I didn't know. . . . " The motif of not knowing, of trying to find out, of finally reaching the truth, becomes the central, extended verbal structure of the story, echoed and repeated through an exhaustive variety of expressions: "Evidently," "I guess," "I wondered," "maybe," "Presumably," "that unknown," "I couldn't make out," "seemed," "I couldn't tell," "Whatever it was," "What looked like," "My imagination had to supply," "You'd almost think," "That puzzled me," "A little at a loss," "You know nothing," "Apparently," "I speculated," "I suspected," "possibly. . . . Possibly not," "I supposed—I don't know."

This litany of doubt is finally replaced by one of conviction: "Then I got it," "I knew what it was now," "I could see," "I knew I'd been right," "A certainty of murder," "a firm belief," "a conviction," "I myself was . . . convinced," "I could tell," "[I] knew," "It had to be." While Jeff comes to know about Lars Thorwald, we still know very little about Jefferies, even by the end of the story. We know the season is warm, that he has trouble sleeping, that he is "stewing in a vacuum of total idleness," that he likes rational explanations of events, that he is tenacious, that, with his African-American servant Sam, he spent an idle time on a "cabin cruiser." But we do not know if he owns the boat or when it was that they "were bumming around," for we are told only that it was "that cabin cruiser" and "that season." We infer that he has sublet his furnished apartment, for he speaks of the books and the clay bust as belonging to "the former owner." He tells us also, surprisingly, that he "never read" books.

In short, we know almost nothing about him, certainly less than we know about Thorwald's activities. What we do know is that Jefferies's life becomes active the moment Mrs. Thorwald ceases to be, that he becomes free to live the moment Anna Thorwald has been killed. Her death is his life. Her murder provides him with the means to escape the confinement of his apartment through the reach of his mind, much as Thoreau escaped his prison cell in "Civil Disobedience." He is a person trapped in his nature but freed through his thoughts, hence so secretive a past and so active a knowing agent. He is trapped by his body and freed by his mind. It is no accident, perhaps, that he escapes being killed by Thorwald's bullet by placing over his head the bust belonging to the former owner so that the head of "Rousseau or Montesquieu," Enlightenment philosophers associated with reflections on the nature of freedom, gets "disintegrated into chunks" and Jefferies lives to tell the story.

The story he tells is an unstated parable of freedom, a theme he alludes to only briefly early in his narrative, after the day has gone and it is evening again. He sketches the lives of the people in the quadrangle outside his rear window: "The chain of little habits that were their lives, unreeled themselves. They were all bound in them tighter than the tightest straitjacket any jailer ever devised, though they all thought themselves free."

If what the story omits becomes what the film includes, and Jeff-[e]ries, women, and violence are all linked in some cohesive and informing way, then we can expect that the theme of freedom touched on briefly in the story will become the focus of the film, and that minor allusions will develop into major structures. For instance, while there is no description of Jefferies's profession in the story, certainly not of his being a photographer, there are allusions that may have attracted Hitchcock to the story and helped Hayes develop his screenplay. The term "unreeled themselves" in the quotation above by itself can suggest fishing or filming; but the climax of the story makes the preeminence of the camera irresistible. Waiting for Thorwald to attack, Jeff muses on the trap he is in, believing he is doomed. "There wasn't time now," he thinks, "for one of those camera-finishes." And when he is rescued in the nick of time, the image returns to him: "The camera-finish after all."

With the allusion to camera in the story becoming the central preoccupation in the film, we can consider other items only suggested in the story but developed in the film. The name "Jeff[e]ries," having little or no connotations in the story, acquires several now that the camera is central, for the second half of his pronounced name, the one left off when his nickname is invoked, is "f[e]ries," pronounced like "frees" as in "the act of freeing," or (if film is paramount) "freeze," as in a "freeze frame." The James Stewart character in the film is frozen in a sterile life from which he is freed by the murder of Anna Thorwald and the love of Lisa Fremont. If the second half of Jefferies's name relates to the theme of freedom, the first half of Lisa's pronounced last name does also, so that it becomes the function of Lisa Fremont to free Jefferies from his sexual fears and anxieties.

The impotent L. B. Jefferies acquires power through his camera: the lens he uses for spying frequently rests on his lap and becomes the potency he lacks. As Stella points out: "You got a hormone deficiency. Those bathing beauties you've been watching haven't raised your temperature one degree in a month."

In the film the linkage of Jefferies, violence, women, and freedom is established in Jeff's apartment, where omission is eloquent. Although there are many photographs on the walls, all of them deal with or suggest violence — accidents, explosions; none of them is of Lisa. There are only two photographs of women — one on the cover of the magazine Jeff works for and the other, which he has framed, a negative of the positive that is the magazine cover. It is clear that Jeff needs to see women as opaque if not invisible, especially Lisa Fremont. For him, she is too perfect.

If the principle of omission is at work, this would then suggest that Jefferies fears his own imperfection, that what Lisa reminds him of is something he does not want to accept — his own inadequacy. This inadequacy, we can infer, is sexual. The songs heard on the sound track act as a marker: for example, "That's Amore," "Mona Lisa," "Lover, When I'm Near You." When Lisa is intimately near her lover (indeed, sitting on his lap), she kisses him repeatedly. He talks. She kisses him again. He talks again. She elicits no response. When Jeff tells her (referring to Thorwald), "There's something terribly wrong," Lisa counters, "And, I'm afraid it's with me." Her frustration echoes her earlier question to Jeff when she makes her first appearance in that riveting profile kiss filmed in a sequence of repeated frames that just misses being slow motion: "[How's] your love life?" Yet it is Jeff who complains — about Lisa.

But when we view and hear Lisa, we encounter none of what Jeff objects to: her money and her "perfection." On the contrary, these obsessions, when they are mentioned by others or Jefferies himself, reflect on Jefferies's insecurities. Lisa's flair for fashion and dining (she arranges for dinner at "21" by having it delivered) earns Jeff's terse accolade, spoken in dismay, about her dinner arrangement: "Lisa, it's perfect — as always." And later, when Doyle, Lisa, and Jeff are discussing the Thorwalds, Doyle informs us that it was his saving Jeff's life during the war that enabled Jeff to have fame, a good job, and money. When Miss Torso is linked with one of her male guests, it is Jeff who announces to Lisa, "Well, she picked the most prosperous-looking one." Again, Lisa, enchanted by the composer's melody (which at the end of the film will come to bear her name), wonders about the source of his inspiration. Jeff's answer acknowledges only monetary considerations: "He gets it from the landlady once a month." The Lisa that Jeff complains about, then, is his projection of his own anxieties.

He fears marriage most of all because such an intimacy would likely cause him to confront his demons. So his demons are projected not only onto Lisa but onto the Thorwalds as well. The major irony of the film is that while the Thorwalds' marriage dissolves and ends in murder, the possibility of marriage for Jeff and Lisa blooms. It is Anna Thorwald's murder and Jeff and Lisa's involvement in bringing it to light that enable another truth to emerge: that Jeff cannot bear to live without Lisa. The turning point that marks this revelation is Lisa's mortal danger at the hands of Thorwald: she is trapped in the murderer's apartment, with Jeff impotent across the courtyard, trapped in his inability to help.

Before that, though, he was merciless in his excoriation of marriage and his treatment of Lisa. When he loses the assignment to another photographer, Jeff speaks of doing something drastic—like getting married and never going anywhere. And he glances at Thorwald when he says this. When Stella voices her opinion that Miss Lonelyhearts will some day find happiness, Jeff adds, "And some man will lose his." It is not until Lisa becomes his potency (assuming a role belonging to Sam in the story) by becoming his legs and getting the name and address of the salesman, that we hear Jeff use his first term of endearment, telling Lisa, "Thank you, dear." This slight change in attitude is noted again the next morning when Stella serves him a superb breakfast and he remarks, "No wonder your husband still loves you." The positive attitude increases when Lisa arrives again. He notices that her hair is different; she has put it up, whereas before—and later—she resembled Mrs. Thorwald: slim, blonde, hair worn down. As Lisa, thinking of Mrs. Thorwald, muses, "It doesn't make sense," Jeff uses a second term of endearment: "I can't guess what you're thinking, honey." Lisa explains about women and jewelry, and Jeff uses still another term of endearment: "I'm with you, sweetie." But the change in attitude is not permanent, for when Lisa decides to spend the night, the cutting edge returns. Lisa speaks of the person who helps the detective, "his Girl Friday"; but

Jeff's riposte is hurtful: "But he never ends up marrying her." Undeterred, Lisa announces a "preview of coming attractions" and later emerges wearing a negligee that links her ever more closely with the late Anna Thorwald, who was seen similarly attired.

When Thorwald attacks Lisa, is he then attacking his wife once more? And when he killed Anna, was this Jeff's projection at work? It is the consensus among commentators on *Rear Window* that the outer world surrounding Jefferies mirrors his inner world; that, for instance, Miss Lonelyhearts, wearing a green outfit that is echoed in a lighter shade in Lisa's tailored suit, who entertains a man not there and fights off a man too much present, is an analogue for Lisa in relation to Jeff and Thorwald. Miss Torso objectifies Jefferies's sexual frustration as Jeff's itch that needs to be scratched at erotically suggestive moments or moments of professional or personal frustration. The first urge to scratch comes while watching Miss Torso limber up when he learns he has lost the photo assignment. Similarly, he has an urge to scratch when Doyle reports that the police intercepted a postcard from the supposedly murdered Mrs. Thorwald: "Arrived okay. Already feeling better. Love, Anna." A similar scene with a nearly identical postcard message appears in the story, but there is no urge to scratch.

This conjunction of inner and outer worlds in the film is facilitated most of all by the camera and the sound track, for many viewers the eyes and ears of L. B. Jefferies. Since the story by Cornell Woolrich is a first-person narrative, such an identification would be appropriate. Indeed, William Kittredge and Steven M. Krauzer, in their introduction to *Stories into Film* (1979), remark upon this device: "The protagonist . . . passes time by observing other people's lives through the rear windows of the apartments around the areaway upon which his own apartment looks. Hitchcock confines his camera in the same way, revealing the other windows only as Jeffries [*sic*] can see them, drawing the viewer to participate in Jeffries's [*sic*] voyeurism" (132).

Yet if the film appears to operate by adding what the story omits and omitting or altering what the story includes, then perhaps the identification of the camera with Jefferies's point of view may not be entirely valid. Before Lisa gives her "preview of coming attractions," she lowers the shades on the windows of Jefferies's apartment. A little later, when the dog is found with its neck broken, she raises a shade. In both cases, the shades are raised or lowered by hand, not mechanically or electronically. Yet when the opening credits are run, the shades move up each to the same height, in sequence, left to right, and of their own accord. Jefferies does not lift them. He is shown later to have been sound asleep. What agent, then, is revealing this series of framed views? It is not the sleeping Jeff. It is not Lisa. It can only be the camera, announcing its autonomy, declaring itself as the most important character in the film, and assuming the function of Woolrich's first-person narrator.[1] And it does so in a manner far more complex than that of the literary narrative; for in revealing the inner and outer worlds of L. B. Jefferies, it takes its cues primarily from us, the viewer. If the rear-window drama takes its character from the projections of Jefferies's fears and desires, then the camera acts as the agent of *our* fears and desires.

Having introduced us to this figure sleeping, the camera satisfies our first desire to learn more about him and therefore pans across the apartment, showing us a thermometer registering ninety-two degrees, his leg in a cast with the inscription that gives us Jefferies's name, a broken camera, shots of an auto race crash, the negative and the positive print of the woman who is not Lisa. Thus, we know his profession and learn about his accident. Since Jefferies is unconscious at this time, the camera becomes to a degree a surrogate consciousness for him. The camera "sees" for Jeff the *external* conditions that brought him to his present, impotent state—confined to a wheelchair. But later the camera helps the audience to see that Jeff is trapped in ways he fails to acknowledge or comprehend. The camera thus becomes his other consciousness, the one that reveals his inner life, the life he has repressed, and the one that will free him from his obsessions. The role of the camera in this connection is a paradox, for it is the *movie* camera that will free Jefferies from the cameras that have become his way of seeing the world and relating to it.

The camera, of course, is our way of seeing the world of the film and of relating to that world. When we wish to hear something better, the camera obliges by jump-cutting closer, as when we cannot quite make out what the sculptress is telling Thorwald. The camera in close, the sound track obliging, our desire to hear satisfied, we readily learn that she is advising him not to overwater his flowers. In reply, he tells her to "shut up," words to be echoed by Jefferies later when Lisa is criticizing his profession, comparing him with a tourist traveling from place to place taking pictures. The important point is that a camera limited only to Jefferies's point of view could not have so obliged us. In the story, there is no camera, but a spyglass — an instrument that brings distant objects near but cannot capture them on film. With film, the image is caught — as Jeff is caught in his world where the chief reality, the chief stimulus, is what he can see through the lens of a camera (or the frame of a window); and as we are ultimately caught in the world of the film, where we can see only what we are shown. The paradox is that we are shown what we want to see.

Part of what we are shown is privileged information — visual information denied Jefferies, who is again asleep when the camera reveals to us a darkly dressed woman with a large-brimmed hat who leaves Thorwald's apartment with him in the middle of the night. That we are uncertain about her identity communicates a significant detail about the camera's function as our agent. The camera, while serving as the agent of our fears and desires, is not entirely pliable. It is a free agent as well, thereby serving the larger themes of the film.

Since, as viewers of a Hitchcock film, we want a murder — if not two or three — the camera perversely obliges by not showing us the murder of Mrs. Thorwald and by forcing us to share Jefferies's anxiety and impotence when Thorwald attacks Lisa. At the climax of this scene occurs the film's most powerfully ambiguous use of the camera because it is not clear whether the audience is agent, Jefferies is agent, or Lisa is agent unawares. Lisa has found Anna Thorwald's wedding ring and, significantly, wears the ring on the appropriate finger of her left hand, which she holds behind her back, moving the ring and pointing to it with her other hand. Jefferies, using his camera's telephoto lens and seeing the ring, cries out, "Look, the wedding ring!" When the camera cuts to the scene it leaves Jefferies's point of view and again gives us a privileged shot — of Thorwald himself responding to the command to see the ring. Jefferies sees Thorwald looking, but is not aware of Thorwald's awakening to the identity of his nemesis. Nor is Lisa. Only the audience is aware. It's as if, having been simultaneously thwarted in witnessing the potential murder of Lisa and satisfied that she escapes unharmed, the audience's appetite for murder has found a new object, one truly helpless and impotent, Jefferies himself. It is the audience signaling

Thorwald, "Look, the victim!" Hitchcock, in satisfying audience desire, has used a complex camera setup, so that an auditory command (from Jeff) evokes a visual response (from Thorwald), which triggers this time an inaudible desire (from the audience) that in turn evokes the climax of the film. It is as if Hitchcock were deliberately invoking a line from the story's buildup to its own climax: "They wanted a body? Now I had one for them."

The complexity of this sequence is underscored by the action in Thorwald's apartment being intercut with an ultimately abortive suicide attempt by Miss Lonelyhearts. Three isolated characters — Lonelyhearts, Thorwald, and Jeff — are markers for each other and for the audience, which is equally isolated since it can do nothing to aid the characters on the screen. The tension and suspense are excruciating, but the true high drama is masked and hidden: while the audience is desperate for a resolution and thinks it has finally been given release, it is being reminded that there is no escape from the consequences of its perverse will — which is simply a marker for the perversity of life.

The departure of Thorwald for Jefferies's apartment is another instance of privileged information and audience perversity. While Stella and Jeff are engrossed in trying to gather bail money for the arrested Lisa, the camera reveals Thorwald glancing in the direction of Jeff's apartment and leaving. Jeff is completely unaware of both the look and its meaning. The audience, perversely desiring and dreading an attack on Jeff, knows it is about to be satisfied once more. And when Thorwald finally appears, his arrival has been prepared for by a series of conscious and extended fades to black. There are about twenty of them in the film as a whole, only one of which, the penultimate one, is apparent and not real. Before Thorwald enters Jeff's apartment, there is an apparent fade to black — a blotting out, as it were, of Thorwald's existence if the audience so desires. But it does not desire his extinction. It wants Jeff's extinction — and at the same time it wants Jeff's extinction to be nullified.

The first indication that this nullification will happen comes with an element of surprise. Thorwald speaks. With his plaintive, "What do you want from me? . . . Say something. . . . Tell me what you want," he nullifies audience antipathy by suddenly engendering audience sympathy. In the story, by contrast, he utters only one word:

"'You—' I heard him grunt to himself. I think it was the last thing he said. The rest of his life was all action, not verbal."

Yet in the film, as in the story, Thorwald attacks. When Thorwald attacks in the film, the camera engages in its revenge on us for wanting Jeff dead. It puts us—albeit briefly—in Jeff's position, so that when Thorwald lunges in anger he is attacking us. We wanted a corpse and got it in Anna Thorwald. We wanted Lisa attacked and got it. Not satisfied, we wanted Jeff attacked, but before he got it, we got it. And in that instant, we no longer wanted it. (Since there is no Lisa in the story, the impact and implication of these developments occur only in the film.)

The camera is witness and agent of our most intense desire in the film thus far, as we desperately want Jeff saved. But first the camera reminds us that we are not yet ready to let go of the desire to have him killed. Thus, we are shown Jeff apparently going over the window ledge headfirst. Jeff's drive to live, his struggle to survive, gains him a reprieve, and now Jeff is going over the ledge feetfirst. The camera, perhaps through our most emotional urgency, leaps the bounds of the confinement of Jeff's apartment and is out in the courtyard. It answers our most pressing needs even more by speeding up the action in the courtyard—the only such occasion in the film—with the entrance of the other neighbors and the arrival of the police. Jeff does fall—our worst desires are satisfied in that respect—but his fall is broken. With the final, genuine, fade to black, we are relieved to learn that Jeff has survived.

After this final fade, the camera announces its freedom from us as agent. It reveals the songwriter and Miss Lonelyhearts together— what the sentimentalist would like; similarly, it reveals a new dog to replace the one killed by Thorwald. In a departure from anticipation, it reveals Miss Torso's boyfriend to be a somewhat pudgy serviceman more interested in food than sex. And it provides a close-up of the now bickering newlyweds, perhaps a foreshadowing of Thorwalds to come. Most of all it exposes a hitherto unexpected Lisa Fremont—legs in blue jeans, torso in red blouse, and determinedly her own person, as she sets aside an apparently recommended book by Jeff on the Himalayas and picks up *Harper's Bazaar*. The one concession to our expectations is that both the sleeping Jeff, with his two broken legs, and the wakeful Lisa are smiling. This concession turns out to have an edge, however, since upon reflection we recognize that the blissfully dozing Jeff in the currently cool weather is unaware of what Lisa is up to. More important, his back is now to the rear window. As a marker of Jeff and the audience, the camera then has turned its back on us as well. In cutting us off from any specific future developments, the camera declares its final autonomy.

While the story provides none of the details for the film's climax (Thorwald shoots at a bust Jeff holds over his head, and there is no attempt to throw Jeff from the window), Woolrich's original does provide an outline for the Hitchcock-Hayes treatment. Jefferies receives a phone call (as in the film). Thinking the call is from his detective friend, he answers "Unguardedly, in my own normal voice . . . I kept giving away samples of my voice." Soon he is alone and trapped. The references to the "camera finishes" appear here. Thorwald's approach is stealthy: "I never heard the door open." The only indicator that Thorwald is present is tactile: "A little eddy of air puffed through the dark at me." When Thorwald fires, "The flash of the shot lit up the room for a second, it was so dark"—the probable source for the flashbulb "shots" in the film. While Jeff does not fall from the window ledge, Thorwald does: "He flung over the sill on one arm and dropped into the yard. Two-story drop. He made it." The film's ironic detachment at the close echoes a similar irony in the story. In the final paragraphs, the story presents a summing up of events: Mrs. Thorwald was buried under the fresh cement floor of the apartment above; Thorwald and his mistress hoped to collect the insurance when his wife committed "suicide"; but Jefferies discovered the plot, and Thorwald is shot and plunges to his death. This leaves Jefferies to face his doctor. Sam announces the arrival of the physician (" 'Here's Doc Preston,' "), who enters, "rubbing his hands, in that way that he has," and declares, in the story's single understatement, " 'Guess we can take that cast off your leg now. You must be tired of sitting there all day doing nothing.' " The "nothing" performed by the passive Jefferies is as active a production as the nothing produced by the film's "passive" camera. The camera and Jeff, in their apparent constrictions, actually create a revealing window on the world of the film—both inner and outer—and on the world of the viewer.

Notes

1. I am indebted to William Rothman's *Hitchcock: The Murderous Gaze* (Cambridge, Mass.: Harvard University Press, 1982), which provided me with a series of suggestive readings of a number of Hitchcock films: *The Lodger, Murder!, The Thirty-Nine Steps, Shadow of a Doubt,* and *Psycho.*

THE SPACE OF *REAR WINDOW*

John Belton

In Book III of the *Republic*, Plato identifies two distinct and opposed modes of representation — imitation (or mimesis) and simple
narration (or diegesis).[1] Contemporary literary theory has inherited
this distinction in the form of mimetic and diegetic theories of narration, which range in sophistication from the simple opposition of
drama, which "shows" a narrative, and the novel, which "tells" it,
to the more complex narrative theories of Wayne Booth and Gerard Genette, which view narration as a fusion of mimetic and diegetic techniques.[2] Though the cinema has traditionally been regarded
as a dramatic form because it presents itself to its viewers as pure
"story" rather than mediated "discourse" (to borrow Emile Benveniste's terms),[3] it clearly mixes narrative modes. Classical narrative
cinema tells as it shows; indeed, it can only tell *through* showing.
Dramatic spectacles are staged for and then "read" by the camera,
and this reading narrativizes them.

Cinematic narrative techniques clearly rely upon certain codes of
representation that were previously developed in the plastic arts, the
theater, and literary narratives. Any notion of "pure" cinema — of
a mode of expression that is unique to the cinema and that has
evolved autonomously out of the singular nature of the medium's
raw materials — must be qualified by the essential impurity of a quasi-

theatrical, quasi-novelistic mode of narration. The figure most frequently identified with the notion of "pure cinema" within classical Hollywood filmmaking is Alfred Hitchcock, who often cites *Rear Window* as his "most cinematic" work because it "is told only in visual terms."[4] Yet *Rear Window* is arguably one of Hitchcock's most "theatrical" films. In what follows, I want to map out the representation of space in *Rear Window* in terms of its quasi-theatrical, quasi-cinematic nature and to suggest that the film, as a limit-text, explores the parameters of theatrical and cinematic modes of narration.

The credit sequence of *Rear Window* is set against three windows whose bamboo blinds rise in succession to reveal a Greenwich Village courtyard and the apartment buildings which enclose it. The film ends (that is, before the current distributor, Universal, replaced Paramount's original logo and end titles with its own) with a similar theatrical effect — the successive lowering of these same shades. Beyond the curtained windows lies a space that serves as both a stage and a screen, a space controlled by the authorial presence of Alfred Hitchcock, who invisibly raises and lowers the bamboo shades to open and close the film's narrative. This space is quasi-theatrical in its pro-filmic unity and three-dimensionality and yet also cinematic in the flat, multi-windowed design of the apartment complex across the way, which resembles nothing other than a series of little movie screens. In front of the shades lies another space that, though architecturally segregated from that of the courtyard, is similarly theatrical and cinematic. The apartment interior is not merely a spectatorial space from which the main action beyond the window is seen, but serves as a space for the playing out of another drama. Both spaces invoke notions of the theater and the cinema and use them as metaphors through which spectators are asked to read the action that takes place within these spaces.

The overall organization of the film, whose action is divided into distinct, temporally continuous units by a series of fades, resembles the act structure of the theater, which breaks down the action into discrete "blocks" of time. In this way the structure of the narrative suggests that of a drama built around scene or act divisions. Even the device of the fade is theatrical, resembling the lighting techniques of the curtain-less theater, which raises and dims the lights in lieu of the raising and lowering of a curtain. The fade is clearly a "filmic" device which draws upon theatrical convention; Hitchcock's use of it here, in the context of other theatricalisms, gives further support to the notion that the film is engaged in a playful acknowledgement of its own constructedness, an acknowledgement which it shares with its audience.

Within the film itself, the shades are once again lowered (and later raised) – this time by a character within the fiction, Lisa, who first announces "show's over for tonight," then picks up an overnight case with her lingerie in it and carries it to an adjoining room to change. Displaying the nightwear to Jeff, she describes it as a "preview of coming attractions." Lisa's dramatic gesture with the curtains and her comments about "coming attractions" function, like the credit sequences themselves which acknowledge Hitchcock's magisterial presence as narrator, to lay bare the film's devices.[5] Hitchcock playfully uses Lisa to unmask the film's status as staged spectacle by having her call attention to the narrative's two central "attractions" – the murder mystery plot that is "playing" across the courtyard (the show that is over) and the love story that is being acted out within Jeff's apartment (the coming attractions) – and to characterize them as "constructions." Not only are the film's two main playing spaces thus metaphorically identified as sites for fictional spectacle, but Lisa consciously identifies herself here (and elsewhere) as a construction similar to that created for the stage or the screen and presents herself as a spectacle for the male gaze. Earlier, her introduction in step-printed close-up as she kisses Jeff in his darkened room presents her as a magical materialization of male erotic fantasy, appearing, as it were, out of the dreams of the still-sleeping Jefferies. Then, wearing an eleven hundred dollar Parisian dress, Lisa introduces herself, dramatically turning on lamp after lamp as she recites each of her three names – Lisa, Carol, Fremont. In both instances, Lisa's self-spectacularization directs Jeff's (and our) attention away from the space of the courtyard and toward that of the interior of the apartment, effectively *opposing* the lure of one space with that of another.

In general, the film's narrative is built around a pattern of alternation from story-space to story-space, from scenes in Jeff's apartment which foreground the action taking place there to scenes playing out across the way, from Jeff as "actor" to Jeff as "spectator." And Lisa herself openly competes for Jeff's attention with the space across the way. Indeed, as she lowers the shades, she jokingly threatens "to move into an apartment across the way and do the dance of the seven veils every hour" in order to catch Jeff's eye. By the end of the film, with Lisa's entry into Thorwald's space and Thorwald's into Jeff's, the film's spaces have been revealed as continuous rather than segregated and its stories as intertwined rather than opposed. The love story can only find resolution *through* the solution of the murder mystery by Jeff and Lisa acting together as a team. Though still object of spectacle for Jeff, Lisa has inserted herself, as spectacle, within the space of the murder plot, i.e., Thorwald's apartment, where she herself is in danger. In a dramatic turnabout, Jeff's space suddenly becomes the object of Thorwald's gaze, and, dangling out of his own rear window, Jeff is himself inserted into this same plot; and, much as he earlier watched helplessly as Thorwald attacked Lisa, so she now watches as Thorwald attacks him, their relationship thus perversely sealed through this exchange of roles and places.

Given this spatial portrait of the film as a whole, I will both examine in greater detail how one part of that larger space — that which is seen through Jeff's rear window — relates to the other and explore that relationship in terms of the film's overall construction and narrativization of space. At the same time, I want to discuss the way in which the film plays with the differences between theatrical and cinematic notions of space and, through this process, calls attention to its own construction of space. In this way, the film explores and lays bare the nature of cinematic space, revealing it to be an amalgam of theatrical and cinematic qualities.

Much as the curtain-effect conjoins notions of theater and cinema (in that both traditional, legitimate theaters and first-run movie houses regularly used curtains to open and close their programs in the 1950's), so are the spaces in *Rear Window* both theatrical and cinematic. I am using the term "theatrical" metaphorically to describe a certain kind of *cinematic* space, a space that resembles but is not identical to that found in classical theater. Traditional theatrical space is the product of architecture; it is defined by the proscenium, beyond which space does not exist for the viewer.[6] Though, as Andre Bazin and Christian Metz point out, the convention of the footlights may tend to separate the spectacle from the spectator, the two, like Jeff and his courtyard within the film, must necessarily share the same overall space.[7] This unity of space is literalized in

Rear Window through its single-set construction, which imposes certain theatrical constraints upon the action.

At the other end of the film's spatial spectrum lies what I would call "cinematic" film space, a space that is "other" for the spectator, who is necessarily segregated from it, physically prohibited from entry into it.[8] Not bound by the Aristotelian unities which dominate the traditional theater, cinematic film space is, with the exception of certain single-take films, such as *Rope* (whose space might be described, using the above distinction, as "theatrically cinematic"), constructed out of flat, temporally and spatially discontinuous images which the codes of classical narrative cinema have taught spectators to transform into an illusorily continuous space.

Rear Window plays with the differences between theatrical and cinematic film space, relying on set design and certain kinds of camera movements to establish a concrete, unified, theatrical space and on editing, framing, and camera movement to construct a more abstract, psychological, cinematic film space. At the same time, the film plays with the psychology of traditional theatrical and cinematic spaces, i.e., with spectators' attitudes towards and understandings of those spaces. In particular, the film exploits traditional notions of theatrical space as resistant to and cinematic space as conducive to manipulation for purposes of narrativization and then collapses the two, rendering both kinds of space equally manipulable and narrativizable, though this is achieved in different ways.[9] The theatrical-cinematic distinction is most commonly articulated in terms of the concepts "showing" versus "telling" (see Booth, or Scholes and Kellogg), mimesis versus diegesis (Plato), and/or spectacle versus narrative (Mulvey).[10] This distinction is in need of qualification in that showing and telling, mimesis and diegesis, and spectacle and narrative are discursive modes which differ in degree, not in essential nature; drama is diegetic as well as mimetic, telling as it shows, and cinema involves "both the presentation of actions and their mediation."[11] But what concerns me here are not so much theories of narration as the psychologies of different kinds of space in terms of their conduciveness to narrativization. In this context, space in the classical theater is, as Eikhenbaum argues, understood as a given, something to-be-filled-in, and resistant (though not entirely invulnerable) to attempts to reshape it.[12] It presents the narrator with an obstacle of sorts which must be overcome by the forceful presence of an authorial voice which directs spectatorial attention within a fixed space. Space in the cinema, inasmuch as it is flat and, through montage, discontinuous, is seen less as a given than as a construction; it is a transformation of the real, bearing the marks of an intervening discursive presence.

Both of the spaces that I wish to discuss are constructed: theatrical film space is a literal construction, a feature of the pro-filmic set design, while cinematic film space is a more figurative construction, the result of medium-specific techniques such as framing, camera movement, and editing.[13] And the nature of their construction determines, in large part, the role these spaces play in the film's production of meaning.

The set on which *Rear Window* was shot consisted of seven apartment buildings, most of which were, at least, five or six stories in height. The apartment houses were built with a slight forcing of perspective in order to enhance, through changes in scale, the illusion of depth. "At least thirty of the apartments worked — that is, they were lit and furnished to suit the characters of their occupants."[14] The sets are designed to satisfy narrative demands. Miss Torso, for example, is provided with a fairly open space because she is a dancer and her movements require it; the shape of her windows permits us to see her dance. The space of her apartment is continuous, unlike that of the Thorwalds. The Thorwald set, though apparently identical to that of the couple with the dog (above them) and that of Miss Lonelyhearts (below them), emphasizes the couple's estrangement; they occupy separate rooms — he, the living room; she, the bedroom; even the color of the paint on the walls of these two rooms differs, which is not the case for walls in any other apartment. The couple with the dog are routinely seen together, on the fire escape for example, while Miss Lonelyhearts, though alone, repeatedly moves from room to room, unifying, to some extent, her space by moving easily through it. Hitchcock's set design and staging turns the Thorwalds' windows into fixed framing devices which dramatize their isolation from one another and their discordance as a couple.

Each working apartment in the elaborate set was individually wired so that it could be lit separately. The lighting board with its control switches was located in Jeff's apartment, behind the camera, enabling Hitchcock to direct the lighting from a central location. The unique nature of the set and Hitchcock's decision to shoot the film primarily from the vantage point of Jeff's apartment forced the director to take unusual measures in his direction of actors. The movements of those actors across the courtyard were directed by Hitchcock—from behind the camera in Jeff's apartment—by using short-wave radios and outfitting the actors with flesh-colored receivers, a communication procedure which permitted Hitchcock to co-ordinate background with foreground action more easily.[15] This production information, together with the overall design of the set, reinforces the notion that the film's space is *centered* around the apartment of its central character. Contemporary theorists who link cinematic space to the codes of Renaissance perspective would view *Rear Window*'s spatial features as a further instance of the "centering" properties of cinematic space in general, which tends to address a subject whose position that space determines.[16] Thus Jeff might be said to occupy a point within the space of the film which identifies him, in a purely spatial way, with the traditional film spectator. At any rate, Hitchcock's art direction here has rendered the "theatrical" quality of the set design "cinematic." The set has been built for the camera and for the cinema spectator, placing them at its central station point.

The set design reproduces the conditions of spectatorship in the conventional movie theater. In this way, it is possible to see the film, as Jean Douchet and others do, as being *about* spectatorship.[17] Jeff functions in one space as a surrogate spectator, watching events on a giant screen or series of mini-screens across the way.[18] The basic desires which spectators bring to the cinema—desires for sex, romance, adventure, comedy, etc.—are realized on these mini-screens. Miss Torso's window, as screen, recapitulates the subject matter of primitive, pre-1905 peep shows which feature women dressing and/or undressing and erotic dancing.[19] Miss Lonelyhearts offers us the woman's picture—a melodrama of romantic longing and isolation of the sort found in *Now Voyager*. The composer's window, barred to symbolize his frustration, reveals, as Robert Stam has suggested, the essential scenario of a success musical, in which the struggling artist is finally recognized.[20] The couple on the fire escape belong solidly to the world of screwball comedy—that is, until the moment of awful truth when their dog is discovered murdered. And on Thorwald's screen plays a noirish crime film which reworks the murderous love triangles of James M. Cain.

In considering the film's set design, one must, of course, remember that Hitchcock, as a former art director and set designer himself, has always paid close attention to matters of design.[21] *Rear Window*, as a project, enables Hitchcock to indulge his passion for design. At the same time, the project poses certain challenges to him as a designer, especially the difficulty of working within the restriction of a single set in a unified space, which are restrictions that he had earlier explored in *Lifeboat* (1943) and *Rope*.

More so than these earlier films, *Rear Window* displays a remarkable coincidence of theme and design. The central character's immobility within the fiction clearly dictates the design of the set as well as the structure of the narrative. Since Jeff cannot leave his apartment, his world is effectively reduced to the immediate visual and aural space around him (except for occasional telephone conversations with off-screen characters, whose voices refer to a source that is actually elsewhere, although the telephone gives them a source within the scene). Everything else is excluded.

The confined space of the courtyard mirrors Jeff's confinement to his apartment and to his wheelchair.[22] As in the theater, there is no space beyond the parameters of the set. The exception which proves the rule is the narrow section of the "outside" world which is seen through the alleyway next to the Sculptress's apartment. Though it suggests access to an "elsewhere," through which we can see traffic and anonymous pedestrians, it is *as contained* a space as that of the courtyard. Indeed, Miss Lonelyhearts's entry into that outside space — she goes to a bar across the street where she picks up a young man — reveals its essentially confining nature; it provides no escape for her but returns her to an even more desperate isolation. The young man's aggressive sexual advances are more than she had bargained for. Though she successfully fights him off, her failure to find "her true love" in this foray into the outside world leads eventually to her decision to attempt to take her own life later in the film.

This spatial restriction and Hitchcock's reliance upon a single, more or less fixed camera perspective, which is firmly rooted in Jeff's apartment for the bulk of the film, would normally tend to limit narrative complexity, preventing, for example, cut-aways to other events taking place elsewhere in the city or preventing entry into other spaces or perspectives which might facilitate narrative exposition or broaden point of view. It would also seem to restrict the role of sub-plots, that is, of other characters and stories which might serve as foils for the central characters and their story. What Hitchcock has done is build his sub-plots into his set design, using the neighbors across the way as foils for his central romantic couple.

At the same time, this fixed camera perspective tends to limit the film's narrative perspectives on the action, such as we might find in the more spatially open work of Renoir or Altman. In *Rear Window*, all other narrative perspectives, such as those of Stella, Lisa, and Doyle, which initially differ from Jeff's in their refusal to believe him, ultimately give way to his perceptions, in large part because their characters are forced to share this spatial position, to see events from the single perspective which is his own. For Jeff, trapped at a fixed station point, there is only one possible way of interpreting what he has heard and seen; his stubborn adherence to his reading of events is partially understood in terms of his immobilization in space, which prohibits him, unlike the other characters, from gaining other perspectives on what is happening. Denied the mobility of others, his position in space forces him to see something that has been, as it were, anamorphically encoded into a larger representation, like the death's head in Hans Holbein's *The Ambassadors* (1533). One might argue, then, that the film presents us with two psycho-spatial systems; by "psycho-spatial," I mean that the spaces exist as perceived from different subjective perspectives—1) Jeff's and 2) that of the characters around him. In this way, Jeff, who is figuratively de-centered in his variance from the perspective of other, more mobile (and thus presumably more "objective") characters, attempts to re-center the views of others around his deviant, de-centered view. Thus the more that the other characters come to share his space—such as Lisa who moves in on him and spends the night—the more able they are to share his understanding of what has and is still taking place across the courtyard.

The film not only overcomes the potential restriction imposed on it by the set's unity of space, but it actually uses that restriction, transforming it into a *productive* limitation, which serves to further reinforce the confined nature of Jeff's perspective and our forced identification with it—without sacrificing the narrative diversity of more conventional screenplays. In short, Hitchcock's script makes the film's spaces and the set design perform double duty: the set both establishes a concrete playing space for the immediate action and, at the same time, functions abstractly, referring to other, unseen spaces. For example, although we never get to see Lisa's fashionable, uptown apartment, it nonetheless exists for us, metaphorically displaced (and down-graded in status) in the apartments of Miss Torso and Miss Lonelyhearts.

As Lisa prepares dinner from "21" for Jeff, Jeff watches Miss Lonelyhearts welcome and toast an imaginary male guest. She drinks alone by herself, starts to cry, and then buries her head in her arms. Unaware of the implicit similarity between Miss Lonelyhearts and Lisa, who is also preparing a dinner for a man (Jeff) who is "not really there" for her, i.e., who has withdrawn from any emotional commitment to her, Jeff comments that "at least that's something you'll never have to worry about." Lisa, acknowledging her kinship with Miss Lonelyhearts, replies: "Oh? You can see my apartment from here, all the way up on 63rd Street?"

Jeff, in turn, likens Lisa to Miss Torso instead, who is entertaining three men in her flat: "No, not exactly," he replies, "but we have a little apartment here that's probably about as popular as yours. You remember, of course, Miss Torso?"

When Jeff cynically comments that Miss Torso has chosen the most prosperous-looking man for her date, Lisa informs Jeff that "she's not in love with him — or any of them."

> Jeff: "Oh — how can you tell that from here?"
> Lisa: "You said it resembled my apartment, didn't you?"

In correcting Jeff's reading of the action, Lisa identifies her own, empty socializing with Miss Torso's, using the latter's space and activity to temporarily "stand in" for her own, off-screen activities. In this way, the courtyard set takes on a metaphorical function, and its spaces become sites for the vicarious playing out of fantasy scenarios projected upon it from another space, that of the interior of Jeff's apartment.

It has become by now a critical commonplace to connect the activities in Jeff's apartment with those in the apartments across the way. Jean Douchet, for example, interprets what Jeff sees in the apartments opposite him as projections of his own desires.[23] Robin Wood views each character or story as functioning to comment on Jeff's relationship with Lisa.[24] The squabbling Thorwalds and the

85

overly amorous newlyweds thus become projected options for Jeff if he were to marry Lisa, and both options are portrayed as equally unacceptable. Hitchcock's direction often supports this notion of projected options. For instance, in their first scene together, Lisa asks Jeff to leave his job at the magazine and the single, vagabond-like existence it promotes. As she seductively pleads "isn't it time you came home," the camera dollies in and reframes the couple to include the newlyweds' closed window in the background, associating her indirect proposal of marriage with them.

By the same token, it is surely no coincidence that the Thorwalds' apartment is *directly opposite* Jeff's and at a level that is approximately the same as his own. Indeed, its frequent presence in the background of scenes that take place in Jeff's apartment subtly colors our reading of those scenes. Most significantly, it provides a crucial point of reference at the conclusion of Jeff's first argument with Lisa, when he refuses to leave the magazine and become a fashion photographer. As Lisa begins to set the table for dinner, Jeff looks at the Thorwald apartment which is also engaged in dinner activity. The mirroring that takes place here is rather complex. Thorwald, who in several respects reflects Jeff's notion of marriage as entrapment and whose plight is compounded by the fact that his wife is an invalid, serves her dinner in bed. She openly rejects this husbandly gesture by tossing aside the flower which he had put on her tray. Meanwhile, Lisa, whom Jeff has just rebuffed, prepares and serves dinner to Jeff, who is also, like Mrs. Thorwald, an invalid. Though Jeff seems to identify himself with Thorwald as the henpecked husband in a bad marriage, Hitchcock complicates this identification by likening Jeff, as ungrateful, cranky invalid, to Mrs. Thorwald. The sequence clearly confounds any simple theory of projection that might reduce the relationship between the film's foreground and background to that of one-for-one allegory.

The use of the newlyweds' and the Thorwalds' apartments cited above represents one way in which Hitchcock can make his set design function meaningfully within the narrative. But in order to achieve this in these scenes, Hitchcock needs to *articulate* a relationship between the spaces of the actual set. In other words, Hitchcock *reconstructs*, as it were, the overall space in order to make it act as a signifier at specific points within his narrative, using camera movement (as with the newlyweds), editing (the Thorwalds at dinner), or some other formal device. Hitchcock narrativizes the space, in part, by drawing it into the temporal continuum of the narrative, giving it associations with specific characters or actions at specific moments. The distinction that I want to make here concerns the difference between construction and reconstruction, between an object, event, or space and a reading of that object, event, or space. For instance, the overall set design constructed by Hitchcock and his art directors sets forth certain absolute thematic ideas, such as the claustrophobia of the enclosed space of the courtyard or the literal spatial opposition between Jeff's and Thorwald's apartment, which might be seen as floating motifs without any fixed place in a narrative sequence. These thematic motifs exist statically within the set *before* filming begins. Their construction and staging have given them a potential for narrative realization that can only be realized by their placement in a temporal sequence.

Their reconstruction begins when characters enter these spaces and events take place within them, that is, when the shooting starts. Camera movement, framing, and editing create the space anew, either realizing ideas implicit in the set, such as the point-of-view editing which links Jeff and the Thorwalds during dinner, or reading the set in a way which elicits a new idea, such as the reframing which positions the newlyweds' window in the background as Lisa obliquely proposes marriage. In this way, concrete space becomes "psychologized," that is, it becomes related to character psychology. By a similar process, the original block of space becomes narrativized, that is, it is made significant for narrative purposes. One example from early in the film will illustrate what I mean.

In the first shot after the credit sequence, the camera dollies out of Jeff's rear window to explore the set. Though somewhat narrativized by the camera movement which "reads" the set, the set exists largely as pure spectacle—something to be looked at and admired before the story proper begins.[25] Subsequently, two elaborate crane shots survey the courtyard, moving from right to left. The first surveys the overall space, and the second introduces specific characters such as the composer, the couple sleeping on the fire escape, Miss Torso, and Jeff. All these characters are engaged in apparently random, morning activities. The camera movement that presents this activity is as much descriptive as narrative in effect. The movement functions merely to describe, as it were, an equilibrium, a state necessary to a narrative but distinct from the disruptive process that sets a narrative in motion.[26] Though the narrative has begun, nothing of major narrative significance has been initiated, at least nothing that implies temporal linearity or involves narrative causality. Indeed, the second crane shot is not continuous but actually *cuts* from the composer to the couple on the fire escape, deliberately eliding the space occupied by the Thorwalds. This enables Thorwald's subsequent entry to *disturb* the film's initial, non-narrativized space with a narrative urgency.

It is important to note that both of these crane shots conclude their "neo-realist" portrait of daily routine with close-ups of Jeff, his back to the window, *asleep* in his wheelchair. Jeff's consciousness will play a major role in *shaping* this space for us. Once Jeff wakes up, the story — and the cutting — begins, as Hitchcock deploys point-of-view and reaction shots to counterpoint Jeff's telephone conversation with Gunnison, his editor at the magazine. What is interesting about the editing here is that although it establishes Jeff's voyeuristic interest in his neighbors (the sunbathers, Miss Torso), it remains rather random in terms of its narrative function. By that I mean that there is no sense of a connection between what Jeff is saying and what he is seeing. The two spaces — that of Jeff's apartment and that of the neighbors across the way — remain separate. That is — until Thorwald enters. As the Willie-Lomanish salesman returns to his hot apartment, looking haggard and at the end of his rope, Jeff, complaining that he has had nothing to do for the past six weeks but look out of his window at the neighbors, tells Gunnison that "if you don't pull me out of this swamp of boredom, I'm gonna do something drastic . . . like get married. Then I'll never be able to go anywhere."

As Jeff and Gunnison talk off-screen about marriage, we see the Thorwalds' apartment in which the tired husband is greeted by a nagging wife. For the first time in the film, the dialogue and the visual action coincide.[27] Thorwald is identified with "doing something drastic," an identification which sticks with him as a character. An expectation is introduced which will soon be realized. At the same time, Jeff's perception of the Thorwalds' marriage as a kind of imprisonment and denial of free movement — "I'll never be able to go anywhere" — relates not only to his present immobility in his wheelchair but also to his potential marriage to Lisa. In other words, the first seeds of the narrative to follow are planted here and made significant for us by a kind of synchronization of word and action. Point-of-view editing and dialogue have begun to narrativize the space, i.e., to create meaningful relationships within it.

There will subsequently be references to the random events and characters seen in these initial crane shots, but, unlike the Thorwald story, their presence here does not introduce narrative expectations. The narrative recuperates, as it were, these events and characters retroactively, developing them into a series of sub-plots tangential to the central narrative. The central narrative — indeed, all these narratives — becomes tied to and organized around Jeff's perception. With one crucial exception, i.e., when Jeff falls asleep as Thorwald exits with "Mrs. Thorwald" on their way to the train station, the events which follow will be understood from Jeff's point of view.

The exception, I might add, is there to prove the rule. The narrative so effectively allies the spectator with Jeff's reading of events that, even though we see "Mrs. Thorwald" leave, we suppress that knowledge, preferring instead to suspend our reading of its significance until another explanation, more consistent with Jeff's logic, is made available to us. It soon comes in the form of Lisa's pat rebuttal to Doyle's evidence from eyewitnesses: "We'll agree they saw a woman — but she was not Mrs. Thorwald. That is, not yet."

The shot of "Mrs. Thorwald"'s departure reminds us of the presence of another narrating agency — that of Hitchcock, whose narrative "consciousness" here exceeds that of the sleeping Jefferies. Hitchcock uses this sequence as a snare to complicate our reading of the film's events and our identification with Jeff. Though apparently full of significance, the sequence refuses to deliver up its meaning to us, in large part because it is not read but merely described, presented to us through the same sort of omniscient crane shots with which the film began. In terms of Roland Barthes' hermeneutic code, this sequence-shot snares, equivocates, jams, and provides only partial answers.[28] Its meaning is incomplete, awaiting the interpretation of some reader figure and, in that way, permitting the spectator to suspend interpretation of it.

Two levels of narration are foregrounded by this sequence-shot — the "subjective" readings of events by Jefferies collide with the "objective" narration by Hitchcock.[29] Moreover, each level is identified with different, aesthetically opposed formal devices. Jeff reads/narrates via point-of-view and reaction shot editing patterns. While also implicitly bound up in this stylistic device, Hitchcock, as omniscient narrator, reads/narrates via camera movement. For example, the film's first act of "narration" occurs while Jeff sleeps, well before the coincidence of dialogue and action discussed above. After one of the initial crane shots which surveys the courtyard, the camera tracks from Jeff's face to his cast and from there to the various objects in his room (smashed camera, action photographs), which serve to explain the cause of Jeff's injury: he presumably broke his leg taking photographs of a crash at a car race when his attempts to get something "dramatically different" brought him too close to the action. Hitchcock's camera movement engages us in a cause and effect logic through which we assemble Jeff's "story." Thus implicated in the logic of detection and positioned/addressed as readers of clues, we readily identify with Jeff's attempt to do the same later in the film. This "narration," however, differs from that which begins with the introduction of point-of-view editing moments later — not only in its privileging of Hitchcock as narrator but also in its essentially *descriptive* function. It tells us about Jeff's character by engaging us in an active reconstruction of past events, of a previous story that will relate only indirectly to the Thorwald murder mystery or the love story. In other words, it does not *cause* these other stories or set them in motion in as direct a way as Thorwald's (or Lisa's) entry does. One might conclude, then, that Hitchcock plays with different kinds of narration, exploring the relationship between omniscient and subjective narrators, which are, in turn, seen in terms of the different "psychologies" of camera movement and editing. His use of these different narrative voices produces a layered narration, which constantly shuttles the spectator back and forth from one level to another and from identification with one narrative voice to that with another. In playing with different kinds of narration, Hitchcock foregrounds the process of narration itself, making us aware of the various mediating agencies through which the story is told.

The interplay between omniscient and subjective narration finds resolution in the final shot of the film, in which the omniscient narrator is seen to contain and over-ride all other narrative voices. The crane shot which surveys the courtyard and those whose apartments open onto it echoes the film's initial crane shots, providing a closure of sorts.[30] Yet that closure is over-determined, characterized by an implausible simultaneity in the resolution of the film's various subplots. The composer and Miss Lonelyhearts listen together to his recording of "Lisa"; the childless couple have a new dog; Miss Torso welcomes home her short, fat, soldier boyfriend; and the newlyweds squabble. Meanwhile, the Thorwald apartment is being repainted; the new paint covers over the bloodstained narrative that is past and presents a fresh surface (a blank canvas, as it were) for the playing out of a new story. The crane concludes its circular survey of the major characters in the film with a return to Jeff's apartment, where he is found asleep and with both legs in plaster casts, a comic doubling which functions as something of a "topper"—a gag which recalls and extends the slow disclosure of the courtyard space and final revelation of Jeff in a cast that structured the crane shot which opens the film. This gag is itself topped by the final image of Lisa, dressed for a globe-trotting adventure and reading (apparently) a book whose title, *Beyond the High Himalayas*, suggests her capitulation to Jeff's way of life. Yet this image is soon revealed as a deception, a piece of theater complete with costume (her "male" attire) and props, which has been staged for Jeff's benefit. She picks up a copy of *Harper's Bazaar*, a magazine identified with the "old" Lisa, and begins to read it. Her "act," which is designed to deceive Jeff, recapitulates the narrator's own "act"-ivity in manipulating/ misleading the film's spectators.

The neatness of the narrative resolutions which we see in the final crane shot becomes something of a joke on Hitchcock's part and draws attention to his own arbitrariness as narrator. Like Lisa who offers Jeff a preview of coming attractions and presents herself as spectacle for his gaze, Hitchcock ultimately spectacularizes his own presence as narrator. It is as much Hitchcock whom we have come to see as it is the story which he tells. The concrete playing spaces of *Rear Window* thus finally refer us to another, more abstract space — that of Hitchcock's narration.

Notes

1. Plato, *Republic*, 393a.
2. See Wayne Booth's "Telling as Showing" in his *The Rhetoric of Fiction* (Chicago: University of Chicago Press, 1961), 211–240; and Gerard Genette's "Frontiers of

Narrative" in his *Figures of Literary Discourse*, trans. Alan Sheridan (New York: Columbia University Press, 1982), 128–143.

3. Emile Benveniste, "Les relations de temps dans le verbe français," *Problemes de linguistique générale* (Editions Gallimard, 1966), 237–250.

4. Alfred Hitchcock, *"Rear Window," Take One*, 2, no. 2 (1969), 18.

5. The film's reflexivity has, of course, been discussed by virtually every critic that has dealt with the film from Jean Douchet and Robin Wood to Robert Stam (*Reflexivity in Film and Literature: From Don Quixote to Jean-Luc Godard*, Ann Arbor: UMI Research Press, 1985) and David Bordwell *Narration in the Fiction Film*, Madison: University of Wisconsin Press, 1985). My interest here lies with the reflexive aspects of the film's activity. Thus, I will treat *Rear Window* largely in terms of its exploration of the nature of cinematic space, hopefully complementing the work of others on the film.

6. Myerhold's Constructivist theater did away with the curtain and the proscenium shortly after the turn of the century, and the modern theater of Brecht and others repeatedly plays with the notion of the proscenium and with Aristotelian unities. I have used the term "traditional theatrical space" to distinguish the classical techniques I refer to here from modernist practice, in which a non-traditional, theatrical space is created.

   I would like to thank Tom Gunning whose comments on the ms. led to a rewriting of the discussion of theatrical space.

7. Andre Bazin, *What Is Cinema?*, trans. Hugh Gray (Berkeley: University of California Press, 1967), 1: 100–102, and Christian Metz, *Film Language: A Semiotics of the Cinema*, trans. Michael Taylor (New York: Oxford University Press, 1974), 9–10.

8. Indeed, only spectators *within* films may enter into it, as in *Sherlock Jr.* and *Purple Rose of Cairo*.

9. Boris Eikhenbaum makes this distinction between the resistance of theatrical space and the conduciveness of cinematic space to manipulation in "Problems of Film Stylistics," *Screen* 15, no. 3 (Autumn 1974), 25–26.

   Eikhenbaum argues the time and space in the cinema are constructions and that the cinema does not merely reproduce the time and space of phenomenal reality, but actively constructs them. In the theater, however, time and space are more or less "naturalistic," i.e., determined by the actual time and space of the performance. Thus, theatrical time and space are *givens*; they are passive blocks of theater which resist all effort to shape them. For him, cinematic time and space are not merely filled but built (through montage, camera movement, and other medium-specific devices).

   Though Eikehenbaum exaggerates the resistance of theatrical time and space to manipulation, his distinction becomes useful in describing the "psychologies" of the different times and spaces in the traditional theater and in montage cinema.

10. Booth, 3–20, and Robert Scholes and Robert Kellogg, *The Nature of Narrative* (New York: Oxford University Press, 1966), 4; Plato, *The Republic*, Book III and see discussions of mimesis and diegesis in Andre Gaudreault's "Recit Scriptural, Recit Theatral, Recit Filmique: Prologomenes a une Theorie Narratologique du Cinema," Doctoral Thesis, University of Paris-III, 1983, 57–138; Bordwell, 3–26; Laura Mulvey, "Visual Pleasure and Narrative Cinema," *Screen* 16, no. 3 (Autumn 1975).

11. Thomas Gunning, "D. W. Griffith and the *Narrator-System*: Narrative Structure and Industry Organization in Biograph Films, 1908-1909," Doctoral Dissertation, New York University, 1986, 36-37.
12. Eikhenbaum, 25-26.
13. Gunning considers the issue of film narration in a way which is relevant here. For him, narration takes place on three levels—the organization and staging of the pro-filmic event, the reading of that event by the camera (framing, distance, angle, movement), and the final reconstruction of this camera-generated footage in the editing. See Gunning, 37-40.
14. Joe Hyams, "Hitchcock's *Rear Window*," *New York Herald Tribune*, 1 August 1954.
15. Frank Scully, "Scully's Scrapbook," n.d., newspaper column in clippings file on *Rear Window* at the Film Study Center of the Museum of Modern Art.
16. See, for example, Comolli's "Technique and Ideology," Baudry's "Ideological Effects of the Basic Cinematographic Apparatus," both in *Movies and Methods*, vol. 2, ed. Bill Nichols (Berkeley: University of California Press, 1985), and Heath's "Narrative Space" in his *Questions of Cinema* (Bloomington: Indiana University Press, 1981), as well as Noel Carroll's section on Renaissance perspective in "Address to the Heathen," *October* No. 23 (Winter 1982).
17. Jean Douchet, "Hitch and His Public," trans. Verena Conley in *A Hitchcock Reader*, ed. by Marshall Deutelbaum and Leland Poague (Ames: Iowa University Press, 1986), 7-8.
18. One person has suggested to me that the array of screens resembles a bank of television sets on display in the window of an electronics store, a display practice that persists from the 1950's to the present day.
19. See, for example, the Annabelle dance films (Edison, 1894), *Fatima* (1897), *From Showgirl to Burlesque Queen* (Biograph, 1903), or *Pull the Curtains Down, Susie* (1904).
20. Stam, 44.
21. Here, I am referring to Hitchcock in a somewhat different way than I have before. His former status as art director has nothing to do with his status as implied author, narrative presence, or enunciator; it is merely part of what David Bordwell would call his "biographical legend." The relevance of biographical information here, like that of on-set production information earlier, can be argued only on a figurative not on a literal level. His biographical legend informs our reading of the film without literally existing within it. By the same token, a critical discussion of the film's set design ought to acknowledge any extra-filmic criteria that led the critic to focus upon it in the first place.
22. The sense of claustrophobia produced by the courtyard design is enhanced by the shooting of the film within the confines of a studio sound stage. Shooting on location (without sets whose perspective has been forced) would have resulted in a less centered space and one possessing less sense of being controlled. Certainly the sound that was recorded during production on location would have had a different, perhaps more open, spatial quality.
23. Douchet, "Hitch and His Public," in *A Hitchcock Reader*, 7-8.
24. Robin Wood, *Hitchcock's Films*, 3rd ed. (New York: A.S. Barnes, 1977), 69-70.
25. A similar conjunction of camera movement and spectacular set design occurs in the Babylonian sequence of *Intolerance*; in both instances, the crane shots have

a descriptive rather than a narrative function. Indeed, Griffith brings his multi-storied narrative to a halt in order to display his fabulous set.

In early cinema, camera movement is initially associated with non-narrative material, e.g., panoramas, and it acquired a narrative function only in the post-1908, Griffith period (though even Griffith, as in the sequence above, continues to recognize its descriptive status and associations with pure spectacle).

26. That is, it is the descriptive element of narrative process, not something that falls outside of narrative itself.

27. This coincidence of dialogue and action immediately follows Hitchcock's cameo appearance in the composer's apartment. Bellour argues that these appearances occur "at the point in the chain of events where what could be called the film-wish is condensed." See Raymond Bellour, "Hitchcock: the Enunciator," *Camera Obscura* no. 2 (Fall 1977), 73. Ruth Johnston made a similar point in her paper on *Rear Window* at the Pace conference on Hitchcock in June of 1986. Hitchcock's gesture of winding the clock here might be seen as a setting of the narrative in motion since it is followed, more or less promptly, by Thorwald's entry.

28. Roland Barthes, *S/Z: An Essay*, trans. Richard Miller (New York: Hill and Wang, 1974), 75–76.

29. Hitchcock's objectivity here clashes with Jeff's subjectivity, where elsewhere the two narrative voices seem to coincide or agree. Interestingly, this "objective" shot initially serves to prevent the audience from seeing the truth of Thorwald's guilt, while Jeff's limited subjectivity provides a more accurate understanding of what has happened. It is important to note, however, that Hitchcock's "objectivity" is ultimately redeemed; we discover that we, like Thorwald's eyewitnesses, have been had; we misread what he saw. In this way, "objectivity" has been revealed to be accessible only through a problematic subjectivity (our own misreading).

30. Closure takes place through two successive gestures, the crane shot *and* the dropping of the bamboo shades, which answer the film's opening and give the film a chiastic (abba) structure.

"THEY SHOULD BE TREATED LIKE CATTLE"

Hitchcock and the Question of Performance

Doug Tomlinson

Walt Disney has the best answer to the actor problem. He makes
cartoons, and if he doesn't like the actors he tears them up.

(Hitchcock, 1962)[1]

In the documentary the basic material has been created by
God, whereas in the fictional film the director is the god; he must
create life.

(Hitchcock, 1967)[2]

In his inimitable way, Alfred Hitchcock generally played to the
oft-repeated myth that actors should be treated like cattle,[3] delight-
ing in the confrontations it provoked with journalists as well as the
attention it ultimately brought his name. Ever the shrewd businessman, Hitchcock acknowledged that such press coverage was effective publicity for his films.

Across his career, Alfred Hitchcock presided over the creation
of hundreds of performances, many of them startling in their depiction of psychological perverseness and/or emotional abnormality.
Throughout most of that career, Hitchcock cast performers capable
of credibly embodying such characters; ingeniously, he sought effec-

95

tive ways to communicate visually the more complex layers of character emotion, psychology, and cognition. Early on, for example, while conceiving the climactic scene from *Sabotage*—and it will be recalled that *Sabotage* was the instance of Hitchcock's intertextual incorporation of a Disney cartoon "Who Killed Cock Robin?"—he made a significant discovery: the effective combination of gesture and montage created a more psychologically precise depiction of the "murder" of Mr. Verloc. While many of the key scenes in *Sabotage* were shot in a manner which foregrounded theatrical modes of performance, in this and similar scenes, a theatrical approach to characterization was inappropriate and perceived by Hitchcock as counterproductive.

Over several decades, Hitchcock continued to experiment with various ways to extend and develop the application of structural and choreographic approaches to characterization utilized in *Sabotage*; by the late 1950s, he had developed a full range of visual strategies which, in combination with synchronized gestural choreography, led to specifically cinematic articulations of character detail. Ultimately, such strategies allowed Hitchcock to *claim* less dependence on the traditional role of projective or theatrical performance in the cinema.

Of the rereleased films, *Vertigo* provides us with the most instructive examples of his predetermined approach to both the use and visualization of performance. These strategies find special significance in *Vertigo* when seen as congruent to the film's central subtext—that of Hitchcock's reflexive exposé of his control over the details of performance: Madeleine and Judy, the characters played by Kim Novak, are manipulated by both diegetic (Gavin Elster) and extradiegetic (Alfred Hitchcock) forces. In addition to the issue of control over the act of performance, *Vertigo* provides further illustration of Hitchcock's fascination with the performer/spectator dynamic that was a central focus in *Rear Window*.[4] In that film, James Stewart plays L. B. Jefferies, the voyeuristic analogue of the cinema's consumer who is hooked on the act of viewing the activities of others, but who, through his insistence on contextualizing and decoding the performed/projected images he sees, is ultimately vindicated. Rather than complacently absorbing the images before him, he analyzes their significance and thus proves his case against Lars Thorwald. In *Vertigo*, as Scottie Ferguson, Stewart is initially that spectator unable to free himself from those illusions created and performed

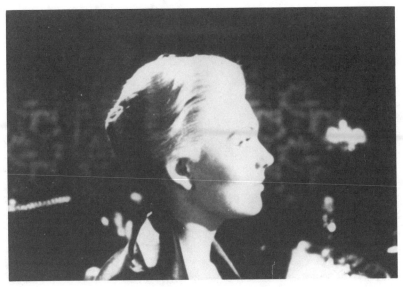

Kim Novak as Madeleine in *Vertigo*.

solely for seductive purpose by a trained actress and her skilled director. Only by freeing himself of his status as a passive/manipulated spectator and reactivating his skill as a detective is Scottie able to unmask the actress and her director as manipulators of human emotions.

Most notable of the many significant examples of Hitchcock's precisely predetermined use and visualization of performance in *Vertigo* are the zoom-in/pull-back process shot to describe the dominance of an attraction/repulsion syndrome in Scottie's acrophobic sensation, and the 360-degree rotating shot with rear-screen projection employed to depict Scottie's emotional journey into the past. In both of these well-known scenes, James Stewart effectively projects a variety of emotional states—from restraint to panic in the first, from confusion to panic and back in the second. Beyond Stewart's choreographed projections are, however, camera-determined and structurally conceived augmentations of performance which more effectively signify Scottie's psychological crisis.

In the first instance, Scottie is visualized as he hangs from the eaves. His gestures in close-up are not, however, the central mode of signification: precisely choreographed and *synchronized* to match

97

Kim Novak as Madeleine in *Vertigo*.

the directional needs of the extenuated montage, the gestural details of Stewart's performance are ultimately superseded in effect by Hitchcock's use of the zoom-in/pull-back process shot, which renders concrete through point-of-view editing the psychological trauma of Scottie's acrophobic seizure.

Later, during Scottie's mental odyssey, Stewart's gestures are once again choreographed and synchronized so as to fit precisely into Hitchcock's cinematically predetermined structure: as the background changes, Scottie's gestures reflect his mental meanderings, his haunting meditation on Judy, Madeleine, and Carlotta, and are choreographed so as to correspond precisely to the locations projected behind him.

Such scenes have generally been viewed as anomalies, as specific instances of Hitchcock's ostentatious foregrounding of technological ingenuity. Most emphatically, they are *not* anomalies, for many other scenes serve to illustrate, albeit more subtly, the director's consistent predetermination of both the use and visualization of performance. Three that illustrate other aspects of this overall strategy are (1) Madeleine's encounter with Scottie after she wakes up in his bed having "fallen" into San Francisco Bay; (2) Scottie's initial encounter with

Kim Novak as Judy in *Vertigo.*

the "completely refurbished" Judy in the moments before the mental odyssey; (3) Scottie's moment of realization that Judy and Madeleine are one and the same person.

Following his resignation from the police force due to the problems created by his acrophobia, Scottie is hired by Gavin Elster to trail his wife, Madeleine. Significantly, this undertaking is distinguished by its analogous relationships to the cinematic experience: on a perplexing odyssey through space (San Francisco) and time (Carlotta's past), Scottie casually observes Madeleine from a distance, his gratification, in the Metzian sense, ultimately residing in the fact that "the object being looked at does not know it is being looked at."[5] This cinematic analogy is, of course, intensified retrospectively by our knowledge that the woman Scottie is spying on is an actress playing a part. As such, Scottie's gratification is falsely determined, for the object not only knows she is being watched, but she, like any actress, functions to direct his (the spectator's) attention. And, like the paradigmatic spectator who indulges in the image as if it were a reality, Scottie pays the price of gullibility: once he embraces the illusion, he is trapped in a vertiginous construct.

Kim Novak and James Stewart in *Vertigo*.

A turning point in the narrative occurs when Madeleine falls into San Francisco Bay, thereby allowing Scottie to break through the "screen" and, by rescuing the object of his fixed gaze, establish physical contact. He then takes her to his apartment.

In a seventeen-shot sequence which begins as Madeleine exits the bedroom, Hitchcock's predetermined approach to gestural and structural signification is precisely indicated by both the consistency of the character's actions and the precise stylization of the editing patterns. Madeleine's highly choreographed, self-conscious "performance" begins as she exits Scottie's bedroom. With a combination of eerie deliberateness and subtly exaggerated sensuousness, she moves toward Scottie. Her uneasy movement through space signals Elster's (and Hitchcock's) choreographic predetermination, her walk representing what Michael Chekhov, in *To the Actor*, calls an "archetypal gesture," one which serves as an original model for all possible gestures of the same kind.[6] The very tentativeness of her step shapes her concomitant gestures: her eyes are wide open; her left arm, bent at the elbow, delicately holds her kimono closed; her lips, slightly parted, connote a luscious vulnerability. At numerous moments throughout the film, her gestures extend this dreamlike persona. Similarly, Scottie's desire is signified by the obsessive quality of his gaze. Initially shown in close-up in shot numbers 2 and 4, his gaze is fixed on Madeleine, his face barely masking enormous pleasure. In shot number 6, his gaze remains compulsively with her even as he (and the camera) moves. In shot numbers 8 and 10, he breaks his gaze only momentarily to retrieve and place the cushions for Madeleine to sit on. In shot number 14, he continues to stare at her intently even while in the process of sitting down. Ultimately, the extent of his fixed gaze is most strikingly reiterated in shot number 17 as Hitchcock continues to visualize Scottie's point of view of Madeleine, even from above and behind as he reaches for the coffee pot. While our understanding of Scottie's obsession is signified by Stewart's enactment of precisely choreographed and synchronized eye movements, that understanding is subsequently and simultaneously *intensified* by Hitchcock's incorporation of those gestures into a shot/counter-shot montage of movement patterns. Shot numbers 6 through 10 and 13 to 15 are most exemplary. As Scottie and the camera move toward screen right in number 6, Madeleine moves toward screen left in number 7, each subsequent shot developing the dynamics of their psychosexual interchange. In shot numbers 13 through 15 Scottie's descending motion is cut into the middle of Madeleine's similar action. Significantly, these sculpted movement patterns invest the sequence with that hypnotic quality of vertigo, and serve to simultaneously symbolize and prefigure Scottie's "fall"; had Hitchcock dropped back to a longer shot and filmed the scene in an extended take, the transmission of that complex character interaction would have relied almost solely on the theatrically projected effects of his performers. Arguably, the scene would have been less compelling, the characters less psychologically individuated.

A pair of scenes, later in the film, reiterate and expand on Hitchcock's choreography of gesture to accommodate structural configurations. Having emerged from the sanitarium suffering from, as William G. Simon has noted, a repetition compulsion,[7] Scottie visits the locations which "revivify" his lost love: at Ernie's he thinks he sees Madeleine, but it is an illusion; at the museum and in front of her apartment building, the same is true; and outside the flower store where Madeleine had purchased her "Carlotta" bouquets, Scottie encounters yet another woman with similarities to his beloved. This one, unlike the others, is dressed in green, a color previously associated with Madeleine; unlike the others, she doesn't lose her similarity when he takes a closer look. In this eleven-shot point-of-view sequence, the performers, especially Stewart, gesture in ways that are clearly choreographed to serve the signifying potential of this psychologically determined structural device: in the odd-numbered shots, Scottie watches the woman in green, his gaze fixed upon her; from the moment he first notices her, he is entranced, his eyes moving only to follow her actions, his posture erect rather than stooped as in previous shots. Significantly, in shot number 6 Hitchcock alters the distance of Scottie's point of view: unlike previous shots in this sequence, we see Judy in close-up; and, significantly, we see her in a profile configuration strongly reminiscent of Scottie's initial subjective view of Madeleine at Ernie's Restaurant. Where the director had rendered previous shots of this young woman in long shot, he here intensifies Scottie's obsessed state with a close-up. It is at this moment that Scottie's necrophilic desire to revivify Madeleine finds embodiment. When she moves off down the street, Scottie blinks as if to initiate a release into action. He immediately pursues the woman; ultimately, she succumbs.

A key scene begins as Judy returns from the hairdresser's. Entering the hotel room, her anxiety manifests itself through an obvious tension in her hands and upper body. When Scottie critically remarks that her coiffure does not match Madeleine's, Judy nervously clutches a comb, insistently moving it through her hair in a downward pattern, in direct opposition to Scottie's proposed scenario of pinning it *up*. Finally succumbing to Scottie's plea for indulgence, Judy's musculature softens as she haltingly moves away from Scottie and toward the bathroom, where the final transfiguration into Madeleine will occur: the rounding of her shoulders and neck suggests her ultimate introspective withdrawal, the defeat of resistance. The inward thrust prefigures the rebirth of the simulacrum — Madeleine.

A series of ten shots precedes the aforementioned 360-degree circular tracking shot which illustrates the culmination of Scottie's emotional and psychological journey. In this ten-shot sequence, Kim Novak's performance as the reconstituted Madeleine and James Stewart's as the obsessed necrophilic are again both highly choreographed for insertion into another precisely determined visual structure. Stewart's presentation of Scottie's traumatized condition is, however, effectively intensified by Hitchcock's deployment of a series of extra-performance strategies: a point-of-view structure, a profile composition, a penetrating camera movement, and an alteration in shot distance.

Visually, the most prominent strategy involves Hitchcock's infusion of a bluish-green haze into Scottie's subjective view of the bathroom door in shot number 1 to heighten the depiction of Scottie's psychological state and specifically to signify his necrophilic desire. As Donald Spoto has pointed out in *The Art of Alfred Hitchcock*: "green is, after all, the traditional stage color for the manifestation of spirits."[8]

In shot number 2, as Scottie hears the sound of the door opening, he cautiously turns to face Judy, pausing partway through this action in that postural configuration which William Rothman has argued Hitchcock used to signify interiority:[9] as Scottie is visualized in profile, we witness his consternation — his head is tipped forward, his brow slightly furrowed, his mouth ajar. As Scottie turns directly toward the camera and Judy, Hitchcock *tracks in* closer, significantly intensifying the impact of the moment on Scottie as projected by James Stewart's altering facial expression. Following shot number 3, in which Hitchcock visualizes Scottie's point of view of Judy enshrouded in that ghostly green haze, Scottie's facial gestures and upper-body posture alter significantly, his anticipation of fulfilled desire signified both by the obsessively focused quality of his gaze and by the accentuated movement of his throat as he swallows (an action which paradoxically signifies both Scottie's fear and desire). In shot numbers 6 and 8 his lips begin to part, his facial muscles begin to relax into a smile. In shot number 10 he girds himself, commits another accentuated swallow, then, parting his lips, moves toward Judy and the camera.

The final strategy Hitchcock uses to intensify Stewart's depiction of Scottie's anticipatory state is the change in shot distance between number 6 and number 8. Altering the shot scale from a medium shot to a tight close-up not only signifies an intensification of the character's thought processes, but serves to deepen spectatorial involvement with Scottie's desire.

Moments later, the history of Madeleine's death begins to emerge. Two lines of dialogue, uttered in seeming innocence by Judy, but having obvious double meaning for the viewer in retrospect, provide an initial key: when Scottie asks for a kiss, Judy replies, "Too late, *I've got my face on*" (the Madeleine mask); when he asks for instructions on how to fasten her necklace, she responds with, "Can't you *see?*"

The ensuing scene provides Hitchcock the opportunity to display yet more technical wizardry: again, Hitchcock starts with a potent persona created by James Stewart, but he succinctly heightens the impact of Scottie's psychological realization of Judy's complicity through a montage of structures: point-of-view editing, zoom shot, match cut, flashback editing, and superimposition. Once again, the centrality of projective performance is minimized while directional systems of signification are simultaneously maximized.

Having secured her necklace, Scottie gazes into the mirror, his face suddenly transfixed by what he *does* see. His eyes blink once as if to refocus, then settle, staring at a fixed point. Signifying interiority, Hitchcock visualizes Scottie in profile: his brow is furrowed, his mouth slightly ajar, his right hand stopped in mid-movement. Hitchcock then *moves the camera in* for a close-up of Scottie in this position, symbolically penetrating his cognitive process. Then, echoing Scottie's earlier discovery at the museum, in which he *detected* that Madeleine did her hair like Carlotta and carried a bouquet identical to the one Carlotta holds in the portrait, Hitchcock *zooms into* Judy's necklace, match cuts to *Carlotta's* necklace in the museum portrait, reverse-tracks to reveal Madeleine seated in front of the portrait, then reverses further to the position in the museum previously established as being held by Scottie. Onto that final visual field Hitchcock superimposes Scottie's face as he stands behind Judy.

Importantly, this action occurs in front of a mirror, Scottie perceiving Judy on that symbolic screen, and thereby recognizing her as a projected image. Significantly, the third, and only, extended shot of this narrative moment is rendered through a reverse camera movement, thereby signifying Scottie's psychological release from the illusion Judy and Gavin created to divert his attention. Another director might have chosen to place the responsibility to communicate this realization solely on the performer, using gesture to signify cognition; here, Hitchcock communicates both the process of cognition as well as the psychological impact through a montage of effects.

Ultimately, this moment precipitates a final visit to the mission at San Juan Bautista and the full blossoming of Scottie's sadistic sensibility. As he forces Judy up the tower, Scottie reveals his knowledge of her deceit; the diatribe that he delivers as they ascend the tower steps includes dialogue that establishes Gavin Elster's and, by extension, Scottie's acts as analogous to the film director's traditional role in creating performance: "You played the wife very well, Judy. He made you over, didn't he. He made you over just like I made you over. Only better. Not only the clothes and the hair, but the look and the manner and the words. And those beautiful phony trances. . . . And then what did he do? Did he train you? Did he rehearse you? Did he tell you exactly what to do, what to say?" Symbolically ascending from the pit of despair as the duped lover to the heights of masculine dominance, Scottie berates the seductress, chiding her for being a pawn in the hands of her creators, and belittling her for destroying the fantasy by becoming an individual with an emotional and psychological makeup other than the one designed for her: the actress is to be all the director insists that she be, not a woman with an uncontrollable and unpredictable artistic personality. For Hitchcock and his surrogate directors (both Gavin Elster and Scottie Ferguson), individual talent is to be applauded, so long as it does not interfere with the predetermined agenda; hence, before the fade out, Judy must pay the price for unacceptable individualism.

Lest it seem that only specific scenes with technological incursions bear the mark of Hitchcock's controlling agenda, scenes with less obvious editing should also be examined. While each of the three scenes I have analyzed provides evidence of Hitchcock's predetermination of the details of performance for insertion into a montage structure, Hitchcock's predetermination of the use and visualization of performance in non-montage scenes can also be detected. An often criticized scene — as Judy writes her letter of confession — serves as perhaps a too obvious, but nonetheless instructive, example. As Robin Wood has noted in his book, *Hitchcock's Films*, "One becomes uncomfortably aware of the director behind the camera telling her 'Now do this. . . . Now do that.'"[10]

While not disagreeing with the criticism that this scene displays some of the potentially negative ramifications of Hitchcock's authorial control, I would argue that, as it now exists, this scene is crucial in its function as a reflexive, demystifying exposé of both Judy Barton and Kim Novak as actresses responding to directorial demands.[11] Unlike the acrophobic montage, or other examples I've analyzed, this scene is *not* highly edited, the performer *not* inherently restricted by the structural demands of Hitchcock's cinematic articulation. Here, I would argue, Hitchcock was intentionally foregrounding his reflexive strategy—his ongoing commentary in the film on acting and directing in the cinema—by revealing Judy's erratic behavior as a reflection of her amateur status as an actress, specifically the confusion between her role as Madeleine and her identity as Judy.[12] Here the performance is controlled so as to signify by analogy the extent to which *all* her actions have been controlled.

The closing shot of *Vertigo* provides a further example of such control of gesture in a performed scene, while the analysis of it epitomizes the benefits of reading Hitchcock's gestural signifiers. Having experienced the devastating results of this return to the cathartic scene, Scottie has *seemingly* been released from his acrophobic condition; while he is able to stand at the edge of the precipice, his posture is symbolically open and vulnerable.[13] In this *postural duplication* of the fall experienced during his post-trial nightmare, Scottie's legs are spread apart in a wide stance, his arms open to the side, his hands loosely distended. As the image fades, Scottie's head tilts upward, as if preparing to fall.[14] Since his nightmare had ended with a violent awakening that ultimately prompted his yearlong incarceration in a sanitarium, one could argue that Hitchcock's reiteration of that posture is meant to suggest Scottie's imminent plunge into a darker, more debilitating despair. Hitchcock, however, fades to black without resolving the future, leaving the spectator in a state of debilitating emotional ambivalence: the fear he'll fall, the desire to see him jump.[15]

When, in 1972, Charles Thomas Samuels accused Hitchcock of making live-action animated films, Hitchcock emphatically replied: "I know every shot we'll end up with because the planning stage has been so complete. What mystifies me is why so many other filmmakers need to see things on the screen before they edit, whereas a musician can hear his music simply by looking at the notes and lines of his score. Why shouldn't we do the same?"[16]

Nevertheless, Alfred Hitchcock was highly appreciative of the art of performance. He admired the great talents of the stage and screen and often invited them to work with him. Perversely, he often downplayed the importance of the professional training and capabilities of the performers he employed. As a director, he tended to consider his performers as employees hired for their professional acumen and status rather than as artists with whom he could actively collaborate, generally relying on both his performer's talent and professional image and the ideal spectator's knowledge of that established persona to create the first layer of a character's meaning. Alfred Hitchcock generally disapproved of his performers indulging in a theatrically based psychological construct; his difficulty with Montgomery Clift on *I Confess* and his subsequent avoidance of Method performers provide direct proof. As Hitchcock complained to Charles Higham, "You can't get them to look the way you want when you want to cut."[17] Through detailed choreography of gesture, often in combination with precisely formulated editing structures and compositional strategies, Hitchcock, in fact, attempted to *create* the more complex aspects of his characters. In certain scenes, he simply needed his performers to embody physically a character whose psychological, emotional and cognitive dimensions he, as director, could control. For some performers, Hitchcock's direction was a lesson in precision; for others it was an insult to their profession.[18]

To the question of whether Hitchcock treated his performers like cattle, the proper response must be a reconceptualization of the myth: the cattle analogy makes most sense if one considers the cinematic frame as an enclosure. As such, the actors are not cattle, but are often subject, like cattle, to a confining structure. Unlike Walt Disney, Alfred Hitchcock could not tear up his actors when dissatisfaction set in; like Disney, however, he could control the precise depiction of significant character detail.

Notes

1. Alfred Hitchcock, interview, "Papa Hitchcock," *Chicago Sunday Tribune Magazine*, 29 April 1962.

    Another version by Hitchcock: "I suppose the best casting man is the novelist. He describes his character minutely and it's always what he intended. But [in film] we always end up with a compromise somewhere." Hitchcock, interview, "Hitchcock and the Dying Art," *Film* (London) (Summer 1966).

2. Alfred Hitchcock, interview, in François Truffaut, *Hitchcock* (New York: Simon and Schuster, 1967), 70.

3. In his remarks before the Cambridge Film Society, Alfred Hitchcock said: "I was once asked 'Is it true that you said actors are cattle?' I said, 'It's a confounded lie. All I said was that they should be *treated* like cattle.'" Here, as elsewhere, Hitchcock, with double-edged wit, both refutes and confirms the myth of his cruelty toward performers.

4. For an excellent discussion of *Rear Window* and the spectator/voyeur dynamic, see Roberta Pearson and Robert Stam's "Hitchcock's *Rear Window*: Reflexivity and the Critique of Voyeurism," *Enclitic* 7, no. 1 (Spring 1983).

5. Christian Metz, "History/Discourse: Note on Two Voyeurisms," trans. by Susan Bennett, *Edinburgh '76 Magazine*.

6. Michael Chekhov, *To the Actor* (New York: Harper and Row, 1953), 76–77.

7. In his paper, "Hitchcock: The Languages of Madness," presented at the 1986 Pace University conference on the rereleased Hitchcock films and included in this volume.

8. Donald Spoto, *The Art of Alfred Hitchcock* (New York: Doubleday, 1976), 328.

9. See William Rothman, *Hitchcock: The Murderous Gaze* (Cambridge, Mass.: Harvard University Press, 1982), and his article on *Notorious* in *The Georgia Review*, (Winter 1975).

10. Robin Wood, *Hitchcock's Films* (London: A Zwemmer, 1965), 97.

11. Vera Miles was originally to have played Madeleine/Judy, but was forced to withdraw because she was pregnant. When Hitchcock began to have difficulty with Kim Novak, he claimed to have had Marilyn Monroe lined up to replace her if the situation persisted. See interview with Hitchcock in *L.A. Mirror-News*, 10 December 1957.

12. Throughout the film, Novak's performance is exceptional in its precise definition of this confusion between self and construct (a confusion no doubt exacerbated by or a reflection of her working relationship with Hitchcock). Regularly her performance verges on exposure: she slips in and out of character, her breathy Madeleine voice giving way to her panicked Judy voice. This slipping in and out of character does not unnerve Scottie: it goes *undetected*. He has accepted the illusion, blind to its inadequacies and contradictions.

13. On the tower steps, Scottie declares himself cured. Significantly, Hitchcock eschews a point-of-view configuration in this final scene, thereby, in retrospect, encouraging an ambiguous response to Scottie's declaration.

14. Scottie tilted his head upward in a similar fashion before an attack of vertigo caused him to fall off the footstool in his experiment in Midge's apartment.

15. In some foreign versions of the film, a final scene exists in which Scottie and Midge hear a radio broadcast detailing Gavin's capture by European police.

16. Alfred Hitchcock, interview, in Charles Thomas Samuels, *Encountering Directors* (New York: Putnam, 1972), 234.

17. Alfred Hitchcock, interview, in Charles Higham, *The Celluloid Muse* (New York: New American Library, 1972), 108.

18. See, for example, Janet Leigh, interview, "Psycho, Rosie and a Touch of Orson," *Sight and Sound* 39, no. 2 (Spring 1970).

HITCHCOCK: THE LANGUAGES
OF MADNESS

William G. Simon

This essay deals with certain central narrational figures in Hitchcock's *Rear Window* and, in particular, *Vertigo*, with a brief reference to *Psycho*. My purpose is partly to describe these figures and
especially to formulate something about the significance of the specific usage of these narrational patterns. My argument will be that
Hitchcock structures certain narrational figures in these films in
such a way as to foreground the central characters' experience of
madness in a privileged way for the spectator, hence my reference
to the languages of madness.

The narrative structuring of *Rear Window* is organized in a very
formal way around three modes of presenting narrative information. One mode, which can be described as authorial or omniscient,
consists of the extended camera movements surveying the courtyard that constitutes the total space of the film. The film's protagonist, Jefferies, played by James Stewart, is usually established as
being asleep during these shots, so they clearly cannot be ascribed
to his or any other character's point of view. There are five or six
of these shots, which punctuate the film at significant moments.

The rest of the film is organized around two alternating modes
of narration, both variations within the classical style of analytic or

continuity editing. One mode is very largely organized around point-of-view editing and features the Stewart character and, at times, the characters played by Thelma Ritter and Grace Kelly, observing the apartments across the way. The basic content of these scenes centers on the series of observations made by Stewart (and, later, Ritter and Kelly) and the conclusions they draw from them. Their critical observation and conclusion, of course, is the suspicion, then assumption, that Thorwald has murdered his wife.

It is important to emphasize for now that these scenes are conveyed almost entirely through point-of-view editing employed to represent the art of voyeurism and that they are largely without dialogue, except for brief exchanges when Ritter and Kelly are participating in the voyeurism.

The other mode of narration, which alternates in a very symmetrical pattern with the point-of-view scenes, depicts the interaction within the apartment between Stewart and the Ritter, Kelly, and Wendell Corey characters (Corey plays Stewart's detective friend). These scenes are handled in a fairly neutral shot-countershot format with some fairly long takes. The essential content of these scenes is conveyed almost entirely through dialogue. The central issue for discussion is an on-going calling-into-question and criticism of the activities in and conclusions drawn from the point-of-view voyeurism scenes. In effect, these dialogue sequences present a series of debates between Stewart and the other characters. Ritter, and then Kelly, subject Stewart's voyeurism to moral scrutiny. When he decides a murder has been committed, they disagree and raise questions about his evidence. Once they are persuaded about the validity of his observations, the detective continues to resist, presenting persuasive counterevidence, usually from outside the sphere of the courtyard.

To summarize, the deployment and interaction of these three modes of narration involve a complex process of modulating the perspective over the course of the film. The authorial shots present us at points with critical information outside the perspective of the central character. The point-of-view scenes strongly foreground the voyeurism, and thus the perceptual and cognitive experiences of the Stewart character, in particular — a perspective which the spectator shares intensively. This happens especially in those scenes when Stewart observes the Raymond Burr character's activity for extended periods of time and attempts to interpret the limited amount of information he has access to through the windows. The more neutral inside-the-apartment scenes pull the spectator out of this experience and, through dialogue, present the spectator with a more discursive evaluation of the Stewart character's behavior, as when Ritter questions the morality of Stewart's voyeurism and Corey questions the validity of his conclusions.

The last point to emphasize about *Rear Window* is that in the debate between Stewart and the detective concerning what Stewart thinks he has seen across the courtyard, the Stewart character turns out to be correct. That is, the conclusions drawn from the voyeuristic activity turn out to be true and the counterarguments, presented through dialogue in a more analytic and rational mode of discourse, prove to be false.

In *Vertigo* there are several important areas of continuity with *Rear Window* in these terms and some crucial divergences. The protagonist, again played by Stewart, is again suffering from a psychological disorder, except that Scottie's complex vertigo/acrophobia/ necrophilia/repetition compulsion is infinitely more extreme and serious than Jefferies's voyeurism. The film is again organized around point-of-view and more neutral analytic scenes, with the point-of-view figure of narration used primarily to represent Stewart's obsessive and increasingly neurotic behavior, especially in the scenes in which he follows and observes Madeleine.

However, the symmetry of the alternation of point-of-view and neutral scenes in *Rear Window* is not as evident in *Vertigo* in that the point-of-view scenes, depicting Stewart's compulsion, occupy more screen time. The neutral dialogue scenes, involving the characters Midge and Elster, while certainly analyzing Scottie's illness in discursive terms, do not carry as much weight as the Ritter/Kelly/ Corey scenes in *Rear Window*. And the analytically edited dialogue scenes between Scottie and Madeleine are so infused with his fascination with the enigma of Madeleine that they reinforce rather than distance the depiction of his compulsive behavior.

The high degree to which the point-of-view scenes are used in *Vertigo* to represent the obsessive-compulsive behavior of Scottie suggests that it is useful to introduce new terms with which to formulate the alternating narrational patterns: terms that more accurately reflect the content, emphasis, and effect of these passages. I suggest rechristening the point-of-view mode as the "experiential register of narration." "Experiential" is meant to suggest that such scenes strongly foreground the subjective experience of the protagonist, that experience in both *Rear Window* and *Vertigo* being obsessively neurotic or psychotic behavior. It is also meant to suggest that the spectator's experience during such scenes involves a privileged access to the character's obsessive perspective and a heightened degree of sharing of that perspective.

The alternating narrational pattern can be called the "neutral" or "analytic register of narration" in that it does not foreground a particular character's experience as strongly and the content of the scenes frequently involves a rational attempt, through language, to come to terms with the irrational behavior represented in the experiential register. For example, in the scenes between Stewart and the Barbara Bel Geddes character, they attempt to analyze and cure his acrophobia, and later she criticizes his compulsive attraction for Madeleine.

In order to appreciate the significance of Hitchcock's treatment of these alternating registers of discourse in his films, it is especially important to consider the magistrate's scene in *Vertigo*.

The scene occurs after Madeleine's apparent death and after about an hour and a half of the presentation of Scottie's obsession, much of it in the experiential register. The action of the scene consists largely of the magistrate describing in words the circumstances of Madeleine's fall and the state of mind of both Scottie and Madeleine leading up to the moment of the fall.

It is, in short, an extreme case of a scene in the analytic register, which conceptualizes and objectifies the action and emotions we have witnessed in the previous extended section of the film. The scene centers on a legal authority's account of the characters' experience. The magistrate is excessively verbose, referring to San Francisco, for instance, as that "great metropolis to the north." He uses ten words where two or three would do.

The resounding impression of the scene, of hearing the magistrate's description of Scottie and Madeleine as being of "unsound mind" or of "Scottie's weakness, his fear of heights," centers on how incredibly inadequate this mode of verbalization of experience is compared to the way it has been represented through the experiential register. There exists a tremendous gap between the representation or language of madness in the experiential register, foregrounding the subjectivity of that experience, and the language of the highly rational figure of law and order. The alternation of registers of filmic narration creates this gap. And clearly, Hitchcock is privileging the experiential register as a narrative mode for representing madness, for representing neurotically and psychotically obsessive behavior. The behavior depicted in the experiential register is understood as the truth of the character's experience in comparison to the magistrate's inadequate verbalization.

To put this point in a slightly different way, I would propose that at the stage of his career exemplified by films such as *Rear Window, Vertigo, Psycho, The Birds*, and *Marnie*, the central impulse or theme of Hitchcock's filmmaking involves an insistence on the centrality of madness or varying levels of irrational behavior in human life. Hitchcock's project is to impress upon his audience the nature and centrality of madness, as well as the possibility of madness in all of us.

There are a number of ways by which he represents this theme, but perhaps the most important is through the rhetorical strategy I have described. In varying ways in both *Rear Window* and *Vertigo*, the subjective experience of neurotic or psychotic activity is privileged through the experiential register of narration. Attempts to understand and conceptualize irrational behavior through language, especially as practiced by authority figures, are demonstrated as inadequate. The authority of legal figures and psychiatrists is bracketed, ironized, even ridiculed for its inadequacy to describe and comprehend the irrational behavior represented in the experiential register. Once again the alteration of the two registers of narration, the two opposing "languages" of madness, is a rhetorical method, a form of address to the spectator to impress upon him or her the reality and power of irrational behavior.

Two other scenes in the Hitchcock canon strongly exemplify the effects of this rhetorical strategy. A little while after the magistrate's scene in *Vertigo*, there is a scene between Midge and a psychiatrist. They attempt to diagnose Scottie's breakdown in psychiatric terms. Again, the dominant impression is the utter inadequacy of their language to represent the reality of Scottie's experience as it has been conveyed to the spectator in the experiential scenes.

This sequence is really a sketch for the more complex and notorious psychiatrist scene at the end of *Psycho*. Briefly, I would suggest that the psychiatrist scene in *Psycho* is bracketed, perhaps even ironized, along the same lines as the magistrate and psychiatrist scenes in *Vertigo*. At the very least, it is not to be taken as a satisfactory explanation or coming to terms with Norman Bates. The psychiatrist's words ring hollow, given the extended presentation of Norman's madness in the experiential register over the course of the film. The scene does not provide *Psycho* with its closure. Instead it is followed by the great shot of Norman which reasserts his experience of madness, as if nothing had been changed by the psychiatrist's diagnosis. The psychiatrist may have clinically defined Norman's psychosis, but that has little effect on the experience and continuity of his madness.

In *Problems of Dostoevsky's Poetics*, Mikhail Bakhtin suggests that Dostoevsky had no sympathy at all "toward the psychology of his day as it was expressed in scientific and artistic literature, and as it was practiced in the law courts." Dostoevsky saw this psychology, Bakhtin asserts, as a "degrading reification of a person's soul, as a discounting of its freedom and of that peculiar indeterminacy and indefiniteness which in Dostoevsky constitute the main object of representation." Bakhtin claims that Dostoevsky was especially critical of legal investigative psychology, which is "at worst simply a lie degrading the individual."[1] These psychological and legal systems fail utterly to grasp the authentic nature of individual character.

A related emphasis is operative in Hitchcock's presentation of his protagonists in relation to psychological and legal systems. Hitchcock deploys the experiential register of narration to foreground the reality of the character's experience of obsessive and irrational behavior. The spectator is thus placed in the situation of sharing the experience, or at least of understanding its unique reality. When representatives of the psychological and/or legal systems conceptualize this behavior in language in more neutral scenes, their attempts resound with the "degrading reification" that Dostoevsky rejects according to Bakhtin. Like Dostoevsky, Hitchcock's "object of representation" is the authentic reality of the individual's experience, an experience that defies conceptualization by psychological and legal systems.

Hitchcock's great achievement in the period of his career exemplified by films such as *Rear Window, Vertigo*, and *Psycho* resides in the ways he adapted the editing procedures he had used throughout his career to the idea of madness. His structuring of the experiential and neutral registers of narration over the course of these films became a means of presenting this central concern to the spectator in an especially forceful and direct way, as well as a means for having the spectator contemplate the significance of the irrational. His mastery of the use of these narrational figures accounts for the power these films still hold for contemporary audiences.

Notes

1. Mikhail Bakhtin, *Problems of Dostoevsky's Poetics* (Minneapolis: University of Minnesota Press, 1984), 61.

HITCHCOCK AND BUÑUEL

Authority, Desire, and the Absurd

Robert Stam

At a Hollywood party in honor of Luis Buñuel, Alfred Hitchcock is reported to have called the director of *Tristana* "the best
director in the world."[1] And in an interview shortly before his death,
Hitchcock again expressed his admiration, specifically citing *Viridiana* and *That Obscure Object of Desire*.[2] Buñuel, for his part,
reciprocated, if somewhat less enthusiastically, Hitchcock's admiration, citing his respect, notably, for *Rope* and *The Birds*.[3] But quite
apart from this mutual admiration on the part of two artists little
given to praising their colleagues' films, clear and deep affinities
make their work an especially suitable object for comparative analysis. The two filmmakers form a pair of doubles, strangers on the
train of film history, rather like the proliferating shadow-selves that
haunt Hitchcock's films. They "cohabit," as it were, the same universe of concern, exploring the same paradigms, posing identical
questions even when their responses to those questions sharply diverge. Their superficial differences — like those of Guy and Bruno —
mask subterranean analogies.[4]

Both Hitchcock and Buñuel display instantly recognizable stylistic signatures. Each creates an idiosyncratic universe crowded with
self-referential icons. Both have spent a professional lifetime work-

116

ing out their personal obsessions, and one encounters fully developed in their later films what was embryonic in their earliest work. The two directors' mature directorial methods are also remarkably congruent: both are known for almost scholastic precision, efficiency, and preplanning. For Hitchcock, the final execution is virtually anticlimactic, while Buñuel has claimed to know, before arriving on the set, "exactly how each scene will be shot and what the final montage will be."[5] Both put their highly personal stamp on a wide variety of source material, and both treat actors and actresses as a blank slate on which to write, showing little patience for the empathetic contortions of Method acting. Even their overall career trajectories are in some ways remarkably parallel. Born only six months apart, both began working in silent film in the twenties. Both were partially inspired to become filmmakers by seeing Fritz Lang's *Der Müde Tod* (Destiny, 1921).[6] Both directed their first films outside their country of origin (Hitchcock in Germany, Buñuel in France) and both collaborated with Salvador Dali (Buñuel in *Un Chien Andalou* and *L'Age d'Or*, Hitchcock in *Spellbound*). And both sustained brilliant international careers into the seventies, "playing the cinema," as Godard said of Buñuel, the way Bach played the organ at the end of his life.

Even doubles have their distinguishing features, however. We would be wrong, therefore, to ignore the many salient contrasts between the two directors. Buñuel's radical anarchist politics are simply not collapsible with Hitchcock's libertarian-conservative views. Buñuel's frontal assaults on authority, with their historical trail of scandal and censorship, find but faint echo in the kind of devious undermining performed by Hitchcock. Hitchcock is merely uncomfortable with power, while Buñuel attacks it directly, provoking it into showing its true face. In technical terms, Buñuel rarely offers those virtuoso montage passages that dazzle in Hitchcock's work. Whereas Hitchcock fosters emotional suspense, Buñuel triggers intellectual surprise, preferring the shocks of recognition to the thrills of empathy. Hitchcock films engender anxiety; Buñuel's provoke doubt. The point, however, is that both directors work within the same "problematic" of the law and desire, authority and revolt, the rational and the irrational, even if their fundamental strategies diverge dramatically. My purpose here is not to prove identity but rather comparability within difference, as manifested in a series of thematically linked films: *The Lodger* and *Un Chien Andalou, Vertigo* and *Viridiana, Rear Window* and *That Obscure Object of Desire, Rope, The Birds* and *The Exterminating Angel*. My interest will be less in proving "influence," than in showing that both Buñuel and Hitchcock are animated by similar obsessions, some broadly disseminated within Western culture and others more particular to the two directors.

A simplistic dichotomy would pit Hitchcock the commercial entertainer against Buñuel the avant-garde artiste. But in reality both filmmakers drank at the fount of the avant-garde just as both labored, generally, within the framework of the commercial film. But while Buñuel drew from French and Spanish avant-gardism (surrealism), Hitchcock drew from the Germanic (expressionism). Which is not to say that Buñuel remained untouched by expressionism—like most of the surrealists, he was an enthusiastic admirer of *Das Kabinett des Dr. Caligari* (1919) and *Nosferatu* (1922)—or that Hitchcock was untouched by surrealism. The dream and fantasy sequences of Hitchcock's films, as the director himself acknowledged, were influenced by such films as *Un Chien Andalou, L'Age d'Or, Entr'acte*, and *The Blood of a Poet*.[7] If *The Lodger* shows the traces of "Caligarism" in its expressionist play of light and shadow, *Vertigo* reflects the "anguish of space-time" (Dali) characteristic of surrealist painting. The art/commerce dichotomy, furthermore, tends to equate Buñuel with his "surrealist triptych," obscuring the fact that the vast majority of his films were made within the commercial mainstream of the Spanish or Mexican industries or with large-scale producers like Serge Silberman. In any case, the frankly commercial Hitchcock, and Buñuel, with his disdain for the banalities of dominant cinema (as well as for the "artsy," impressionist avant-garde), have produced surprisingly similar bodies of work. Nor is it accurate monolithically to contrast the "classical realist" Hitchcock with the reflexive modernist Buñuel. For a critical generation raised on Brecht and modernist art cinema, more preoccupied with reflexivity than with storytelling virtuosity, it is easy to discern a modernist dimension in Hitchcock's work—foregrounded especially in some of the films withheld from release by Hitchcock himself—one which subtly undermines both the premises undergirding the institutional apparatus (such as the voyeuristic interpellation of the spectator) and the narrative conventions of realist narrative.[8]

The real relation between Hitchcock and Buñuel is not one of either simple identity or contrast, but rather of complementarity. To the gothic underside of Buñuel — witness the horrific ambulatory hand of *The Exterminating Angel* — corresponds the quiet surrealism and sense of the "marvelous" of much of Hitchcock. The extroverted Spanish surreality of *L'Age d'Or* is echoed by the understated "English" absurdism of *The Trouble with Harry*. The dystopian banquet and spatial confinement of *Rope* are recapitulated in *The Exterminating Angel*. Hitchcock's obsession with dream, his Bretonian *humor noir* and his love for narrative implausibilities qualify him as at least a crypto-surrealist. At the same time, his persistent questioning of conventional ways of shooting — one thinks, for example, of the long takes of *Rope*, the claustrophobic spatial restrictions of *Rear Window*, and the "structural" use of electronically generated sound in *The Birds* — reveals a director eager for technical challenge and formal experimentation.

The play of correspondences between Hitchcock and Buñuel operates from their earliest films. At first glance, the surrealist short *Un Chien Andalou* (1928) and the suspense feature *The Lodger* (1926) seem wildly dissimilar, yet their affinities range from trivial coincidences to basic strategies and concerns.[9] Both films deal with doubles, with androgyny, and with the link between sex and violence. Both directors make cameo appearances which are at once violent and self-referential: Buñuel as the man with the razor (the man who does the cutting), and Hitchcock as a newspaper "editor" and as a member of a lynch mob. (Indeed, while virtually all critics are aware of Hitchcock's cameo appearances, few have pointed out that Buñuel too "signs" his works with shrewdly apt and overdetermined personal appearances.)[10] That Buñuel wields a razor and Hitchcock participates in a lynch mob betokens the aggressive thrust of their "cinema of cruelty." Buñuel called *Un Chien Andalou* a "desperate appeal to murder" designed not to please but "to offend," while Hitchcock, masquerading as a mere entertainer, practices a more disguised and in some ways more insidious aggression in *The Lodger*.

The opening sequences of *The Lodger* and *Un Chien Andalou* already intimate shared themes and common strategies. Both open with a "prologue" revolving around an aggression staged against the body of a woman. The first shot in *The Lodger* communicates extraordinary violence: a blonde woman, backlit and framed in de-centered extreme close-up, screams in silent terror. The horror is decontextualized; we do not know where we are, who the woman is, why she is screaming, or whose viewpoint we share. *Un Chien Andalou* withholds its equivalent act of aggression until the tenth shot: a man razors a woman's eye. Here too the act is shorn of all context. We are given no clue as to the man's motivation and no explanation for the woman's blasé attitude toward her imminent mutilation. But already here we discern difference of approach within complementarity. The visible contagion of horror in the Hitchcock film fosters feelings of pity and terror, while the deadpan response in Buñuel favors an almost comic distance, underlined when the woman reappears subsequently with eyes intact.

Impressed by *Un Chien Andalou*, Hitchcock asked Dali to design the dream sequence for *Spellbound*, where, in an act of creative self-plagiarism, the painter "paraphrased" the earlier film by having an oneiric figure scissor eyeballs painted on the curtains of a gambling den. But quite apart from this somewhat fortuitous collaboration and coincidence of imagery, it is noteworthy that Hitchcock and Buñuel often aim their aggressions at the eye, one of the most vulnerable of organs and the one most deeply implicated in cinematic process. I leave it to psychoanalytically inclined critics to illuminate the unconscious association of the eye and of vision with other forms of dismemberment, especially castration, and with the role of the eye in the primordial cleavage of self and other; my purpose here is simply to point to the frequency of such images in the work of the two directors.[11] Their films are rife with injured looks and broken glasses: they are pervaded by the sense of sight wounded, menaced, or impaired. At times, this motif takes the form of direct aggression on the eyes. The razored eyeball and the empty donkey sockets of *Un Chien Andalou* and the scissored orbs of *Spellbound*, in this sense, presage the sightless face of Farmer Fawcett in *The Birds*, the hollow sockets of Mrs. Bates, and the myriad blind men of Buñuel's subsequent films. (*Tu me mirabas*—you're looking at me—reads the plaque on the cart of the peripatetic blind man in *Los Olvidados*.) Elsewhere, we find vision disturbed or impaired: Marnie losing control at the sight of the color red; Alicia's vision blurred by drugs; Thorwald's vision blanched by Jefferies's flashbulbs; Francisco, in *El*, hallucinating the priest's mockery; Mathieu straining to see the very images which torment him: Conchita doing her striptease or making love to another man. Time and again, it is as if the spectators themselves were being reprimanded for looking. Ocular laceration becomes the talion punishment for what Stella in *Rear Window* calls a "race of Peeping Toms." The hero of *Death in the Garden* thrusts a pen into his jailor's eyes. Francisco in *El* inserts a needle through a keyhole to puncture the prying eyes of an imagined voyeur. An angry Pedro in *Los Olvidados*, tired of the condescension of his guardians, lobs an egg at the camera lens, and by extension at the complacent bourgeois spectator. At times the ocular references are purely verbal: "Why don't you have a look around," the car dealer tells Marion Crane, "and see if there's something that strikes your eyes," his words anticipating the close juxtaposition of eyeball, drain, and blood that ends the shower sequence. And an anonymous woman in a restaurant in *The Birds,* looking directly into the camera, accuses us, on whose eyes the fiction depends, screaming: "You're the cause of all this! You brought this on!"

If both *The Lodger* and *Un Chien Andalou* are perverse in their visuals, they are also perverse in their delight in misleading the audience. Both films, in this sense, form veritable mine fields of miscues and false leads. Hitchcock crowds *The Lodger* with red herrings — Ivor Novello's gothic appearance, his half-scarved face, his fixation on Daisy's hair — which prod us to project guilt onto the wrong-man protagonist. Buñuel's red herrings, in contrast, are less narratival and characterological than spatiotemporal and linguistic. If Hitchcock is perverse in his hermeneutics, Buñuel is perverse in his syntax. The intertitles of *Un Chien Andalou*, for example, outrageously jumble the accustomed categories of narrative time, mixing the nebulous atemporality of fable ("once upon a time") with the reportorial precision of "three in the morning," while undercutting spatial coherence by a plethora of calculated mismatches and *faux raccords*.

The two directors' "ouverture" films also touch on a theme common to both directors — the problematic and unstable nature of identity in general and gender identity in particular. Both films feature "double" characters — literal in *Un Chien Andalou* and symbolic in *The Lodger.* The theme of androgyny and transvestism, meanwhile, is quite explicit in the Buñuel film: the male protagonist dressed in maid's clothes over his suit, his wild careening between behavior socially encoded as "effeminate" and assertive macho behavior, the androgynous pedestrian dressed in skirt and jacket run over in the street. In the Hitchcock film, the theme of ambiguous gender identity remains implicit, taking the form of hints at possible homosexuality in the protagonist — "At least he's not keen on the girls" says Joe the detective; "He is a bit queer" says the mother — and, again, the alternation of an "effeminate" swoon with decisive "masculine" behavior. Transvestism and androgyny continue to be themes in the later work not only in Buñuel — for example, the bearded-woman-devil-Christ figure in *Simon of the Desert* or Don Jaime and the beggar dressing up in the first wife's wedding clothers in *Viridiana* — but also in Hitchcock, most strikingly in the figure of Norman Bates masquerading as his mother.

The two ouverture films also explore what is to become a kind of dominant fantasy at the very kernel of the two directors' work — the obsessive intertwining of the imagery of love and death. Buñuel's account of his childhood as marked by a "profound eroticism" and a "permanent consciousness of death" pinpoints the subject which most deeply fascinates both directors. The love-death obsession took slightly different turns with the two directors, however, more morbid in Hitchcock's case and more utopian-romantic in Buñuel's. While Hitchcock was obsessed with the reality of murder, Buñuel, like many of the surrealists, was enthralled by the idea of suicide. Early in life Hitchcock became fascinated by murders with clearly misogynistic overtones, for example, by the brides-in-the-bathtub murderer, and by Christie, the impotent mild-mannered man who murdered eight women and who could only achieve climax by strangling women while having sex. Buñuel, in his formative stage, was more fascinated by a Spanish couple who committed suicide in the name of the unbearable happiness of their reciprocal love.

Love-death imagery, in any case, pervades the two ouverture films. Key moments in *Un Chien Andalou* — the man's sexual excitement triggered by the spectacle of death in the streets; the bloodied carcasses hauled toward the inaccessible object of desire; the protagonist's clutching at a nude woman during his dying fall; the final necromantic image of the half-buried lovers — highlight the lethal union of Eros and Thanatos. *The Lodger*, meanwhile, connects love and death by eroticizing murder. Indeed, Detective Joe's parallel summary of his deepest desires — "to put a rope around the Avenger's neck and a ring around Daisy's finger" — apart from implying a sinister equation (frequent in Hitchcock) between marriage and legal execution, also encapsulates the typical movement of Hitchcock's double plots: one ("the rope around the neck") involves the bringing of a killer to justice, while the other ("the ring around the finger") entails the constitution of the couple. One narrative is quickened by Eros, the other controlled by death. Homicide and matrimony are intimately linked. The opening and closing sequences, with typical Hitchcockian circularity, stress this link in their orchestration of repetition and difference. The electric sign flashing "Tonight Golden Curls," associated with murder at the beginning of the film, evokes wedding-night consummation at the end.

The mediating term between love and death, for Buñuel at least, is religion. Whereas Hitchcock surrounds sexuality with guilt, Buñuel suffuses it with religiosity, exploiting religious prohibition in order to intensify what the prohibitions are designed to prevent — desire. Religion becomes an aphrodisiac, a trampoline for passion. Sexual pleasure, for Buñuel, as an "exciting, dark, sinful, diabolical experience," only exists in a religious context.[12] Religion (the Law) thus anoints sex with a halo of tantalizing interdiction. Buñuel cites with approval Saint Thomas's idea that sex even in marriage is a venial sin: "Sin multiplies the possibilities of desire" and speaks of a "positively voluptuous" feeling of sin.[13] Lacan could hardly have said it better: the Law catalyzes desire. Indeed, innumerable passages in Buñuel fuse religious law and sexual desire in a kind of transcendental pornography. Francisco becomes enamored of Gloria's feet during Mass; the blasphemous debauch of *L'Age d'Or* is conducted by a Jesus Christ look-alike; the orgy and rape of *Viridiana* take place to the sounds of the Hallelujah chorus.

The "feeling of sin" in Hitchcock, meanwhile, is more melancholy and sinister than voluptuous. At times sexuality in Hitchcock becomes a prosecutable offense. The murder charge against Father Logan in *I Confess* becomes intimately linked to the question of a possible past affair with Ruth Grandfort, as if the priest were being prosecuted not for murder but rather for the crime of sexuality itself. Asked whether the two did in fact have an affair, Hitchcock once answered that he certainly hoped so, then added, with typical ambivalence: "But far be it from me as a Jesuit to encourage that kind of behavior." Hitchcock's response counterpoises the desire for sexual liberation with the tongue-in-cheek disavowal of that very desire. Hitchcock the Victorian clearly infuses sexuality with a guilt he himself finds oppressive, and much of the special poignancy of the "wrong man" theme in *I Confess* doubtless derives from this double attitude. Surrounded with guilt, sex remains at the same time one of the few radically innocent activities available to human beings. Hitchcock feels the guilt, and adroitly plays on the culturally instilled guilt of his audience, yet he seems quietly outraged that such guilt should ever have been instilled.

The most striking biographical bond between Hitchcock and Buñuel consists in their shared Catholic upbringing and Jesuit education. The implacable logic and inexorable punishment associated with the Jesuit order can be traced not only in the premeditated exactitude and artful symmetry characteristic of both directors' work but also in the motif of guilt, which serves as a common generator of fascination. Indeed, both Hitchcock and Buñuel can be said to be profoundly Catholic directors, not in a narrowly ecclesiastical or theological sense, but in a deep quasi-anthropological sense of working out the contradictions of a religious-cultural tradition. The religious obsession is close to the surface in Buñuel — there is scarcely any Buñuel film which does not proliferate in visual or aural references to priests, nuns, crosses, religious chorales, or theological disputes — while in Hitchcock this obsession is more discrete, driven underground, rather like Catholicism in Hitchcock's own Protestant-dominated England. Buñuel's Catholicism is of the Southern European, carnivalesque variety, while Hitchcock's is Northern, of the post-Reformation, post-Cromwellian puritan variety. Their response to a shared Catholic heritage is marked, furthermore, by a number of paradoxes. While critics such as Rohmer and Chabrol see Hitchcock as a quintessentially Catholic director, there is biographical as well as textual evidence of emotional ambivalence, of a "kicking against the pricks." Spoto reports that Hitchcock loved to throw stolen eggs against the windows of the Jesuit residence and then blame the dirtied glass on the passing birds,[14] and John Russell Taylor recounts Hitchcock's refusal to go through with a scheduled visit with the pope, on the pretext that the Holy Father might warn him to play down all the "sex and violence."[15] The anecdote, while not explicitly anticlerical, at least betrays a feeling on Hitchcock's part that the impulse which drives his films is not one of which the church would approve.

Buñuel, meanwhile, plays out the obverse side of the same paradox, mingling outspoken hostility for religion with secret affection.

Thus the repressed anticleric in Hitchcock corresponds to the closet believer in Buñuel. Buñuel's public stance toward Catholicism, of course, has always been one of provocation and sacrilege. As an adolescent, he and Garcia Lorca would shave closely, powder their faces, and masquerade as nuns in order to flirt with male passengers on streetcars, a piece of biographical evidence that merely confirms the omnipresent anticlericalism of the films. On another level, however, Buñuel's relation to the church is parasitical, almost vampirish; it feeds on what it attacks. His insistent desacralization depends on Christianity as a source of imagery and fount of inspiration.

Religion, pervasive in Buñuel, also subliminally informs much of Hitchcock. His "wrong men" recapitulate—at times comically (Roger Thornhill), at times tragically (Father Logan)—the Golgotha of their exemplary prototype: Jesus Christ. The full name of the protagonist of the paradigmatically entitled *Wrong Man*, drawn from his real-life model, "happens," in a marvelous instance of the "definitive by chance," to evoke the incarnation: the Christ in Christopher, the Man in "Manny," and God, etymologically present in the Hebrew roots of "Emmanuel." (The celebrated dissolve from Manny bowed in prayer before an icon of Christ to the face of the actual thief epitomizes, through its "substantial fusion, magical transmutation, mystical efficacy" the religious thrust of the film.) Indeed, both Hitchcock and Buñuel show a certain disabused affection for Christlike figures such as Manny, Father Logan, Viridiana, Nazarin. *I Confess* and *Nazarin*, in fact, can both be viewed as cinematic variations on a single premise: What would happen if Christ's teachings were strictly carried out in the contemporary world? The priest-protagonist of *Nazarin* literally follows Christ's example, while Father Logan obeys to the letter an obscure point of the canonical code—the rule of priestly silence—and responds with immaculate purity to a battery of temptations. But their *imitatio Christi* proves to be futile. Both protect murderers, and both are vilified. Father Logan's religiously sanctioned silence leads to the loss of innocent life, and Nazarin's unassuming charity is greeted with howls of execration. In both cases, strict adherence to religious principle leads to catastrophe, and in both cases the authors underline this failure by having antagonistic double figures deride their useless sacrifice: "I am alone . . . like you. You are alone. You have no friends," the dying Keller tells Logan in the climactic scene, in the same way that the thief mocks Nazarin:

"You're on the side of good and I'm on the side of evil, but neither of us is any use for anything." Thus both directors highlight the fearful symmetry of saint and sinner.

Both *Nazarin* and *I Confess* score the repressive antisexuality of the church. Pursued by passionate women, the protagonists of both films are too spiritually absorbed to respond to them as sexual beings. The ideal of celibacy, criticized in *Nazarin* and hysterically lampooned in *Simon of the Desert*, is subtly undermined in *I Confess*. Hitchcock's pairing of Montgomery Clift and Anne Baxter as leading man and lady inevitably stimulates certain erotic expectations in the audience. Hitchcock even offers a tantalizing "bracketed" sample of a possible romance—a subjectivized idyll complete with libidinous thunderstorm and a phallic gazebo—only to withhold its culmination. The film as a whole, similarly, withholds the satisfying closure of final marriage and implied conjugal bliss. Thus Hitchcock frustrates the hopes and desires of the spectators, who must ultimately blame the church for what seems a sad waste of amorous star talent and the denial of a legitimate cinematic expectation.

Love in occidental art, de Rougemont observes, thrives on obstacles. Romance comes into existence only where love is fatal, frowned upon, doomed. Buñuel's work, especially, both laments and celebrates *l'amour impossible*. Love in *Un Chien Andalou, L'Age d'Or*, and *That Obscure Object of Desire* becomes a tragicomic obstacle course leading only to protracted frustration. Modot and Lya Lys's clumsy attempts at lovemaking in *L'Age d'Or* are in this sense paradigmatic. Burlesque comedy and high tragedy meet as the twosome stumble over chairs, bang their heads on flowerpots and are interrupted by music and distracted by statues. The music evokes passion (etymologically "pathos," suffering), a constantly swelling unfulfilled desire, a perpetual tumescence never reaching climax. Love and pathology become indistinguishable. At times, Buñuel's exalted vision of love-death, almost utopian in its religious aspiration, recalls the sublime pornography of Bataille, where "orgasms ravage faces with sobs and horrible shrieks," and where eroticism is apocalyptic and danger an aphrodisiac. *L'Age d'Or* achieves the cinematic equivalent of Bataille's vision by having Modot, his face bloodied, ardently embrace Lya Lys as he murmurs "mon amour, mon amour." In *The Exterminating Angel*, Beatriz and Eduardo, in homage to Buñuel's admired suicide couple, make soft-focus *amour fou*, with a corpse at their side for inspiration, invoking the language of death ("the rictus . . . horrible . . . my love . . . my death!") while in the throes of orgasm. Death goads sensuality and aggravates desire. The only possible next step in this amorous escalation is mutual suicide (or is it reciprocal murder), illustrating de Rougemont's observation: "Sometimes even, [death] aggravates desire to the point of turning into a wish to kill either the beloved or oneself, or to founder in a twin downrush."[16]

The entire oeuvres of Hitchcock and Buñuel can be seen as variations on the theme of the *liebestod*—love and death. De Rougemont traces this occidental fixation back to the medieval myth of Tristan and Isolde, and it is significant that both directors make frequent allusion to Wagner's musical version of the myth. Wagner was one of Buñuel's favorite composers and *Tristan and Isolde* one of his favorite compositions. Recordings of the "Liebestod" accompanied the first screenings of *Un Chien Andalou* and the orchestra plays it during Modot and Lya Lys's inept trysting in *L'Age d'Or*. Buñuel returned to it in *Cumbres Burrascosas* (*Wuthering Heights*) as commentative music for one of the classical novelistic treatments of the love-death theme. Hitchcock, for his part, also returned to this Wagnerian theme throughout his career. In *Murder*, the piece is played over the radio. Herrmann's score for *Vertigo*, similarly, constantly alludes to the "Liebestod" (without ever quoting it directly), suggesting death as love's devoutly desired consummation. In *North by Northwest*, when Eva Marie Saint, double agent of murder and marriage, encounters Cary Grant on the train, still another variation on the "Liebestod" underscores their tantalizingly dangerous flirtation. And in *The Birds*, a reiterated shot frames Melanie Daniels, a record player, and a lone album cover—Wagner's *Tristan and Isolde*.

Since fetishistic love thrives on obstacles, death, as the ultimate obstacle, is the perfect spur to love. Love in Hitchcock and Buñuel, therefore, often takes on a decidedly necrophilic cast. The male protagonists of both *Viridiana* and *Vertigo* are obsessed with deceased love objects, in films which concatenate sex, death, and religion— the convent, the nun, the crown of thorns in *Viridiana*; Mission Dolores, the San Juan Bautista chapel, the nun in the bell tower in *Vertigo*—in a holy trinity of desire. Both films are actually two films in one—*Viridiana*'s first half ends with the suicide-death of Don Jaime and resumes with the entrance of Jorge and Viridiana's in-

127

volvement with the beggars; *Vertigo*'s first half ends with Madeleine's apparent suicide and Scottie's breakdown and picks up with his search for Madeleine and discovery of Judy — and it is the first part of *Viridiana* that resembles the second part of *Vertigo*. Don Jaime is haunted by the memory of his first wife, who expired in his arms on their wedding night. Just as the heartbroken Tristan weds a second Isolde in order to sustain the memory of the first, so Don Jaime attempts to transform Viridiana, the physical double of his spouse, into a reincarnation of his former love. He dresses her in his wife's wedding clothes, drugs her, and beds her, caressing her ankles and running his hands along her satin gown to the accompaniment of Mozart's *Requiem*.[17] The intense sensuality of his unilateral caresses clearly suggests necrophilia. Viridiana resembles a corpse, and Don Jaime's clumsy gestures toward consummation remain incomplete, as they must, for he is in love with death itself. (His personal history of unconsummated weddings thus repeats itself, first as tragedy and then as farce.) Later, he smiles enigmatically as he pens the suicide letter which binds Viridiana to him after death through the inheritance he leaves her. With a kind of sadistic self-slaughter, he achieves the legalistic version of the courtly ideal of a love that reaches beyond the grave.[18]

The necrophilic overtones of *Vertigo* are equally clear and insistent. The protagonist, Hitchcock told Truffaut, "wants to go to bed with a woman who's dead; he's indulging in a form of necrophilia."[19] Both Madeleine and Judy, while not literally dead, enjoy what might be called a privileged relationship to death. "Madeleine" appears to be possessed by the deceased Carlotta Valdes, and is thus her "ghost," just as Judy, in turn, is the "ghost" of Madeleine. Like Don Jaime, Scottie shows a morbid predilection for the deceased; he can only respond to a flesh-and-blood woman after she has been transformed into a spectral repetition of a lost love. Like Don Jaime, he plays God/Pygmalion by creating a "new" woman, coaxing a reluctant surrogate into masquerading as a deceased beloved, and again like Don Jaime, he prefers the threat of the abyss to life-affirming pragmatism (Midge in *Vertigo*, Ramona in *Viridiana*). The film continually associates Madeleine with ghostlike ethereality, with tombstones and suicide, and the fascination she exerts is clearly that of death, oblivion, and annihilation, a yearning for final release. This yearning is cinematically realized by morbidly eroticized camera movements.

The lure of the abyss is rendered by the subjective track, which buries the dreaming Scottie in Carlotta's grave. And the subjective shots depicting Scottie's vertigo combine a backward track with a forward zoom, a double movement of attraction and repulsion whose kinesthetic in-and-out is analogous to the sex act itself.

The coincidences between *Vertigo* and *Viridiana* range from apparently trivial coincidences to fundamental strategies and preoccupations. Both feature Spanish or Spanish-American settings and decors: cloisters, missions, bell towers, nuns. Both feature "offstage" wives, key characters who are never seen on-camera or appear only briefly, as in *Vertigo*, as a corpse. In both films, flowers are surrounded with funereal associations. Madeleine carries with her a bouquet on her tour of death-haunted landmarks, and later tears at the petals and tosses them into the bay. In Scottie's nightmare, the bouquet spirals and swirls and centrifugally pulls itself apart in his delirium. In *Viridiana*, Don Jaime keeps his dead bride's bouquet and at one point throws it onto the same bed where Viridiana will soon deposit a basketful of ashes. Both *Vertigo* and *Viridiana* focus on sexually problematic males, and both foreground structures of voyeurism via point-of-view editing (a feature generally rare in Buñuel's work). Both films create a dreamlike atmosphere, although they realize that atmosphere by different means. The first part of *Vertigo* is fashioned after a dream, and the second part is borne of a nightmare, and the film as a whole has the estranged temporality of the oneiric. Eerily slow and quietly gliding tracking shots in a scene without dialogue emphasize Scottie's dreamlike search for a wandering wife. Diffuse focus blurs and mutes the phantom of desire called Madeleine, while fog filters in sunlight produce an other-worldly effect, underlined by Bernard Herrmann's hypnotic score. In *Viridiana*, meanwhile, film and dream are entwined in the surrealist manner, which prefers to present implausible dreamlike events—the wedding veil, the crown of thorns, Rita's reported dream of a black bull, the somnambulating Viridiana depositing ashes on the bed of her benefactor—with clarity and precision, the superficial realism of the scene masking the madness of the conception.[20]

If we turn our attention from the male protagonists to the female protagonists, meanwhile, we find that *Viridiana* merits comparison with another Hitchcock film, *Marnie*, in that both films anatomize the psychic damage done by sexual guilt. Superficially, the two female protagonists are polar opposites: Viridiana is a contemporary saint; Marnie is a liar and a thief. Viridiana's vocation is charity, the art of giving; Marnie's avocation is kleptomania, the crime of stealing.[21] Yet there is a radical Genet-like innocence about Marnie's desperate attempt to "help herself." Both protagonists evolve from extreme sexual reticence to a highly problematic "normality." Initially, both are repulsed by sexuality. Viridiana recoils in disgust from the phallic cow udders, just as Marnie shrinks from Mark's "degrading" and "animal" touch. And both films trace the religious etiology of this sexophobia—Catholic in Viridiana's case, fundamentalist Protestant in Marnie's. Viridiana, after rebuffing Don Jaime's advances, ultimately "plays cards" with his son Jorge, just as Marnie, after angrily rejecting Mark's embraces, moves toward acceptance and implied fulfillment. Both are readied for this "normality" by a process of symbolic as well as literal rape. Viridiana is first symbolically raped by Don Jaime, then literally raped by the cripple. Marnie is symbolically raped by Mark's predatory interrogation and by a coerced marriage, and then literally raped on their "honeymoon." In both films wedding-night consummations are surrounded with morbid associations. Don Jaime restages the wedding-night death of his first wife with Viridiana as surrogate corpse, and her subsequent rejection of him triggers his suicide. Marnie's wedding-night, meanwhile, very nearly literalizes the sex-death connection evoked in their free-association word game, in which "sex" is followed by "death." Hitchcock renders their sexual encounter as a kind of living death, with Marnie's body rigid and her face expressionless as Mark advances in menacingly outsized close shots. And sex is followed, the next morning, by near death, in the form of Marnie's attempted suicide.

In both *Marnie* and *Viridiana*, the men exercise patriarchal power over the women, Don Jaime by virtue of his role as Viridiana's benefactor, Mark by virtue of his wealth and his knowledge of Marnie's kleptomania. The recognition of the female protagonists' sexophobia should not blind us to the psychosexual problems of their male counterparts. Don Jaime is not only a necrophilic but also a transvestite, fetishist, and voyeur. Mark's love for Marnie, similarly, is shot through with neurosis, pithily summarized by Marnie as a "pathological fix on a woman who's a thief and who can't stand for you to touch her." He belongs, along with L. B. Jefferies in *Rear Window* and Scottie in *Vertigo*, to Hitchcock's overcrowded gallery of sexually problematic males. His generosity, deeply involved with fantasies of domination, begins with a kind of rescue fantasy: he saves Marnie from joblessness by persuading her prospective employer to overlook her lack of references. He then blackmails her with his secret knowledge in order to gain proprietary rights. His pretext for taking "legal possession" by marriage recalls the ancient rationale for slavery: the vanquished owes all to the victor who has spared his or her life. The same patriarchal power that "normalizes" the female protagonist also generates a humiliating dependency.

The title of Buñuel's last film points to the theme that so obsesses both Hitchcock and Buñuel — *That Obscure Object of Desire*. Here again, Buñuel anatomizes desire as pathology. Just as Mark is attracted to Marnie's frigidity, Mathieu fetishizes Conchita's virginity. Playing out a widely disseminated double bind, the aging protagonist cannot attain his desire without destroying it. His love of a virgin, or at least of the idea of virignity, is foredoomed and ephemeral by definition. Indeed, *That Obscure Object of Desire* demonstrates a kind of Zeno's paradox of passion: the space between two potential lovers is infinitely divisible. While Mathieu enjoys the sterile plenitude of physical proximity — the same house, naked in the same bed — Conchita remains as spiritually remote as a medieval damsel locked in the castles of courtly love. The scene is partially set in Seville, historically one of the centers of the Provençal poetry often cited as the source of courtly love. Provençal love poetry drew on the Arabic culture pervasive in Andalusia, and especially on a kind of poetry which idealized love as the humble (and usually unrewarded) service from afar to a lady. The Buñuel film visualizes this inaccessibility by placing between the lovers bars, fences, grillwork. Mathieu, in a chromatic version of the obsessions with confinement in film noir, is framed as the prisoner of desire. His vision is repeatedly barred as he is subjected to cruelly seductive revelations of Conchita's flesh. The bars become a metaphor for the treadmill of desire — always tantalizing, always unfulfilled, perpetually on the brink — both confronting and generating its own longed-for obstructions.

Both *That Obscure Object of Desire* and *Rear Window* qualify as what Patricia Waugh calls "metafictions," that is, works constructed on the principle of a fundamental and sustained opposition between the construction of a fictional illusion (as in traditional realism) and the laying bare of that illusion, where the two processes are held together in formal tension.[22] In both films, an illusionistic story exists in creative tension with a kind of allegorization of the cinema and spectatorship. *That Obscure Object of Desire* allegorizes its own procedures and its own mechanisms of fascination through a story about a man fascinated by the image of a woman. The film constitutes a protracted joke on the spectator, a narrative striptease that refuses to strip, whose very title designates our own position as desiring spectators. Just as Conchita consistently eludes Mathieu's desiring grasp, so the film playfully foils our desire, never delivering on the abstract erotic promise of the title. We too are cruelly locked out of the spectacle, subjected to an infinite regress of spectatorial frustration. Instead of stimulating desire, Buñuel holds the mirror to our own psychic fix on films themselves. He analyzes, as if on a movieola, the most mystified moment in our culture — the moment of sexual surrender — and scrutinizes our phantasmatic relation to the spectacle, exposing desire as a cultural cinematic construct.

Like Hitchcock, Buñuel inscribes the spectators within the diegesis in the form of Mathieu's rapt listeners in the train compartment, a collective interlocutor which, not unlike the audience of a film, poses questions and speculates about motivations and outcome. And if *Rear Window* is not, generally, so narrowly focused on specifically sexual desire, it too, like *That Obscure Object of Desire*, explores the complexities of cinematic spectatorship. By its insistent inscription of scenarios of voyeurism, as Roberta Pearson and I have argued elsewhere, the film poses the question that so preoccupies contemporary film theory and analysis: the question of the place of the desiring subject within the cinematic apparatus.[23] Rather than ask, "What does the text mean?," film theory asks the question: "What do we want from the text?" Thorwald says to Jefferies, "What is it you want from me? . . . Tell me what you want!" His question, ostensibly addressed to the protagonist, might as well have been addressed to us. And to this question, *Rear Window* offers a complex and multileveled response. The spectators in the film — Jefferies, Lisa, Stella, even Doyle — want first of all to see, to peek into the private corners of the lives of others. The technical instruments at Jefferies's disposal — binoculars, telephoto lens — come in answer, as it were, to this primordial desire. Beyond that, these spectators want to identify with the human figures within the spectacle. When Lisa enters into the space of the spectacle — Thorwald's apartment —

Jefferies's "investment" in spectatorship becomes clear. Most of all, these spectators want to experience certain "subject effects." They want to find themselves in a heightened state of pleasurable absorption and identification. Jefferies begins as a listless and apathetic spectator, but he gradually "comes alive" through what he sees. He shares the experience, furthermore, with others within a kind of ephemeral *communitas* of spectatorship. His metamorphosis from distant observer into excited participant "allegorizes" the transformation engendered in us by the narrative procedures and identificatory mechanisms of Hitchcock's cinema, and even that engendered by *Rear Window* itself.

Rear Window dismantles the structures of scopophilia and identification operative in Hitchcock's own films even while exploiting those very structures. Jefferies and the apartment complex taken together prefigure the "cinematic apparatus," that is, the instrumental base of camera, projector, and screen, as well as the spectator as the desiring subject on which the cinematic institution depends for its object and accomplice. Jefferies, in his state of inhibited mobility and exacerbated perception, embodies the situation of the immobile cinematic viewer who absorbs everything through the eyes. Binoculars and telephoto lens grant Jefferies the illusory godlike power of the "all-perceiving subject." *Rear Window,* as many commentators have pointed out, constantly underscores the voyeuristic abuse of which the cinema is so often susceptible. An early shot in the film epitomizes this attitude. Two women on a rooftop, presumably Greenwich Village "bohemians," discard their clothes to sunbathe. A helicopter approaches and hovers overhead, with the clear implication that those aboard the helicopter are spying on the women. The helicopter provides a perfect "vehicle" for the spectatorial desire to enjoy a fantasy omniscience, to go everywhere and see everything, and especially for the socially nurtured desire to see women in states of undress. The helicopter evokes the technological resources available to the cinema and enlistable in the service of the scopic drive. Yet Hitchcock withholds the "payoff" of these resources by denying us the point-of-view shot from the helicopter. We never see the women; we become aware, rather, only of our desire to see them. The desire is not fulfilled but only marked and exposed.

Both *That Obscure Object of Desire* and *Rear Window* feature sexually perturbed male protagonists. But while Mathieu is fleeing toward an impossible love, Jefferies flees from a possible love; while claiming that it is impossible ("too perfect" as he puts it), Jefferies provides a quintessential exemplum of what Stella calls "a race of Peeping Toms." His profession of photojournalism already assumes a kind of voyeurism by which he observes the world's catastrophes from what is usually a safe distance, while at home he indulges, from his rear-window post, in what Metz calls "authorized voyeurism." Jefferies's voyeurism goes hand in hand with an absorbing fear of mature sexuality. Indeed, the film begins by hinting at a serious case of psychosexual pathology. A radio commercial allusion to that "run-down listless feeling" is followed by a series of comments by both Stella and Lisa that might be taken to refer to sexual impotence: "You're not too active," "How's your leg?" "Is anything else bothering you?" Stella calls him "reasonably healthy" but wonders about a "hormone deficiency." The complement of Jefferies's voyeurism, at least at the beginning of the film, is a certain passivity. While avoiding relationships with friends and lovers and neighbors, he is passionately absorbed in the spectacle of his neighbors' lives. Indeed, his involvement with people exists in inverse proportion to their distance from him. He would rather watch Miss Torso than touch the flesh-and-blood woman next to him. The tension between the attraction to distant spectacle and close-at-hand reality even takes the form of a physical tussle concerning the direction in which Jefferies's wheelchair will face: out the window toward Miss Torso and, metaphorically, the cinema, or inward toward the apartment, Lisa, and "reality."

Both *Rear Window* and *That Obscure Object of Desire* touch on the issue of the sexual politics of looking. Voyeurism in *Rear Window* is largely defined as a masculine activity, even though the principal object of that voyeurism, through a kind of displacement, is rendered as male. The cinema, by analogy, is defined as the product of the male auteur/spectator/voyeur who at best enlists some women as accomplices in his voyeuristic activities. (Only Jeff, significantly, is allowed to look through the phallic telephoto lens.) But while Lisa and Stella, at least in the beginning, look directly at Jefferies, he looks away toward women and men transmuted into spectacle. And when the women turn their eyes toward the spectacle, they see differently, showing enhanced capacities for empathy and comprehension, especially in relation to other women. Lisa understands instantly that Miss Torso is not in love with the man she kisses on the balcony and knows, without ever having met her, what Mrs. Thorwald would or would not have done. While Jefferies regards the world as a kind of private panopticon, Lisa is less concerned with spying and exercising voyeuristic control over the lives of others. The female spectator-in-the-text, in sum, demonstrates a sensibility and approach quite distinct from that of the male.[24]

That Obscure Object of Desire, meanwhile, stresses the impaired vision of its male protagonist. By having two actresses who do not even especially resemble each other play the single role of Conchita, Buñuel stresses the blindness of a "sexual idealist" who does not even perceive that he is dealing with two women. The substitution of actresses undercuts Mathieu's indignation and discourse of victimization by "la pire des femmes." Since what he is really after is an abstraction, a phantom, a phantasmatic incarnation of desire, rather than a real woman, he sees only his phantasies falsely unified into one figure. At the same time, Buñuel mocks our habits as spectators. Accustomed to expect that a character who answers to the same name and who serves the same function in the narrative must be played by a single actor or actress, we find it hard to believe that a director would so abuse our confidence as to use two players for the same role. In either case, the device works. If we do *not* notice that there are two actresses, we are shown to be as blind as Mathieu, while if we *do* notice, we are distanced from him, obliged to "see" critically the impairment of his vision.

In her study of surrealist film, Linda Williams briefly contrasts the perpetually deferred quest, and the train as "teasing interruption," in *That Obscure Object of Desire*, with the completed phallic quest of *North by Northwest*, and the final train as metaphor for that quest. Her aside points to a fundamental difference-within-similarity between Hitchcock and Buñuel. The Lodger and Daisy, Roger Thornhill and Eve Kendall, do consummate their marriage; the protagonists of *Un Chien Andalou, L'Age d'Or*, and *That Obscure Object of Desire* presumably do not. Hitchcock's narratives achieve orgasm; Buñuel's practice systematic coitus interruptus. If films such as *North by Northwest* are shorn of their final shots, however, their narratives begin to resemble those of Buñuel films. Both *North by Northwest* and *That Obscure Object of Desire* posit picaresque itineraries — Buñuel might have entitled his film *North by*

Northeast—in which desire's pursuit of its receding object is set against a background of international terror. In both films, middle-aged men, successful in the world but infantile in love, pursue younger women. An oedipal configuration, analyzed by Williams herself in relation to *That Obscure Object of Desire* and by Raymond Bellour in relation to *North by Northwest*, links both narratives, with the difference that Buñuel leaves Mathieu's trajectory incomplete, while Hitchcock has Thornhill accept civic and marital responsibility. Thornhill is "cured," but Mathieu prefers the disease to the cure.

The women, in both cases, are portrayed as dangerously and mysteriously double. This doubleness of women, common in the films of both directors, is made literal in Buñuel by having the two actresses, dubbed by a single voice, play the same role. The two Conchitas, meanwhile, form a compendium of contradictory images, at once passionate and frigid, modest and brazen, assertive and submissive. Hitchcock's heroine is similarly bifurcated: saint and temptress, madonna and whore. The actress's name, in another instance of aleatory good fortune, incarnates these dualities: the fallen Eve, the Virgin Mary, the canonical saint. In both films, death is concatenated with desire. Terrorist explosions "punctuate" each of Mathieu's and Conchita's erotic encounters, and Eve Kendall and Roger Thornhill speak of murder during their first kiss. Both Conchita and Eve could, as Thornhill says, "tease a man to death without half trying." In both films desire is enhanced by inaccessibility and by barriers of class conflict or political tension. Both women become damsels trapped in imaginary castles. In both, the woman participates in a subtext of prostitution. Conchita is the recipient of Mathieu's interested generosity and is kept, ironically, in every sense except the sexual, while Eve, in her role as double agent, is kept by a powerful pimp called the CIA. And if Eve wields sex as a "flyswatter" against America's enemies, Conchita wields virginity as a terrorist weapon against Mathieu and the bourgeois order he represents.

Both *North by Northwest* and *That Obscure Object of Desire* flaunt their fundamental implausibility. The narrative action swirls around an empty center: the conundrum of Conchita's virginity in the Buñuel film, and vague international intrigues in Hitchcock. *North by Northwest* glories in fantastic coincidences and impossible situations. Narrative implausibilities—the couple's amorous badinage while clinging to the granite face of Mount Rushmore—are mirrored by self-referential devices (Vandamm's malevolent "this matter is best disposed of from a great height" triggers an abrupt shift to a high angle), extraordinary camera setups (the extreme high angle shot of Thornhill running from the UN) and audacious *faux raccords*. The splice which takes us, spatially, from Mount Rushmore to a hurtling train, and temporally from singledom to marriage, demonstrates a flair for discontinuity no less dazzling than that of Buñuel, whose splices magically substitute one actress for another.

It would be misguided, I suggested earlier, to pigeonhole Hitchcock as the classicist master-of-suspense and Buñuel as the disruptive avant-gardist. More and more critics are perceiving the "modernist" Hitchcock who constantly plays with spectatorial expectation and with generic and cinematic convention. Both *North by Northwest* and *That Obscure Object of Desire*, in this sense, can be seen as reflexive films. Their authors, in both cases, appear in self-deflating cameo roles; Hitchcock has a bus door close in his face, while Buñuel plays the well-dressed man on his way to the bank who is blown up by terrorists. The crucial difference between Hitchcock and Buñuel, in the final analysis, is in the degree of audacity of their reflexivity. Hitchcock's narrative trains ultimately do run on time, while Buñuel's are constantly derailed and never arrive. Although Hitchcock keeps the spectator in the dark during the first third of *North by Northwest*, after that the double series of enigmas — the espionage series and the romance series — proceed smoothly and finally coincide. Hitchcock ultimately does unravel his enigmas, even if reluctantly and only in the final reel. Buñuel, in contrast, frustrates our "epistemophilia" as well as our scopophilia. *That Obscure of Desire* leaves its central enigmas as intact as Conchita's putative virginity. What drives her to act as she does? Did she actually make love to El Morenito? The film elicits hypothetical answers to these questions and then swiftly subverts them, leaving us with a core of irrationality.

This "core of irrationality" is common to the two directors, and Hitchcock too is no stranger to the absurd, which he practices, as he told Truffaut, "religiously." Hitchcock's most explicit exercise in the absurd is *The Trouble with Harry* (1955), a film whose release coincided with the heights of the absurdist theater of Beckett and Ionesco in France, and which was, predictably, better received in Paris than in London and New York. The film's macabre humor belongs to the more subdued English strain of the carnivalesque tra-

137

ROBERT STAM

dition of "laughing at death," a tradition which inflects both directors' work. Death in Buñuel often takes comic or at least distanced
form — one thinks of Gloria's ephemeral "death" and "resuscitation"
in *El*, or of the inconvenient corpse in the restaurant of *The Discrete
Charm of the Bourgeoisie* (or of Fernando Rey, under attack by guer-
rillas, reaching for that final piece of beef). Hitchcock too takes
what one might call a playful approach to murder, thinking up, as
he told Truffaut, "fun ways for people to die." *The Trouble with
Harry* brings this tendency to its paroxysm, in a film where a corpse
becomes a comic prop, secretly buried and disinterred at least three
times before it is determined that the death was in fact due to natural
causes. Here even the sex/death trope takes comic expression, as flirtation is performed over the corpse — Miss Gravely invites Captain
Wiles for blueberry muffins, then steps lightly over the corpse — and
the film's final innuendo about a "double bed" is followed by a shot
of the corpse.

   The Trouble with Harry bears comparison to Buñeul's *The Criminal Life of Archibaldo de la Cruz* (1955), not only in its comic
approach to death, but also in its central issue of characters who
imagine themselves responsible for murders they did not actually
commit. Archibaldo invariably fails in his plans to murder a number
of people, yet his targets die from other causes immediately subsequent to his failure. The police chief in the Buñuel film articulates
a theme quite common in Hitchcock's films — the spectators' own
potential capacity for murderous thoughts and for identifying with
criminals. "To imagine is no crime," says the police chief. "If I arrested everyone who thinks of murder the jails would be overflow-
ing." Linked to this murderous capacity is the projection of guilt.
Archibaldo thinks himself responsible even for the murders he did not
commit if only because he wanted to commit them. In *The Trouble
with Harry*, similarly, all the major characters have some reason for
feeling responsible for Harry's death, and they imagine themselves
guilty, with that obscure object, the corpse, becoming a kind of
Rorschach test. The hunter imagines having killed him with a care-
less gunshot, the ex-wife imagines having hit him too hard with a
bottle, and so forth. What surprises in the film is the lighthearted
tone with which death is treated; all the characters react to the discovery of the murder with a level of anxiety more appropriate to a

138

misplaced letter than to an accidental murder. "Will he get better?" Jennifer's son asks. "Not if we're lucky," replies his mother. The painter discovers the corpse only after he has painted its feet into his landscape, after which he asks the corpse if he would mind "getting out of my pictures."

But quite apart from its flip, absurdist approach to death, *The Trouble with Harry* practices the absurd on a linguistic-discursive level as well, and in this sense the film merits comparison with Buñuel's *Exterminating Angel*. The Buñuel film carnivalizes social etiquette through provocative misalliances of language, as evidence of grave ruptures in the fabric of bourgeois society. "You smell like a hyena, madame," one socialite tells another in an improbable mixture of the polite and the impolite, the noble and the vulgar. The film proliferates in such absurd discursive encounters: "Allow me to introduce . . . ," begins one socialite in Spanish. "I don't understand Greek," interrupts another. "Just keep introducing yourselves," adds a third. A doctor confides to a friend that one of his patients will soon be "completely bald," a Spanish expression roughly equivalent in crudity to "croak" or "kick the bucket," yet later he announces her death with an exaggeratedly dignified, even sacrilegious, consummation *est*. In *The Trouble with Harry*, the non-sense has less to do with the subversion of social decorum — although the offbeat characters in the film do seem to form a kind of utopian community of artists and eccentrics as opposed to the "no-nonsense" people like the sheriff — than with a kind of domesticated surrealism reminiscent of the aleatory verbal techniques of the "Surrealist games," in which nonsensical affirmations were formed, for example, by joining "if" clauses written by one person to "then" clauses written by a second person unaware of the first clause. Jennifer's son, who has, as his mother says, "his own timing," systematically confuses the word "yesterday" with "today" and "today" with "tomorrow." When the painter promises to come visit him "tomorrow," the son asks, "When's that?" to which the painter replies, "The day after today." "That's yesterday," corrects the boy, "today's tomorrow." *The Trouble with Harry* exhibits every variety of verbal humor: understatement (the corpse is referred to as "our little problem"); euphemism ("horrible masculine sounds" to refer to oaths and curses); sexual innuendo ("there are some things I prefer not to do by myself"); non sequiturs ("If you, an artist, think the worst, what are the police going to think?"); and inappropriate responses (Jennifer answers the painter's announcement that "your husband's dead" with a cool, "Is your lemonade sweet?").

An excellent test case for both the parallels and contrasts between Hitchcock and Buñuel is provided by an instance when the two directors work similar themes, in comparable genres, at the same point in their careers: *The Birds* (1963) and *The Exterminating Angel* (1962). The parallels begin with their titles, both of which refer to winged creatures seen as meting out justice on human beings. The scourge, in both instances, carries overtones of the Apocalypse. The exterminating angel executes a mission of social justice, an apocalyptic laying low of the noble and the powerful, while the characters in *The Birds* are collectively the victim of a kind of judgment day, a theme sounded explicitly in the Biblical citation of the drunk in the restaurant: "The Lord said, I will devastate your high places. . . . It's the end of the world." Both *The Birds* and *The Exterminating Angel* can be seen as proto-disaster films in which respectable people become "castaways" in situations of extreme pressure where ordinary social conventions no longer apply.[25] As the social contract breaks down, the pathological politeness of bourgeois etiquette disappears. This fragility of social convention is imaged by broken glass and destroyed homes in both films. In *The Exterminating Angel*, the mansion is destroyed from within, by the residents, while in the Hitchcock film, it is destroyed from without, by the birds.

The apocalypse, in both cases, has resonances of the absurd in that the central premises—the inexplicable entrapment of a pride of socialites, mass avian attack on human beings—are as calculatedly implausible as those subtending many Beckett or Ionesco plays. Both films elaborate the theme of entrapment that so obsessed the theater of the absurd. In *The Exterminating Angel*, the human characters are barred from crossing a magical threshold, while animals move about freely. *The Birds*, meanwhile, as many critics have pointed out, operates a similar inversion, moving from a situation in which the birds are caged and the people are free to one in which the people are caged—in houses, telephone booths, cars—and the birds are free. The situation in *The Exterminating Angel* would seem at first to be more claustrophobic, but in fact *The Birds*, apparently more spacious and airy, offers a more frightening, global entrapment, a theme sounded in the film's opening shot, where bird cries are superimposed on the turning globe of the Universal logo. The birds cover the earth like a roof, prefiguring a situation in which the whole earth will become a trap. The theme is touched on again in the dazzling aerial view of Bodega Bay, clearly from the birds' perspective, and sealed by the final shot, again from the birds' point of view, showing the human beings beating a cautious automotive retreat, as the birds, the permanent residents, watch them leave.[26]

Because of a curious critical double standard, Buñuel was never belabored for the improbabilities of his film — one expects such things from an avant-gardist — while Hitchcock was ardently pursued by his nemesis "the Plausibles." "Why didn't the schoolchildren hide in the cellar?" critics asked, and "Why didn't Melanie die of bird bite?" (Because it would be *boring* for Melanie to die of bird bite, Hitchcock might presumably have answered.) Both authors refuse coherent, cause-effect, logical explanation. Hitchcock accepted Truffaut's account of the film as a "speculation or fantasy" without "specific explanation," while Buñuel's prefatory note to the first Parisian screening of *The Exterminating Angel* warned that the "only explanation is that there is no explanation."[27] This deliberate refusal to explain does not deter certain of the characters in the films, like certain critics, from seeking plausibility where none exists. Hitchcock's policeman advances commonsense explanations — "the children provoked the birds" — just as Buñuel's positivist doctor pleads for scientific analysis, but in both films the rationalists are discredited. The ornithologist, who at first haughtily dismissed the very possibility of mass bird attacks, is left cowed and trembling. We are left with a core of mystery and the incomprehensible.

Having signaled the parallels between the two films, it is equally important to note certain salient contrasts having to do with their basic modes, and the consequences of these modes for spectatorial positioning and for politics. The mode of *The Exterminating Angel* is ultimately comic, ironic, carnivalesque. Structured according to the comic formula of a slow descent into anarchy, the film derives much of its humor from the burlesque comedy that Buñuel so admired. The mode of *The Birds*, meanwhile, despite its comic underside, is ultimately tragic, taking us through pity and fear to catharsis. ("Comic" and "tragic" are here used in their Brechtian senses: the question is one of spectatorial positioning.) Hitchcock enlists all the cinematic codes — camera movement, framing, editing, color — in the service of an identificatory response. His predilection for point-of-view editing, in this sense, is but the most clearly marked instance of a general subjectivization. Buñuel, on the other hand, works in the opposite way. We identify with no one in *The Exterminating Angel*; we merely observe critically. Buñuel consistently refuses empathy-inducing techniques, eschewing point-of-view editing, shot-countershot structures, eyeline matches, commentative music, and the like. The camera, meanwhile, exhibits its own autonomy, exploring walls and weaving through the partyscape without following individual characters. Even dreams offer no pretext for subjectivization, for they are collective rather than individual, thus anticipating *The Discrete Charm of the Bourgeoisie*, where members of the same social class dream one another's dreams.

These differing modes and strategies are correlated with very distinct political impulses. Although both *The Birds* and *The Exterminating Angel* attack complacency, that attack takes strongly divergent forms. Although Hitchcock could perhaps subscribe to Buñuel's summary of the final sense of his films — "to repeat, over and over again . . . that we do not live in the best of all possible worlds" — the import of this subscription would hardly be identical. *The Birds* makes a broad humanistic statement about human caring; its categories are moral rather than social or political. *The Exterminating Angel*, in contrast, radicalizes burlesque and avant-garde topoi by linking them to the carnivalesque theme of the "world upside down." The film's critique is structural; its logic is to reduce its upper-class protagonists to the miserable condition of the very people normally oppressed and forgotten — "los olvidados" of the slums.

Our comparison, which has strategically downplayed certain obvious contrasts between Hitchcock and Buñuel, here touches on a critical arena of difference — politics. Buñuel, even while critiquing the bourgeoisie from within, never forgets *los olvidados*; he consistently places in the foregrounds the realities of physical hunger and social class. While he never stoops to vulgar proselytizing, his commitment is everywhere evident. While Hitchcock thinks in the psychological singular of the subjectivized monad, Buñuel thinks in the social plural of class. And while it would be a mistake to underestimate the social critique performed by a film like *The Wrong Man*, where the ordinary workings of justice are revealed to be deeply flawed, it must also be acknowledged that Buñuel's social critique is far more thoroughgoing and radical.

What is true of politics in general is true of sexual politics in particular. The verdict of the place of women in Hitchcock is in dispute. Where some critics, such as Donald Spoto and the early Robin Wood, see the "therapist" putting his heroines through "humanizing" ordeals, others, such as Raymond Bellour and Jacqueline Rose, see "the rapist" punishing "the desire that speaks in a woman's look." Whether we see Hitchcock as one or the other largely depends on our angle of vision. I concur with Tania Modleski's judgment that the question as to whether Hitchcock is sympathetic toward women or misogynistic is fundamentally unanswerable because he is both, and because the misogyny and sympathy are actually connected in complicated ways with one another.[28] Buñuel's work, on the other hand, is less ambiguous on the subject of sexual politics; his films, especially if one sets aside the "surrealist triptych," form an unending indictment of patriarchy and machismo. While whatever critique of patriarchy exists in Hitchcock has to be disinterred, read "against the grain," in Buñuel it is close to the surface. *The River and Death* (1954) treats the theme of the social pathology of machismo through parody and black humor. *The Young One* (1960) interarticulates the issues of sexism and antiblack racism. Many Buñuel films crystallize the nature of machismo in crude gestures clearly marked as repugnant: in *The Exterminating Angel*, Jorge examines the maid Ramona's teeth before pouncing on her, exactly as a master might look at a horse, or a slave, and Buñuel further points to the asymmetry of their relationship by juxtaposing their act with the image of a cat pouncing on a mouse. While women are seen as double in both Hitchcock and Buñuel, the emphasis in Buñuel is on the men's seeing double. While Hitchcock has a certain sympathy with the female outlaw, and while he identifies with the very women characters he is torturing, Buñuel is more clearly sympathetic to his women characters and less invested, I suspect, in violence against them. What spectator can observe the behavior of Gloria and Francisco in *El*, Evie and Miller in *The Young One*, and Viridiana and Don Jaime in *Viridiana* without realizing that these "couples" exist in a relation of oppression and that this oppression forms part of a general configuration of power? (The indictment is less clear in *That Obscure Object of Desire* only because Conchita is little more than a phantasm of what Linda Williams calls a "figure of desire," enlisted in Buñuel's critique of Mathieu's masculinist vision.) The story of *El* is narrated in flashback by Gloria, from her point of view. Although Lacan was fond of screening the film for his students as a case study in paranoia, it might as well have served as a quasi-documentary study of patriarchal violence. Buñuel treats his protagonist with what he himself called "entomological" distance: The hero interests me, Buñuel remarked, "rather like a beetle or a malarial mosquito." The third-person masculine pronoun of the Spanish title, mistranslated and romanticized in the English *This Strange Passion*, underlines the fact that Buñuel is addressing a general social pathology. Francisco is a sadomasochist, a voyeur, a fetishist, and a sexual puritan, and he is clearly mad, an impression clinched by his final zigzagging down the monastery walkways. The film portrays a situation in which a psychotic man has virtually all the rights and the woman none and yet where virtually all of the voices of respectable society—including Gloria's own mother—condemn her and support him, and where the spectator has not the slightest doubt that she is in the right. Indeed, Buñuel radicalizes his critique by making his protagonist to all appearances a model husband, the quintessence of social charm and grace, and by having him played by the prototypical Mexican "gallant," Arturo de Cordova. Francisco embodies the two sides of sexism: its good cops and bad cops; its chivalric, protective side, and its violent, sadistic side. Francisco's attitude toward Gloria is proprietary throughout, and it is no accident that Buñuel depicts Francisco as a quintessential "owner," a quasi-feudal character whose origins go back to the conquistadores who stole the land from the Indians, a man obsessed with property in both the literal and the figurative senses.

The focus of Buñuel's attack has one name—the Law—and many surnames: Patriarchal Power, Authority, God the Father, the Pope, the Generalissimo, the Pater Familias, but also Certainty of Origin, Mastery of Meaning, Dominant Cinema. Unlike Hitchcock, Buñuel offers a profound critique of the symbolic structures of partiarchal thought, a critique at once political, economic, cultural, religious, and even anthropological. If Hitchcock's world is an unending labyrinth of guilt, Buñuel's is one of constant change and revolt. If both directors linger on the illicit pleasures of voyeurism and fetishism, Buñuel indulges them less and for a different purpose. If Hitchcock excites emotions to their paroxysm, Buñuel short-circuits them by a quasi-Brechtian "theater of interruptions." Hitchcock concentrates on the moral inferno within, while Buñuel brandishes the camera-eye in order to set the world on fire.

Notes

1. See Francisco Aranda, *Luis Buñuel: A Critical Biography* (New York: Da Capo, 1976), 248. Buñuel reports in his autobiography that Hitchcock especially admired the amputated leg in *Tristana* — "Ah, that leg . . . that leg . . . ," Bunuel reports him as saying. See Luis Buñuel, *My Last Sigh* (New York: Random House, 1984).
2. See David Freeman, "The Last Days of Alfred Hitchcock," *Esquire* 97, no. 4 (April 1982), 92.
3. See Aranda.
4. This essay is a modified version of an essay which first appeared in *Studies in the Literary Imagination*, no. 16 (Spring 1983), here revised with a view toward giving more attention to the five rereleased Hitchcock films that are the primary focus of this volume.
5. Interview with Carlos Fuentes published in *The New York Times Magazine* 11 March 1973, and anthologized in Joan Mellen, *The World of Luis Buñuel* (New York: Oxford University Press, 1978).
6. See Virginia Higginbothan, *Luis Buñuel* (New York: G. K. Hall, 1979), 18.
7. See Donald Spoto, *The Dark Side of Genius: The Life of Alfred Hitchcock* (Boston: Little, Brown, 1983), 40.
8. Barton Palmer identifies two contrasting portraits of Hitchcock, one which is psychoanalytic and poststructuralist and sees Hitchcock as "classical realist," and another which sees Hitchcock as modernist and reflexive. Palmer argues convincingly that both views discern elements within the work which in fact exist as a source of creative tension. See R. Barton Palmer, "The Metafictional Hitchcock: The Experience of Viewing and the Viewing of Experience in *Rear Window* and *Psycho*," in *Cinema Journal* 25, no. 2 (Winter 1986).
9. Although *The Lodger* was not technically Hitchcock's first feature, it was, according to the director himself, the first "true Hitchcock movie." See François Truffaut, *Hitchcock* (New York: Simon and Schuster, 1967), 30.
10. Buñuel appears in *Belle de Jour* as a Spanish tourist, thus pinpointing his situation as a Spaniard making films in France. In *Phantom of Liberty*, he dons a beard and a monk's frock and has himself assassinated, thus marking his ambivalence toward Catholicism; doing violence against a symbolic representative of the church, he also does violence to himself.
11. For psychoanalytic analyses of the assault on the eyes in Buñuel, see Paul Sandro, *Diversions of Pleasure: Luis Buñuel and the Crises of Desire* (Columbus: Ohio State University Press, 1987), and Linda Williams, *Figures of Desire* (Urbana: University of Illinois Press, 1981). For a psychoanalytic analysis of disturbed

vision in Hitchcock, see Tania Modleski, *The Women Who Knew Too Much* (New York: Methuen, 1988) and Kaja Silverman, *The Acoustic Mirror: The Female Voice and Psychoanalysis in the Cinema* (Bloomington: Indiana University Press, 1987).

12. From Interview with Carlos Fuentes, in Mellen, 69–70.
13. Ibid., 70.
14. See Spoto, 31.
15. See John Russell Taylor, *Hitch: The Life and Times of Alfred Hitchcock* (New York: Pantheon, 1978), 310.
16. See Denis de Rougemont, *Love in the Western World* (New York: Harper and Row, 1977), 53.
17. Midge plays Mozart as therapy for Scottie in *Vertigo*, but to no avail.
18. Love beyond the grave at times acquires incestuous overtones in Hitchcock, notably in *The Lodger*, where Ivor Novello's potentially murderous hand is guided by his deceased mother, and in *Psycho*, in the form of Norman Bates's oedipal relation to a mother who also has a privileged relationship to death.
19. See Truffaut, 185–86.
20. I would like to thank Connie Milner for sharing her perceptions on *Vertigo* and *Viridiana*.
21. Marnie's double life as compulsive thief and dutiful daughter in some respects recalls Severine's double life as faithful wife and debauched prostitute in *Belle de Jour*.
22. R. Barton Palmer argues this point concerning *Rear Window* in "The Metafictional Hitchcock." Patricia Waugh develops her theory of metafiction in *Metafiction: The Theory and Practice of Self-Conscious Fiction* (London: Methuen, 1984).
23. See Robert Stam and Roberta Pearson, "Hitchcock's *Rear Window*: Reflexivity and the Critique of Voyeurism," *Enclitic* 7, no. 1 (Spring 1983).
24. Modleski elaborates on the gender determinants of spectatorship in *The Women Who Knew Too Much*.
25. The castaway situation is also treated in Hitchcock's *Lifeboat* (1943) and in Buñuel's *Death in the Garden* (1956) and *Robinson Crusoe* (1952).
26. Interestingly, Hitchcock contemplated a double-trap structure that would have been even more parallel to that of *The Exterminating Angel*. The foursome were to have driven to San Francisco only to encounter the Golden Gate Bridge covered with birds. The endings of both films, in any case, are highly ambiguous. Buñuel leaves his characters trapped in a church; it is for us to imagine subsequent events. In Hitchcock the reconstituted "family" apparently makes a safe exit, yet we have no evidence that the birds will not attack again elsewhere. Hitchcock wanted to forego the normal closure of "The End," but trial audiences misinterpreted the lack of an ending as a projection breakdown, and Universal was obliged to overlay final titles on all prints in circulation.
27. See Truffaut, 216.
28. Modleski argues that in Hitchcock's films men's fascination and identification with the feminine undermines their efforts to achieve masculine strength and this triggers their violence toward women. See Modleski, 5.

POSTMODERN *VERTIGO*

The Sexual Politics of Allusion in De Palma's *Body Double*

Ann Cvetkovich

I feel about Hitchcock the way I feel about Freud. There's no better way to understand our culture's constructions of sexuality and desire, and the difficulty of distinguishing the normal from the perverse, than to examine their work as both symptom and analysis. It seems pointless to decide if they are sexist because, whether critical of relations between the sexes or not, they provide valuable insight into the pleasures and dangers of desire, and their sensitivity to the often bizarre workings of the unconscious is a caution against overly hasty prescriptions for the elimination of patriarchal social relations. Yet, however relevant the lessons of Freud and Hitchcock continue to be, it is important to historicize their work, and to remember that the processes they explore, no matter how entrenched, are not universal.

Brian De Palma's *Body Double*, a film which, although influenced by and derived from Hitchcock's work, is also relentlessly contemporary, provides an opportunity to gain historical perspective on his predecessor. I'd like to pose the problem of the continuity and discontinuity between the two directors in terms of the paradigm for cultural history offered by recent speculations on postmodernism.[1]

This discourse often circles endlessly around the distinction between the modern and the postmodern and is forced to define a new Zeitgeist because the modernist period seems finally to have been superseded by something else. Because postmodernism is invariably seen as a response to modernism, it is often criticized for being parasitic on the earlier period and thus failing to be new or revolutionary; in a similar double bind, if De Palma has to be read in relation to Hitchcock, he appears to be derivative and repetitive rather than contemporary. I would argue that it is no accident that De Palma has been criticized both for slavishly imitating Hitchcock and for depicting violence against women. (Of course the man who exploits Hitchcock also exploits women.) Whereas Hitchcock, like Freud, has been rescued by feminists as interestingly revealing, in part because his work is seen as formally complex, De Palma's status is more questionable.[2] Aesthetic and political evaluation are closely linked in discussions of De Palma's work, such that the former serves as a cover for or displacement of the latter. De Palma can be scapegoated as a bad artist, thus taking the blame for a sexism that extends far beyond his films.

If there exists such a thing as "postmodern" culture, *Body Double* would seem to be an instance of it. The film's incessant allusion to Hitchcock's films, specifically *Vertigo* and *Rear Window*, exemplifies the most frequently cited characteristic of postmodern culture, which, in the words of Frederic Jameson, "randomly and without principle but with gusto cannibalizes all the . . . styles of the past and combines them in overstimulating ensembles."[3] In keeping with the views of, for example, Jameson and Habermas that postmodernism represents a crisis in cultural production, the prevalence of remakes and allusions among recent Hollywood releases might be taken as a sign of the exhaustion of form in the contemporary cinema, as directors ransack the golden age of Hollywood with a combination of nostalgia and empty cleverness. Indeed, De Palma's critics often accuse him of mindlessly imitating Hitchcock without creating anything new or original.[4]

But not all remakes are the same. Jameson uses the film *Body Heat* to develop the theory that postmodern works cite the past through pastiche as opposed to parody, and that they efface any genuine historical reflection by ignoring contemporary referents and quoting a past that only existed in fantasy form.[5] This analysis would not apply to *Body Double*, which foregrounds contemporary culture by depicting recent architecture, videos, television, shopping malls, and joggers. It thus seems possible that De Palma's translation of Hitchcock's work into images stamped clearly as made in 1984 might operate as a comment on his predecessor and as a register of what separates the eighties from the fifties.

In suggesting this, I'd like to question the tendency in discussions of the postmodern to treat the culture of an earlier period as more authentic or original. What do we make, for example, of the status of Hitchcock's films as "rereleases"? The distinction between originals and remakes becomes confusing when *Vertigo* and *Rear Window* reappear within the same year as *Body Double*.[6] The celebration of Hollywood's past is as much a postmodern phenomenon as the quotation of it. The nostalgic reception of Hitchcock's fifties' films tends to fetishize him as a lost figure of high culture: the movies are treated as timeless originals (after all these years they still seem fresh and contemporary), or as rediscovered classics (only now can we truly appreciate Hitchcock's artistic greatness), or as the masterpieces of a bygone era (no one makes films the way Hitchcock did anymore, and we're better off watching his movies rather than the trash Hollywood currently puts out). But, like a lot of postmodern art, Hitchcock's work renders problematic the distinction between high and low culture, since he was always both popular and aesthetically ambitious. It may be that Hitchcock fascinates us because it's easier to talk about fifties' culture as our own than it is to face the unpleasant and still perhaps unreadable revelations of eighties' culture.

The task of reading the present is the problem that confronts theorists of the postmodern. The discourse of postmodernism should be read, I think, not as a description of a set of cultural phenomena or a historical moment, so much as a theoretical investigation haunted by the difficulty of defining a politically correct cultural practice. "Postmodernism" sometimes becomes the name for a cultural production which has capitulated so completely to the demands of late-monopoly or postindustrial capitalism that it is incapable of critique or radicalism. Art is one more commodity, subject to the demands of the marketplace; it is no longer possible to pretend that the artist's hands are less dirty than the capitalist's. In the wake of this recognition, some postmodern theorists call for a return to the spirit of modernism in order to give back to culture its capacity for critique.

Those who view modernism with more suspicion, as an aesthetic project that failed precisely because it refused to recognize the elitist nature of the assumption that the artist has a privileged critical position, use the name "postmodernism" as a banner under which to propose that a radical cultural production must take new forms because the rhetoric of the avant-garde is no longer applicable to present economic conditions. These economic and political conditions are such that, at least in Western society, political intervention might be possible only through cultural activity or the production of signs. Yet even those who find something to celebrate in the postmodern remain obsessed with ferreting out the many ways in which aesthetic resistance can be domesticated or contained. Critical suspicion often has to stand in for a positive aesthetic project.

My purpose in invoking the discourse of postmodernism in order to situate De Palma is not to classify him as postmodern in relation to Hitchcock as precursor, nor to decide whether he is radical or conservative, a postmodernist of the corrupt school of art or a postmodernist on the cutting edge. Rather, the tensions in the debate about postmodernism suggest that what might be more important to consider is how his work opens questions about the complexities of cultural critique and commentary in the 1980s. Film, as the form of mass culture par excellence, is a particularly important medium in the discourse of postmodernism, one of whose most persuasive claims has been that mass culture cannot be immediately dismissed as either aesthetically bad or politically suspect. The De Palma–Hitchcock connection is significant in that Hitchcock is often celebrated by critics who define his films as high art. If, on the other hand, the value of his work can be recognized as a function of its status as mass culture, then De Palma, too, must be accorded similar recognition.

I would like to argue that *Body Double*'s use of quotation, rather than being simply an imitation of Hitchcock's films, registers two historical developments that mark the difference between the fifties and the eighties: feminism and the rise of visual forms, such as video and television, that have displaced film as the dominant form of mass culture. These two developments need to be linked because, although women have made advances both culturally and economically since the heyday of the nuclear family in the fifties, one of the primary indications of a persistent sexism and a neoconservative backlash against feminism is the continued portrayal of women as sex objects and the use of female sexuality as a means of commodification in visual media such as advertising, television, films, and pornography. Feminist film critics have asked whether the gaze is inherently male, and have attempted to conceive of a cinematic practice in which vision would not be constructed as a form of domination or in which women might appropriate the power of the look rather than being its object.[7] Laura Mulvey's constantly cited and pivotal article on "Visual Pleasure and Narrative Cinema" uses Hitchcock's *Vertigo* to describe how the dominant cinema capitalizes on the processes of fetishism and voyeurism to entertain and reassure its male audience.[8] Her work implies that we are not necessarily in a post-Hitchcock era, but if this is the case, it would be on the grounds that Hitchcock's use of cinematic processes is no less problematic in terms of gender than De Palma's.

Furthermore, if narrative pleasure is not always suspect or avoidable, as challenges to Mulvey's position have suggested, then De Palma's sexual politics, like Hitchcock's, are not immediately decidable. De Palma has been criticized as much for his treatment of women as for his debt to Hitchcock;[9] both criticisms share a misperception of his use of quotation, failing to see how he is reflecting on both Hitchcock and images of women rather than literally repeating these sources in films that are derivative or pornographic. Hitchcock proposes an analogy between libidinal and visual processes; De Palma takes this analogy and shows how its exploitation by mass culture results in the increasing displacement of experience by images. In Hitchcock's films, life or romance operates like the viewing of a movie; in De Palma's film, the consumption of images has become the form that life or romance takes. De Palma's use of allusion reveals how what was once a metaphor has become a reality as he depicts the eighties via Hitchcock's images.

The cross-fertilization of feminism and postmodernism provides another perspective on De Palma. Postmodernism is often said to reveal a new subjectivity, as the "alienation of the subject" is displaced by the "fragmentation" or "decentering" of the subject, which leads to the "waning of affect" (in Jameson's formulation again) in postmodern works.[10] Following this logic, the fact that we have so little investment in De Palma's characters would be a sign, not of his debasement of Hitchcock's psychodrama, but of the fate of subjectivity in our culture. Whereas Hitchcock's exposure of the neurosis that lies behind the easygoing bachelor ways of the characters Jimmy Stewart plays makes our response to him interestingly ambivalent, Jake Scully's anxieties only make him a rather uncompelling wimp. His authority is undermined in a way that Scottie's or Jefferies's never was, beginning with the scene in which he finds his girlfriend cheating on him. Rather than worrying about marriage, he's caught up in the world of postmodern love, trying to manage a live-in arrangement or at least to get laid. The difference between Hitchcock and De Palma is registered in *Body Double*'s rewriting of Scottie's acrophobia as Jake's claustrophobia. The vertical becomes the horizontal; the phallic symbol becomes a vaginal one. Whereas Scottie's masculinity is threatened by his own inadequacies, Jake fears being swallowed up by women who are more powerful than he is.

Jake's troubled authority is a sign of the heightened stakes of maintaining gender roles in a postfeminist era. For the feminist critic, it might be a relief not to feel coerced into identifying with Jake's problems, and to be given enough critical distance even to be able to laugh at him. The decentering of the subject, rather than being a universal phenomenon, might only be a problem for white bourgeois men faced with the challenge to the dominant culture posed by marginal voices. This line of argument is the other pole of postmodern theory, one which valorizes contemporary art for its critical and politically subversive potential. Craig Owens, in a discussion of feminism and postmodernism, suggests that postmodern culture's tendency to rework previous forms can be a radical political strategy, representing a rejection of the modernist faith in revolution through formal innovation: "It is precisely at the legislative frontier between what can be represented and what cannot that the postmodernist operation is being staged — not in order to transcend representation, but in order to expose the system of power that authorizes certain representations while blocking, prohibiting or invalidating others."[11] While De Palma may be neither a feminist nor a political radical, this description of the postmodern project provides for a more sympathetic view of both his use of allusion and his treatment of his male hero.

Although Jake's weakness may silently register the effects of feminism in our culture, *Body Double* also reveals how even in the eighties feminism is both fended off and ignored. The voyeurism and fetishism that Hitchcock reveals to be so closely allied with male desire continue to play a role in the representation of women in pornography, rock videos, and other forms. I'd like to look closely at some of De Palma's visual quotations of Hitchcock to consider what they have to say about how sexism still pervades the production and consumption of images.

One of the more crucial instances of *Body Double*'s debt to *Rear Window* is Jake Scully's observation of his anonymous neighbor's nightly masturbation ritual, made possible by the conveniently placed telescope in his friend's house. A cross between a spaceship and a panopticon, the structure is a scopophiliac's dream house, with a sweeping and safely removed panorama of the city outside and a revolving bed oriented toward a television as the centerpiece inside. In *Rear Window*, Jefferies discovers the possibilities for voyeurism created by his Greenwich Village apartment almost accidentally. Bored and frustrated by his confinement to a wheelchair, he finds distraction in the spectacle provided by his neighbors, whose proximity makes them virtually impossible to ignore. In the hills of Los Angeles, on the other hand, it requires both intention and technology to be a voyeur; Gloria's postmodern glass house provides ample opportunity for observation, but the rich can afford gates and fences to surround the large lots that guarantee their privacy. In a city where neighborhoods don't even have sidewalks, Gloria is Jake's neighbor only in the loosest sense of the term.

Rear Window explores the nature of the crowded urban landscape and the distance and alienation even the intimate space of a rear courtyard creates between people. The courtyard residents live so close to one another that they can only preserve their privacy by actively ignoring their neighbors. When, for example, people emerge from their apartments in response to the cries of the woman who has discovered her dog lying dead in the garden, they react with indifference, as if seeking to avoid the uncomfortable recognition that they share the space with others. In De Palma's Los Angeles, on the other hand, suburban residents are spatially isolated from one another and linked by technologies that bring the world into the home in the form of images.

The institutionalized nature of voyeurism in the eighties, a crucial example of which is pornography, might explain why what Jake sees seems so prepackaged and formulaic when compared with what Jefferies sees. Jefferies's voyeurism consists in transforming his neighbors' random everyday activities into narratives that are projections of his anxieties about marriage and women. The pleasure and power he derives from looking depend on his subjects' unawareness that they are being observed. *Body Double* ups the ante of the ambiguity between that which is displayed for a viewer and that which seems private by presenting as Jake's object a woman who is masturbating. Jefferies's pleasure in Miss Torso's body seems harmless compared to the way Jake and Sam Bouchard gloat lasciviously about their discovery in a moment of male bonding. And in Hitchcock's film the object seems more innocent, too; Miss Torso displays her body in a carefree way as she goes about her household chores in skimpy clothing, while Gloria Revelle/Holly Body's choreographed show is the stuff of pornographic films. Jake's susceptibility to the scene, his belief in its reality, comes from his inability to recognize it as a conventional genre designed for male consumption. Whereas Jefferies makes the mistake of projecting his own fears onto his neighbors' activities, turning reality into a script of his own making, Jake reads a constructed show as natural and unscripted.

De Palma's depiction of voyeurism might seem crude compared to Hitchcock's because it's so much more sexually explicit. Jake's introduction to the object of his desire, unlike Scottie's introduction to Madeleine in *Vertigo*, consists of watching a woman's nearly naked body. Sexual desire remains the latent subtext of Scottie's pursuit of Madeleine; before he even lays eyes on her, his interest is aroused by Gavin Elster's story about her mysterious fascination with Carlotta Valdes, and once he begins to follow her, he is spurred on by the glamour of her wealth and social position, as signified by her clothing, tastes, and manner. There is a narrative to disguise the erotic. Jake's access to Gloria as a sexual object is direct and unmediated by narrative, much like the viewer's relation to pornography, in which plot is simply a pretext for the presentation of sexual activity. In fact, it doesn't seem to matter finally that it is really Holly Body, and not Gloria, that Jake is watching; it's crotch he's after, not the woman herself, as indicated by his sheepish admission to Sam that he didn't even see her face. But the dispensability of narrative is also indicated in *Vertigo*, when, for example, Midge sees through Scottie's interest in the Carlotta Valdes mystery by skeptically asking about Madeleine, "Is she pretty?"

Another way to understand why *Body Double* reveals what *Vertigo* conceals is in terms of the recent trend in pornography toward increasingly explicit images of the female body. In a pair of articles in *Screen* magazine, John Ellis and Paul Willemen attempt to explain this phenomenon, which would seem to contradict the theory that pornography allays castration anxiety by constructing the female body as a fetish object in order to disguise the ugly secret that the sight of the female genitals would expose.[12] Willemen argues that the explicit display of the body, and the prevalence of scenes of masturbation or lesbian sex that appear to exclude men, works to manage male anxiety about increasing pressures to respond to female demands for pleasure. The viewer's privileged visual access to a woman's pleasure or genitalia ultimately provides him with control over her sexuality. In *Body Double*, we can see how Holly Body's performance, while ostensibly a private act, is designed to be viewed. Her body is elaborately decorated with jewels and tantalizingly veiled by a negligee. She incites the scopophilic drive by being not quite open to view; Jake has to work hard at the controls of the telescope to focus the image. Holly's self-absorption serves not to shut him out but to guarantee that he won't be seen. He is able to plumb the mysteries of the female orgasm, free from any anxiety about his own performance. Thus, De Palma uses Hitchcock to speculate not just on how voyeurism in general domesticates the threat of female sexuality, but on how the institution of pornography does so and has become so pervasive that its images become the form experience takes. Jefferies turns real life into an image, whereas Jake's reality *is* an image.

Once his interest in the woman he thinks is Gloria Revelle has been aroused, Jake begins to pursue her, but unlike Scottie's attraction to Madeleine, his sexual desire is always made explicit. Jake never seems to be falling in love with Gloria; he just wants to fuck her. And in fact, he almost gets what he wants without even having to take the trouble to seduce her. He doesn't have to play the hero; Gloria rescues him rather than vice versa after his bumbling attempt to fend off the crazy Indian psychokiller ends with him being convulsed by claustrophobia in a tunnel that is a horizontal version of the mission bell tower.

Once outside the tunnel, Gloria falls into his arms without any introduction at all. She seems quite willing to conform to Jake's pornographic fantasy about her sexual availability. The sequence is filmed in a quotation of the 360-degree tracking shot Hitchcock uses in *Vertigo* to depict the culmination of Judy's transformation into Madeleine. Judy emerges from the bathroom in a haze of light, having just submitted to Scottie's final command that she put her hair up in order to resemble Madeleine in every detail. As Scottie proceeds to embrace her, the music builds to a climax and the camera makes a full circle around the couple, prolonging the moment and heightening its dramatic intensity. Hitchcock's shot is a stand-in for sexual consummation; the scene cuts to a clearly postcoital conversation as Judy/Madeleine dresses for dinner. Once again De Palma's version of the scene is more explicit. This is no demure or tentative embrace, but full-on sexual foreplay. Gloria writhes in excitement and turns her body to the camera to reveal her unbuttoned dress. The camera work also exaggerates Hitchcock. De Palma carries the shot to ludicrous extremes, as the camera revolves not once but three times around the lovers, leaving the viewer in a state of vertigo. He emphasizes the discontinuity of the moment from any narrative that precedes it by breaking the 180-degree rule at the beginning and end of the sequence. We are in a cinematic fantasy space, the trompe l'oeil mural at the tunnel's entrance emphasizing the illusory nature of the moment.

However, a similar perspective is implicit in Hitchcock's use of the 360-degree shot. We would like to believe that the scene between Judy and Scottie is the real thing, and the camera work both allows this suspension of disbelief and demonstrates the illusions upon which the romance depends. The shifting of the background to the scene in the mission stable suggests a continuity between Scottie's past encounter with Madeleine and his present encounter with Judy-as-Madeleine, but the clearly artificial nature of this shot, made possible only by the powers of special effects, reveals this continuity to be Scottie's fantasy. The scene ends with the lovers suffused in green light, enclosed in the intimate circle of the viewer's all-embracing perspective. But the fact that they're so cut off from any context indicates that the transcendence of the moment cannot be sustained, that their love doesn't exist in a real world. There is a tragic poignancy in this climax of Scottie's quest for Madeleine. De Palma, on the other hand, never allows the viewer to get sentimental in the illusory nature of romance, but in De Palma's world of casual sexual encounters, the illusion doesn't even have to be believed in order to exert its visual attraction.

When Jakes does finally meet Holly Body in the flesh, the 360-degree shot is used again. The artifice of the sequence is even more pronounced than before because it occurs as part of a film within a film, a porn flick that looks like a rock video. The Frankie Goes to Hollywood song, with its sexually explicit lyrics ("Relax, don't do it when you wanna come"), and the leather bar setting emphasize that pornography is everywhere, incorporated into all forms of mass culture. That one of the film's most sexually explicit episodes takes the form of a rock video alerts us to the fact that problematic representations of sexuality are not local to pornography, which becomes the genre scapegoated for both representing and causing violence against women.

At stake in Jake's discovery of Holly Body is the way in which television, even more so than film, caters to voyeuristic desires. Life consists of the consumption of images. Whereas Jefferies alternates between the flesh-and-blood Grace Kelly filmed in close-up and the more distant show provided by his neighbors, Jake alternates between one image and another, between his television and Holly Body's pornographic performance taken as reality. With the aid of his remote-control device, he has total control over the screen. In a bit of detective work reminiscent of the scene in *Rear Window* when Jefferies uses slides to verify that the flower bed has been tampered with, Jake discovers the body double when, idly watching the porn channel on television, he recognizes Holly Body as the woman he saw masturbating. His access to Holly Body's image is made possible by the fact that pornography is one more option provided by the riches of cable television, not a marginalized form distributed in underground networks. The preview for Holly Body's newest film is advertised in the way that all movies are, with a series of clips and with press reviews superimposed over the images. Jake has the option of buying the tape version of the film at the all-night video store where adult movies are just one more genre in a store that caters to all tastes. The clerk, as if listing sexual preferences, assures him that the tape is available in "VHS, whatever you want, half-inch, three-quarter, Beta." Jake can watch the video in the privacy of his own home and, with the help of the fast forward, slow motion, and freeze frame controls, find exactly the image he wants. The technology and distribution of video makes pornography more accessible, and images increasingly substitute for direct contact with the world. Even when Judy is playing Madeleine, Scottie is at least spending time with a real woman; in *Body Double*, the middle woman is eliminated and Jake need only watch a screen, identifying Holly Body because of the easy reproducibility of images.

The rock video sequence contains an allusion to the scene in which Scottie follows Madeleine into the florist's shop. Once again what was latent in Hitchcock is rendered explicit by De Palma. The flowers that suggest female sexuality and genitalia are replaced by the real thing; Jake gets to meet the leather-clad Holly Body, her trademark ass exposed and framed for emphasis. He goes through a door marked "Sluts," guiltily looking around to see if he's being observed before he furtively enters. Scottie does the same thing in the dark passageway between the street and the store, looking very much like someone on a secret visit to a pornshop or a prostitute. As Jake opens the door, the mirror on the back of it reflects Holly Body, just as Madeleine is reflected in a mirror as Scottie watches her. Hitchcock's shot reveals in a single image the nature of the voyeuristic process. We focus on the viewer, and what he sees is represented in the form of an image, a reflection of his fantasy. The contact between subject and object is indirect, mediated by an image which provides the distance that guarantees the voyeur's power and safety. However, instead of Judy dressed as Madeleine, we have Holly in leather. The role of clothing as fetish is made explicit, since Holly's leather signifies sex much more blatantly than does Judy's grey suit. It might seem that De Palma has ruined the subtlety of Hitchcock's revelation that sexual desire is a function of dress rather than undress. But the same principle is at issue; the libido finds its object in images rather than in direct sexual contact.

De Palma goes one step further, however. The mirror's real revelation about how images mediate reality comes when it reflects the camera, after it has reflected the woman. Suddenly the viewer's relation to this moment as real is entirely undercut. Just as the breaking of the 180-degree rule in the beach scene reveals the artificiality of the 360-degree tracking shot, the second use of the shot is preceded by an exposure of the scene as a fiction. Once the scene has been framed as artifice, the possibility of our seeing Holly and Jake's embrace as a moment of romance or even genuine sexual activity is removed. This is show biz and the aim is to get a come shot, not to convey psychological passion. Rather than remaining focused on the couple's heads, the camera moves down to show Holly removing Jake's pants and Jake grabbing the real object of his quest, her ass. The camera's emphasis is on the body from the waist down, not faces or psyches. As it spirals around the two of them, and cuts back and forth between Gloria Revelle and Holly Body, the distinction between original and repeat no longer matters. Holly is no more or less important than Gloria; both women are just bodies conforming to generic images. We have only the latest in visual commodities, a glossy production spiked with the raciness of porn and the barest suggestion of narrative. De Palma shows how Hitchcock's principles can be adapted by mass cultural forms so technically sophisticated and seductive that they don't need to depict psychological relations to be compelling. The episode poses the problem of the relation between high and mass culture that pervades the discourse of postmodernism: if mass cultural forms can appropriate all the formal techniques usually used to celebrate and identify contemporary high culture—disruption, lack of narrative, allusions to previous works, self-reflexivity—how is one to locate a formal strategy whose political correctness is guaranteed? If this is not possible, then the field is open for any formal strategy to carry various political valences, and De Palma cannot be dismissed simply for quoting Hitchcock.

Holly Body and Jake's encounter is not loaded with the same psychological and emotional intensity created in *Vertigo* by the drama of Scottie's desire to recapture the lost Madeleine and of Judy's conflict between wanting to please him and wanting to be loved for herself. However, its superficiality allows Holly Body to escape Judy's fatal investment in the man who pursues her. Her continual resistance to Jake and her streetwise toughness give her a strength and charisma that make for a feminist moment in the film. As a woman who sells her sexuality, she remains in control of her body as commodity, never susceptible to making the exchange an emotional one. She matter-of-factly tells Jake what kinds of scenes she will and won't perform, and by openly acknowledging that she is playing a role maintains an emotional distance unavailable to Judy in her disguise as Madeleine. In *Body Double*, it is Jake who has to masquerade; he adopts the persona of a sleazy porn producer in order to trap Holly Body into confessing her deception. When she does finally admit that she played Gloria Revelle, it is without guilt, and Jake is forced to defend himself for having deceived her. Judy, on the other hand, is bullied and victimized by Scottie's angry accusations as he drags her up the stairs of the bell tower and, oblivious to his own creation of a masquerade, blames her for having played the role of Madeleine in Elster's murder plot. Her hopes of winning Scottie now completely shattered, Judy submits helplessly when he forces her to replay the murder scenario in order to cure his own impotence. Rather than palely imitating Hitchcock's drama, De Palma downplays his characters' psychological involvement in order to focus on the manipulation of images and the commodification of sexuality, and in the process he reverses the balance of power between the sexes.

The final moments of *Body Double*, in which Jake barely manages to rescue Holly Body from murder, pinpoint again the impotence of the American male and the potential for a feminist resistance. The last shot before the epilogue shows Jake standing helplessly at the side of the womblike grave in which Holly sits, only her face visible. His posture echoes Scottie's stance in the last moment of *Vertigo* when he stares down at Judy's body from the bell tower. But Jake's Judy doesn't get sacrificed for the sake of his cure; Holly may be in a grave, but better that than trust Jake's helping hand. "Don't touch me. I'm not dead yet," she screams. "Are you going to stay in there the rest of your life?" Jake asks. This is the unanswered question; as long as the visual relations the movie has exposed exist, the only thing Holly can do is say no, resist being sucked in by nice guys who turn out to harbor perverse impulses. It may not be the high tragedy of *Vertigo*, but the image reveals the still perilous state of relations between the sexes, without giving us a dead woman.[13] To denigrate De Palma's work for its superficiality or lack of pathos is to overlook the way his allusions can be a strategy for critique, a strategy he shares with others who have a more overt investment in cultural politics. And reading Hitchcock in light of De Palma's revisions of him allows us to avoid the danger of placing Hitchcock's work in a past from which we shouldn't be too quick to separate ourselves, or in an eternal present that would be a nightmare for women.

The task of discussing Hitchcock and De Palma together should not be to decide who is the greater director, nor to identify a history of styles or culture; it would be a mistake to displace the questions of sexual and cultural politics their work raises onto questions formulated as though aesthetics were an autonomous realm. The problems posed by representations of women and sexuality are not local to De Palma's work, just as they are not local to pornography. While De Palma may not be a subtle artist or a subtle thinker about women, his work reminds us that the dangers and pleasures of representation are both readily visible and sometimes quite ominously invisible.

Notes

1. See, for example, *The Anti-Aesthetic: Essays on Postmodern Culture*, ed. Hal Foster (Port Townsend, Wash.: Bay Press, 1983), especially, "Modernity—An Incomplete Project" by Jurgen Habermas, and "The Discourse of Others: Feminists and Postmodernism" by Craig Owens; Frederic Jameson, "Postmodernism or the Cultural Logic of Late Capitalism," *New Left Review*, no. 146 (Fall 1984), 53-92; Mike Davis, "Urban Renaissance and the Spirit of Postmodernism," *New Left Review*, no. 151 (Winter 1985), 106-13; Jean-François Lyotard, *The Postmodern Condition: A Report on Knowledge* (Minneapolis: University of Minnesota Press, 1984); Jean Baudrillard, *In The Shadow of the Silent Majorities* (New York: Semiotext(e), 1983) and *Simulations* (New York: Semiotext(e), 1982).
2. For a discussion of Hitchcock's usefulness for feminist film theory, see Tania Modleski, *The Women Who Knew Too Much: Hitchcock and Feminist Theory* (New York: Methuen, 1988).
3. Jameson, 66-71.
4. See the following reviews: Vincent Canby, "De Palma Evokes 'Vertigo' in 'Body Double,'" *The New York Times*, 26 October 1984; Richard Corliss, "Dark Nights for the Libido," *Time*, 29 October 1984, 102; Jack Kroll, "Flesh and Fantasies," *Newsweek*, 29 October 1984. For a defense of De Palma's films as they relate both to Hitchcock's work and to contemporary sexual politics, see Robin Wood, *Hollywood from Vietnam to Reagan* (New York: Columbia University Press, 1986).
5. Jameson, 61-64.
6. For examples of the mass media's recent canonization of Hitchcock, see "The Master Who Knew Too Much," *Time*, 26 March 1984, 77-78; Janet Maslin, "'Vertigo' Still Gives Rise to Powerful Emotions," *The New York Times*, 15 January 1984; Andrew Sarris, "Hitchcock's Split Vision," *The Village Voice*, 8 January 1984. Sarris says of *Vertigo*, "If Hitchcock had made only this one movie, he would be stamped forever after as one of the incontestably and luminously major artists of the medium," "Return of the 'Missing' Hitchcocks" *The Village Voice*, 23 August 1983.
7. For discussions of this issue in recent feminist film criticism, see E. Ann Kaplan, *Women and Film: Both Sides of the Camera* (New York: Methuen, 1983); Jane Gaines, "Women and Representation," *Jump Cut*, no. 29; E. Ann Kaplan, "Feminist Film Criticism: Current Issues and Problems," *Studies in the Literary Imagination* 19, no. 1 (Spring 1986), 7-20.

8. Laura Mulvey, "Visual Pleasure and Narrative Cinema," *Screen* 16, no. 3 (Autumn 1975), 6–18.

9. See Marcia Pally, "'Double' Trouble," *Film Comment* 20, no. 5 (September-October 1984), 12–17, an article and interview with De Palma that provoked a series of responses about pornography and film. See also "Pornography: Love or Death?" *Film Comment* 20, no. 6 (November-December 1984), 29–49.

10. Jameson, 61–64.

11. Owens, 59.

12. John Ellis, "Photography/Pornography/Art/Pornography" *Screen* 21, no. 1 (Spring 1980), 79–108, and Paul Willemen, "Letter to John," *Screen* 21, no. 2 (Summer 1980), 53–66.

13. The image of a porn star as resisting woman resembles the strategy of Bette Gordon's *Variety*, a film which the director describes as an attempt to remake Hitchcock in feminist terms. In *Variety*, a woman who sells tickets in the box office of a porn movie theater gradually acquires control of the sexual marketplace and her own desires by playing the role of prostitute and arranging a liaison with the rich businessman about whom she fantasizes. Influenced by the pro-sex position on pornography and feminist film theory, and attempting, in opposition to Mulvey's project, to explore the potential for the female spectator to experience narrative pleasure, Gordon seems closer in spirit to De Palma than to antipornography feminists. Gordon's revision of existing systems of representation resembles the strategy of the feminist critic of De Palma; just as one need not reject narrative in pursuit of utopian formal alternatives, one cannot ignore Hollywood or male directors in order to focus on avant-garde cinema or women. Feminism must proceed on multiple fronts and the work of critique is crucial. Gordon describes her project in "*Variety*: The Pleasure in Looking," *Pleasure and Danger: Exploring Female Sexuality*, ed. Carol Vance (Boston: Routledge and Kegan Paul, 1984).

THE CONCEPT OF THE FANTASTIC IN *VERTIGO*

Ann West

Throughout his American filmmaking career, Alfred Hitchcock employed the conventions of the evolving genres of the suspense thriller, family melodrama, spy drama, and comedy that he employed in England. But his expressionist camera work and composition, as well as his use of ironic plot devices, often contributed to the sense of the fantastic and the absurd. It is suggested here that Hitchcock used the concept of the fantastic not only to enhance the development of the action but also to startle his audience by altering the formula of the traditional realist genre, a goal he shared with the postmodernists.

Hitchcock seemed especially conscious of the magical qualities of women.[1] He often characterized women's powers as bordering on the supernatural. In the film *Vertigo* Hitchcock employs the theme of the dead woman who is virtually present in the shape of an image in a painting. A prominent characteristic of the story is the evocation of the dead by means of a channeling through a living person.

The presence of such overtones of the supernatural contributed to Hitchcock's popularity both on television and at movie theaters. Hitchcock conveyed a special awareness of the relationship between films and the spectator. His remarks at the start and conclusion of his television films reflect a delight in amusing the audience by making puns about the advertisements and by calling attention to the horrifying devices for punishing or murdering that he used in his teleplays. In his comments on *Rear Window*, Hitchcock spoke of a film's message as dual, as a story told in realist detail yet containing clues about itself as a visual contrivance.[2]

Because of this duality, R. Barton Palmer suggests that Hitchcock's work is metafictional, for it is neither realist nor modernist, but a combination of both conventions, and thus a form of postmodernism.[3] Palmer refers to the work of Patricia Waugh, author of *Metafiction: The Theory and Practice of Self-Conscious Fiction*, who states: "Metafiction is a term given to fictional writing which self-consciously and systematically draws attention to its status as an artifact in order to pose questions about the relationship between fiction and reality."[4] Metafiction, considered a form of postmodernism, tends toward the "exaggeration of the tensions and oppositions inherent in all novels: of frame and frame-break, of technique and counter-technique, of construction and deconstruction of illusion."[5]

Hitchcock appears to have used his cameo appearances for this purpose — as a humorous means of reminding the viewer of the illusional nature of film and of his own role as a film director. Hitchcock's appearance on-screen has the effect of interrupting the story and of deconstructing the illusion for the spectator.

Palmer hypothesizes that Hitchcock films such as *Psycho, Rear Window, The Birds*, and *Vertigo* are metafictional works because they are not only a form of traditional realist fiction but also a form of deconstruction, that is, statements about the ways that genre affects the expectations of the spectator and about the process of the construction of the illusion. I believe that Hitchcock specifically employed the concept of the fantastic for metafictional purposes to call attention to realist fictional conventions and to subvert generic formulas.[6]

Writing about the fantastic, Tzvetan Todorov suggests that it is the "hesitation" or "doubt" on the part of the reader of fantastic fiction as to whether events can be explained by natural or supernatural phenomena which is the reason for referring to that type of fiction as the fantastic.[7] It is perhaps these elements of hesitation and doubt that not only enhance the suspense of certain Hitchcock thrillers but also tend to deconstruct the illusion that is created. His stylized sound effects, music, and cinematography implicate the spectators, posing them in the position of readers of fantastic fiction, requiring them to decide if an event should be interpreted as ordinary or extraordinary. And like those American and Italian detective novels considered postmodernist, of which Stefano Tani writes in *The Doomed Detective,* certain Hitchcock films contain a "destruction of the traditional [and taken-for-granted] relation of trust between the reader and the text," or between the viewer and the director; just as the spectator relaxes and accepts one or the other option (ordinary or extraordinary), the story concludes without resolution.[8]

Vertigo is a notable example of Hitchcock's use of the fantastic to call attention to and subvert traditional genres. The film is a reflexive statement about how film is a contrived illusion designed to manipulate audience reaction. Hitchcock creates the illusion during the first half of the film, deconstructs the illusion by revealing the nature of the illusion, and then self-consciously creates doubts about the illusion during the final segment by ending it with an unpredictable conclusion.

In the plot of the film, Scottie (James Stewart) is hired by her husband to follow Madeleine (Kim Novak), whose wanderings take her to museums and famous historical sites from which she seems to receive guidance, as if from the world of the supernatural, from her long dead great-grandmother Carlotta Valdes. During his surveillance of the wandering Madeleine at these sites, Scottie becomes obsessed with her and her association with death. Interestingly, Hitchcock said in his interview with Truffaut that *Vertigo* is based on the concept of necrophilia.[9] As Todorov suggests, the love of someone in the form of a statue or painting, as for a place of historical meaning or a shrine, represents a kind of love of the dead or necrophilia, which is a common theme of the fantastic. In *Vertigo* it is both the male hero's fascination with the possibility that the heroine is a reincarnation of the great-grandmother, as well as the heroine's apparent compulsion to visit places of historical significance (and especially a museum that contains a painting of the long-dead woman), which can be said to represent the sources of necrophilia.

In his essay "The Uncanny," Freud discusses the notion of immortalization and preservation of the spirit from extinction through the creation of monuments, museums, and mummies from permanent materials that house the spirit — in other words, the use of doubling to preserve ordinary and everyday things.[10] In one of Hitchcock's later films, *Psycho*, Norman stuffs birds, just as he preserved the corpse of his mother, entombing her in the mausoleum of their Gothic house. Here in *Vertigo*, as in *North by Northwest*, the shrines are museums and monuments that have national and historic significance, but they exude the same aura of the fantastic, making a colorful tourist setting seem ordinary, yet strange.[11]

We do not always attach supernatural or spiritual meanings to obsessions such as Madeleine's with figures from other times in history. But throughout the first half of the film, Hitchcock compels the viewer constantly to experience doubt and to reevaluate whether Madeleine's wanderings to such places are really guided by the supernatural, by excessive sentimentality, or by a mental disturbance of some sort. During the second half of the story, of course, we are made aware of the contrived nature of the story about the supernatural.

Throughout the early part of the film, subjective tracking shots place Scottie in the position of the spectator as he follows Madeleine through San Francisco to a florist's shop, to Carlotta's grave at the Mission Dolores, and to a seat before Carlotta's portrait at the Palace of the Legion of Honor. The distance from which we observe Madeleine is the distance Scottie maintains as he observes her, his vision sometimes partially obscured by tombstones, by trees, or by the distorted effect of a combined point-of-view–mirror shot, as at the florist's shop. Such subjective shots enhance the otherworldly quality of Madeleine, as do her dreamlike movements and her attitude of remoteness.

In addition, some of her actions clearly border on the fantastic. When she visits the McKittrick Hotel, where Carlotta once resided, Madeleine and her car seem to disappear. When questioned by Scottie, the concierge says that she's not even seen Madeleine enter the building, yet Scottie has seen Madeleine walk toward the building and later push open the curtains of an upstairs window, a shot that makes Madeleine's character seem distant, otherworldly, not quite real. By showing the spectator only the shots of Madeleine approaching the building, then appearing at the upstairs window, Hitchcock seems to be suggesting that the spectator has no reason to assume that Madeleine actually walked by the concierge sitting at the desk on the first floor. Hitchcock is not only telling the story but also hinting at the nature of its construction as an illusion.

This mysterious quality of Madeleine is further emphasized by the unusual nature of what she says. For example, in the forest of sequoias with Scottie, she says, "I don't like it — knowing that I have to die." They look at an ancient felled tree and she remarks, pointing to the different rings within the trunk's core, "Somewhere here I was born, and there I died. It was only a moment for you; you took no notice."

When Madeleine walks away, she soon disappears from view, and her absence from the lingering point-of-view shot that follows seems to emphasize, as Robin Wood states, the brief nature of human existence.[12] Yet Hitchcock seems once again to be making a comment about the world of pretense and camera tricks.

A more obvious visual trick is played on both the spectator and Scottie when Madeleine apparently dies by jumping from the San Juan Bautista church tower. She goes up the stairs, out of Scottie's sight (in other words, off camera), but a double, the murdered wife of Elster, is seen falling through the air, like a stunt person. Because the falling woman is seen wearing the same outfit and appears to have the same hair style and hair color as Madeleine, it is assumed by the viewer, as by Scottie, who does not go to see for himself, that she is Madeleine.

Hitchcock said that editing allows such acts of the imagination to occur and affords to the director the freedom to create such illusions. Hitchcock is perhaps referring to the process of "supplementary visualization," whereby a reader or viewer adds detail, whether of a factual of visual nature, to embellish a story or to complete the image.[13]

Christian Metz refers to this type of visual trickery, whereby a stunt person is used as a double, as "imperceptible *trucage*."[14] The viewer may suspect that a stunt person is used as a double yet suspends disbelief during the film. Metz says that when a special angle is used to flatter an actress, or when special shoes are worn to give height to an actor, it is also considered to be a form of imperceptible *trucage*. At the other extreme of the spectrum is, of course, montage, the most conspicuous example of manipulated images which serve to control the viewer's response.

Soon after the death of Madeleine, an emotionally distraught Scottie has a nightmare, which is subjectively shot in the form of an animated montage sequence. The filmic conceptualization of dreams is often done in animated form, but the colorful, cartoonlike quality of the montage tends to emphasize its fictional nature in *Vertigo*. Because he is subsequently seen at a sanitarium, it is unclear whether the montage is intended to represent simply a bad dream, a kind of psychotic experience, or a message from the afterlife. The doubts are created in part because the images of the nightmare reflect not Scottie's obsessions, except for the vertigo, but the obsessions of Madeleine.

The first shot of the montage sequence is that of a bouquet like the one Madeleine earlier pulled apart and tossed onto the water — an image only she and the spectator could have seen before she jumped into the bay in an apparent attempt to commit suicide. The following image reminds us of her act of plucking apart the posy: it is a cartoonlike bouquet of paper flowers which then also comes apart.

A brief glimpse of Carlotta Valdes dressed in the gown she wears in the painting is seen next, posed between Elster and Scottie, suggesting something else that Scottie could not have known: either that Carlotta's spirit is still present or, since Carlotta faces Elster in a kind of collusion, that perhaps her paranormal possession of Madeleine is merely a fictitious story. Yet how could Scottie know or suspect this at the time of his nightmare? Only Madeleine might have known.

When Scottie subsequently plunges downward in his dream, as Robin Wood asserts, he "achieves identity with Madeleine, first by sinking into her grave (as described by her earlier in the scene by the sea), then by falling onto the roof."[15] Wood refers to the scene by the sea earlier in the film, when Madeleine told Scottie of her recurring dream in which she sees an open grave, her grave, with a new gravestone, waiting for her at the end of the corridor. That dream seems to represent a kind of foreshadowing of Scottie's own subsequent nightmare. The images in the nightmare suggest that, in his dream life, Scottie seems to have become a channel for Madeleine, just as she, in both her wanderings and dream life, appeared to be a channel for Carlotta.

Hitchcock deliberately continues to foster such confusion in the mind of the spectator when, after Madeleine apparently dies, Scottie returns to the places where he had seen her before—outside her apartment building, at the museum, in the restaurant—and sees women whose appearances bear an uncanny resemblance to Madeleine's (her clothing, her hair color and style, her posture and walk), all forms of imperceptible *trucage* deliberately employed by Hitchcock to emphasize the distinction between what is imagined and what is real.

Later, when Scottie is looking through a flower shop window at a bouquet similar both to the one Madeleine had purchased and the one in the portrait of Carlotta, Judy coincidentally walks by, and he looks up to see her. Scottie then follows Judy to her hotel, where she reappears at the upstairs window, just as she had done earlier as Madeleine at the McKittrick Hotel. Her gesture of standing at the window, portraitlike, links her not only to Madeleine but also to the framed museum portrait of Carlotta. The character of Judy thus appears to be a channel for both Madeleine and Carlotta. The sense of coincidence in connection with her appearance seems designed to suggest the aura of the fantastic, but our feelings of wonder are then dissipated when we hear Judy's side of the story through flashback, a visual memory that commences with her direct and deliberate stare at the spectator.

Unaware of Judy's complicity in the crime, Scottie tries to recreate Judy in Madeleine's image. Judy at first resists, but eventually relents. He buys her the same grey suit and shoes that Madeleine wore. Finally, when her hair is dyed platinum blonde and she emerges from the bathroom with her hair in the same style as Madeleine's, Judy appears as a kind of filmy wraithlike apparition in the distance; she is now truly a ghost of Madeleine. When she and Scottie kiss and the camera rotates around their embrace, Scottie sees projected behind them the setting of the livery stable, where he last kissed her. It is as if time has stood still and the original Madeleine is restored to him, as she was just prior to her death, wearing the same grey suit.

Hitchcock is once again not only telling the story but also hinting at the deliberate nature of its construction as an illusion. He is perhaps alluding to the suspension of disbelief that naturally occurs among viewers of a film. That is, once Scottie has recreated his fantasy of Madeleine in terms of her dress and appearance, he even begins, Hitchcock suggests, to imagine seeing her in the last place they kissed: the livery stable. Again, the line between reality and fantasy disappears, both for Scottie and the viewer.

The resolution of the film, however, seems to be explained by normal events, rather than by the supernatural: when Judy puts on the necklace, which is a copy of the one worn by Carlotta in the museum portrait, Scottie finally learns that he has been tricked. The combined point-of-view–mirror shot that is then superimposed over the shot of the portrait of Carlotta emphasizes Scottie's dawning sense of recognition.

The subjective montage of backward tracking shots that follows parallels an earlier montage of forward tracking shots toward Madeleine and the portrait of Carlotta at the museum.[16] In the montage we see Carlotta staring back at the viewer, a shot that seems intended by Hitchcock to be a kind of metaphorical statement about the illusionary nature of cinema.

In addition, the combined point-of-view–mirror shot of Madeleine and Scottie echoes the earlier shot in the florist's shop, where Scottie faces the mirror into which Madeleine looks, a shot that creates a distorted sense of space and distance.[17] Both series of point-of-view–mirror shots are reflexive statements that also serve to deconstruct the illusion. The second is, of course, more decisive in terms of representing Scottie's dawning sense of recognition about the "real" nature of events.

Afterward, Scottie drives Judy to the church at San Juan Bautista, where he confronts her with his knowledge of her complicity in the crime. As she struggles to get away, Scottie accuses her: "You were the counterfeit. . . . He made you over just like I made you over. . . . Did he train you? Did he rehearse you?" Scottie's remarks seem designed both to remind the viewer not only of his sense of final release from the illusion of Madeleine but also of the director's complicity in the creation of the fiction. Yet Scottie then exclaims: "I loved you, Madeleine," a statement that creates doubts for the spectator as to whether Scottie is really free of the fictional illusion or not.

And equally fantastic, at the top platform of the tower, by a strange stroke of fate, Judy leaps to her death, just as Elster suggested Madeleine would do at the beckoning of Carlotta. Judy is startled by the approaching form of a nun who enters silently and appears wraithlike in the dark tower. Although she is a nun and not a spirit from the afterlife, the nun's garb and the spiritual nature of her work suggest that Hitchcock may have wanted to establish a reference to the afterlife. However, because Carlotta is not necessarily a good spirit, a feeling of incongruity and confusion perplexes the viewer.

But the conclusion is still so shocking that it represents a final instance of Hitchcock's destruction of trust with the viewer, an essential element of postmodernist fiction. For even by his earlier introduction of both Midge's comic painting of herself as Carlotta and the unlikely character of Judy into the plot, Hitchcock seems to have been gently calling attention to the idea of plot as contrivance and foreshadowing the unpredictable conclusion.

Yet Judy's character is an appropriate postmodernist character. In her book *Metafictional Characters in Modern Drama*, Jane Schleuter refers to the "relativity of identity."[18] She suggests that in postmodernist texts the individual is "constantly donning masks to play the role demanded" of him or her.[19] Such characters reflect the search for an identity that is always shifting, just as in real life.

> The metafictional character, whether he be game-playing, role-playing, or involved in any number of variations, possesses two distinct fictive identities, between which we are forced to distinguish, accepting one of the fictive identities as "real" and the other as "fictive." At times the metafictional character is the embodiment of one portion of its duality, and at other times the embodiment of the other portion. Ultimately, though, these two aspects of reality and illusion are both embodied in the same character, giving the playwright the perfect opportunity to confuse them once he has distinguished them.[20]

Thus, by the conclusion of the film, it is apparent that the two characters Kim Novak plays, Madeleine and Judy, are indistinguishable. By falling from the tower, Judy/Madeleine not only shocks the audience by the unexpected conclusion, but the "real" and "fictive" characters also confuse the spectator in regard to whose identity is dominant, and who has really died. Also, the question inevitably poses itself as to whether Judy/Madeleine really acted as a channel for the dead Carlotta after all. Is it especially strange, the audience must ask itself, that Judy/Madeleine should be confused and driven to her death by the emergence of a ghostly apparition?

Nonetheless, we, as spectators, are meant to share Scottie's sense of horror and disbelief, for it is only a misperception—not an actual force from the spiritual world—that unaccountably confuses and distorts Judy and/or Madeleine's sense of reality. But there still lingers doubt as to whether such a strange development can be explained by natural or supernatural phenomena; there is no resolution.

Thus the spectator, like Hitchcock's anti-hero Scottie, must simply react in shock, trying to interpret events, not as an agent in charge of those events, but simply as an onlooker who is powerless to change the course of those events. Scottie is a true postmodernist detective who "gets emotionally caught up . . . and is torn apart between the upsurge of feelings and the necessity for rationality," as Tani states in *The Doomed Detective*.[21] Scottie's vertigo, his temporary emotional disturbance, and his obsession with changing Judy all constitute some form of the postmodernist detective's angst. These states can be said to parallel those of the spectator, who not only sees through Scottie's eyes as he follows Madeleine early in the film, but also shares the same sense of hallucinated space when he experiences vertigo, the same desire to change Judy later in the film, and the same sense of shock at the conclusion. The confusion experienced by the spectator is partly explained by Laura Mulvey, who writes that "Hitchcock uses the process of identification normally associated with ideological correctness and the recognition of established morality and shows up its perverted side."[22] But also, as Tani states, "The reader [or spectator] gets involved in the mystery and in the detection to be only partially or not at all rewarded by a plausible denouement."[23] Thus, the jolting experience of watching Judy fall from the tower at the conclusion of the film, which leaves the audience unsettled and wondering, is perhaps the most obvious example in *Vertigo* of the fantastic being used for postmodernist purposes.

Just as Hitchcock often divorced himself from genre conventions by humorously ridiculing his program's sponsors or the gruesome methods used for committing a murder during his teleplays, so in the film *Vertigo* he seems to be highlighting reference, though somewhat obliquely, to the distinction between pretense and reality through his refusal to supply a satisfying conclusion and a coherent explanation of the film's fantastic events.

Notes

1. In the 1960s Hitchcock wanted to film the play *Mary Rose* by J. M. Barrie (author of *Peter Pan*). A story about the supernatural, *Mary Rose* tells of a young woman who mysteriously disappears while on an island in the Hebrides with her husband and a friend. She returns briefly twenty-five years later to find her family much older; subsequently, she returns again as a ghost to visit her son as a mature man. See John Russell Taylor, *Hitch: The Life and Times of Alfred Hitchcock* (New York: Pantheon Books, 1978), 273.
2. Alfred Hitchcock, "Rear Window," in *Focus on Hitchcock*, ed. Albert LaValley (Englewood Cliffs, N.J.: Prentice-Hall, 1972), 40.
3. R. Barton Palmer, "The Metafictional Hitchcock: The Experience of Viewing and the Viewing of Experience in *Rear Window* and *Psycho*," *Cinema Journal* 25, no. 2 (Winter 1986), 4–19.
4. Patricia Waugh, *Metafiction: The Theory and Practice of Self-Conscious Fiction* (New York: Methuen, 1984), 2.
5. Waugh, 2.
6. For a discussion of the different types of fantasy fiction, see Dieter Petzold, "Fantasy Fiction and Related Genres," *Modern Fiction Studies* 32, no. 1 (Spring 1986), 11–20. Unlike the alternative mode (utopian literature), the desiderative mode (fairy tales), and the applicative mode (political allegories), the subversive mode does not depart from reality as apparently or radically as the other modes. In the subversive mode the author creates an atmosphere that merely threatens the "reader's [or viewer's] concept of reality and his sense of security based on it." The subversive mode (elements of which are employed by Hitchcock) results in the following: "Typically, such worlds seem 'normal' or 'realistic' until some strange, inexplicable element disrupts their quiet surface. Indeed, texts of this kind often take great pains to appear noematic [realistic] to represent 'the true' (though partially occult) reality. We are here in the realm of the uncanny and the fantastic in Todorov's sense. Typical genres in which a subversive relation to reality dominates are the Gothic and the horror story, typical authors include Poe, Hoffmann, and Kafka."
7. Tzvetan Todorov, *The Fantastic: A Structural Approach to a Literary Genre*, trans. Richard Howard (Ithaca, N.Y.: Cornell University Press, 1975).
8. Stefano Tani, *The Doomed Detective: The Contribution of the Detective Novel to Postmodern American and Italian Fiction* (Carbondale: Southern Illinois University Press, 1984), 130.
9. François Truffaut, *Hitchcock* (New York: Simon and Schuster, 1967), 186.
10. Sigmund Freud, "The Uncanny," *The Standard Edition of the Complete Psychological Works of Sigmund Freud*, trans. and ed. James Strachey et al. (London: Hogarth, 1953), 17: 217–52.
11. See, for example, Raymond Bellour's discussion of the Oedipal journey of Roger Thornhill in *North by Northwest* in "Le Blocage Symbolique," *Communications*, no. 23 (1975), 235–350.
12. Robin Wood, *Hitchcock's Films* (New York: A. S. Barnes, 1976), 83.
13. Simon Lesser, *Fiction and the Unconscious* (Boston: Beacon Hill Press, 1957).

14. Christian Metz, "*Trucage* and the Film," in *The Language of Images*, ed. W. J. T. Mitchell (Chicago: University of Chicago Press, 1980), 151-69.
15. Wood, 86.
16. Wood, 94.
17. Edward Branigan, *Point of View in the Cinema: A Theory of Narration and Subjectivity in Classical Film* (New York: Mouton Publishers, 1984), 117-19.
18. Jane Schleuter, *Metafictional Characters in Modern Drama* (New York: Columbia University Press, 1979), 11.
19. Schleuter, 11.
20. Schleuter, 14.
21. Tani, 42.
22. Laura Mulvey, "Visual Pleasure and Narrative Cinema," *Screen* 16, no. 3 (Autumn 1975), 15.
23. Tani, 45.

FRAGMENTS OF THE MIRROR

Self-Reference, Mise-en-Abyme, *Vertigo*

Katie Trumpener

In the films of his British and early American periods, Hitchcock develops techniques of narrative and visual self-reference that
reenforce his status as the all-powerful auteur of each movie even as
these techniques call into question the institutional power of illusion-
ist cinema, with its potential to act both as a normative and a destructive force. In technique and in purpose these self-referential strategies are crucially different from Hollywood's self-congratulatory
self-depictions, its celebration of itself in films that treat the origins
of the movies, the discoveries and careers of movie stars, the trials
and tribulations of show business. Such movies tend to be visually
unobtrusive — using minimal camera movement and virtually invisible editing — and narratively conservative, moving toward a closure
in which the Hollywood work ethic is validated: the best man wins,
the show must go on.[1] Hitchcock's propensity for self-reference, on
the contrary, seems meant to unsettle the spectator as much as to
perpetuate the hegemony of the studios. For his films constantly
denaturalize themselves, calling attention to the components of film
production, in order to point up the "enunciated," discursive, constructed quality of film story.[2]

Such self-revelation begins with what Raymond Bellour has called

"Hitchcock's signature system,"[3] his famous habit of appearing for a few frames of each of his own films. Even before the opening credits of *North by Northwest*, for example, Hitchcock has already made an appearance as a character who tries in vain to board a city bus and thus become part of the motion (the chase, across country, by foot, car, train, and plane) that the movie is about. In *Strangers on a Train*, a movie about doubles, equivalence, and cross-cutting, Hitchcock puts in a "double" appearance, as a character who tries to push onto the train a huge double bass, a purveyor of art of the same size and shape as himself.

These cameos have proved an effective device for asserting directorial authority. Audiences wait from the first moment of the movie for his appearance: "Look, it's him, it's Hitchcock. Hitchcock always appears in Hitchcock!" Immediately their frame of reference has expanded from the work itself to the entire Hitchcock oeuvre. "Hitchcock," the extra with the characteristic silhouette, functions as a metonymy for "Hitchcock," a long series of suspense films, whose trademarks are a characteristic use of visual motifs, a characteristic kind of stylistic twist. Yet the director's appearance as a character on the fringes of his own creation also serves to remind the audience of the precariousness of their own safety, as spectators out of the reach of, and unaffected by, the murders and pursuits they watch on the screen. As he appears among his own characters, the auteur's position, during such moments, is similarly precarious.

These moments are meant as a demonstration of mastery in which Hitchcock, as Sandy Flitterman puts it, "makes explicit the fact that the film, as discourse, is proceeding from somewhere, that it is he who is organizing the fiction . . . Hitchcock disrupts [the filmic] flow momentarily in order to reassert his total control of the images."[4] But the metonymy—the whole encapsulated in a part, the part replacing the whole—threatens constantly to go dangerously out of control, increasing the scope of its disruption, turning into a mise-en-abyme which, like a self-consuming black hole, sucks the rest of the movie in after it.

Metonymy and Mise-en-Abyme

Hannay: What are the thirty-nine steps?

Mr. Memory: The Thirty-nine Steps is an organization of spies, collecting information on behalf of the foreign office
of. . . .

Standing on the music-hall stage from which he has fielded an assortment of more or less serious questions, Mr. Memory is forced to reply to a question on whose answer both the spy plot within the plot and the movie we are seeing depend. "What are the thirty-nine steps?" demands Hannay, expecting (as is clear from his use of the plural "are") that the thirty-nine steps will be a flight of stairs somewhere, a hierarchical progression of thirty-nine small levels. But as Mr. Memory makes clear in his answer, the thirty-nine steps "is" a word, a name, a relationship between a group of men bound by a common purpose, is as intangible as the collection of facts stored inside Mr. Memory's memory. The physical space Hannay has been searching for throughout the movie has become a concept, a plot with the same name as the movie he is in. The tangibility of the movie, too, is called into question at this moment in which the movie's mystery is solved, and Hitchcock must act quickly to prevent this proliferation of mirroring levels. Even as he is recounting the plot of the plot from memory, Mr. Memory, the man Hithcock is shooting for his movie, must be shot, before everything is given away.

Sabotage (1936) is constructed on similarly dizzying principles: the intangible is made visible; the questions of filmmaking and reception are displaced, by a metonymic sliding, back into the "real life," the pro-filmic events which provide the subject matter for cinema. The film thus becomes an illustration of what Metz, paraphrasing Jakobson, calls the basic characteristic of cinema, that it "'transforms the object into a sign'; the film mobilizes fragments of the world but turns them into the elements of a discourse in the very act of 'ordering' them."[5] *Sabotage* centers around a saboteur who operates a movie theater as a cover for his treasonous activities. He lives with his unsuspecting family in an apartment behind the movie screen: to get to the entrance of the apartment the family must constantly pass through the movie theater, along the edges of the audience. Only once, very late in the movie, do we actually see either the watching audience or the film being shown on the screen; instead, *Sabotage* shows us what goes on behind and around the movie image.

The constitutive elements of film itself — visual image, verbal messages, light, acting, sound, the movie-going consumers — are shown to us in terms of their function in the Verlocs' movie house: in the opening power failure and the threat it poses to the ticket sales that put the Verlocs' bread on the table, and in the movie sound tracks that penetrate into the Verlocs' dining room. Having moved off the movie screen and through the everyday life of the rooms behind it, these filmic elements and concerns continue to move onto still more distant levels of the movie: out into the city surrounding the movie house and into the narrative, symbolic, and thematic codes of the movie's plot. The components of movie-making (consumption by a mass audience, images, dialogue, music track) reappear finally in displaced form, as the ordinary objects of the outside world and as the elements of the saboteurs' plot, in the form of food, crowds, written and visual signs, the message of bird song.

The theme of consumption is introduced on the pavement outside the movie theater by the ticket-buying public waiting to consume this week's movie. Then it moves by stages to the grocery store next door, where a Scotland Yard detective, working undercover as a grocer, tries to get information out of Verloc's wife, wooing her with heads of lettuce and meals in fancy restaurants. Food in turn is connected to explosives (one saboteur keeps his dynamite in the larder in a bottle of tomato paste), explosives which in turn become reconnected to film, reconnected to consumption and effect. A film canister labeled "Bartholemew the Strangler" proves in fact to contain not a film reel but a saboteur's bomb, which explodes, killing a busload of people. "That's a film tin, isn't it?" a reporter asks at the scene of the tragedy. "No, sardines," is the sardonic reply. Beginning in the movie theater, Hitchcock separates the movie illusion into its constituent parts, then follows it back into the real life the movies come out of and ostensibly reproduce. If art is daily life reordered, rearranged, elevated, then the mundane objects that fill the frames of Hitchcock's movie are imbued with the messages and the potential power of art — bird cages with messages hidden in them, sauce bottles, like film tins, containing explosives. *Sabotage* examines the relationship of the technical processes and the commercial distribution of film to the finished work of art the audience sees on the screen.

The original 1934 version of *The Man Who Knew Too Much* plays similarly with the construction of plots. Before the opening credits we are shown a pile of vacation brochures, hands shuffling through them, holding up pictures one by one for the camera. A locale is being chosen: finally the camera rests on one picture, then cuts to exactly the same view being filmed. The image, like a still photograph, sets the locale: now motion is added, the speed, as we watch a man skiing down a mountain, almost hitting a young girl. A crowd gathers to watch, and then the trapshooting begins, a competition between the girl's mother and a professional assassin. There will be almost continuous shooting or brandishing of guns from now until the final shoot-out in the last minutes of the picture, crowds again gathered to watch the rematch between the assassin and the girl's mother, played out this time over the life of the child.

There is, then, a metonymic and punning correlation in the movie between the amount of time devoted to gunfire and the shooting time of the movie itself. The film's plot itself is organized around a series of small substituted or metonymic objects. In the hotel dance scene there is the unraveling piece of knitting attached, as a prank, to the back of an unsuspecting dancer who entangles himself, his partner, then gradually all the other dancers in ever longer lengths of yarn; shot suddenly by an unheard, unseen assassin, he falls to the ground and dies just as the knitting runs out. There is the room key he hands Betty's mother before he dies, and the "too much" he dies for knowing, a paper (hidden inside his shaving brush) covered with cryptic phrases, pictograms that the movie will decode step by step. There is the kidnapping note, the telltale cigarette case that Betty's father loses in the kidnappers' hideout, the kidnapper's watch that chimes to mark the hour, a noise that in the end betrays his hiding place to the police. And finally there is the child's tiny pin of a skier, which the assassin wordlessly and threateningly hands to her mother at the Albert Hall to remind her that the kidnappers still hold her child.

These metonymic relationships, the film's reproduction of people in objects and as objects that can be passed from hand to hand, continually lead these people into danger, the danger of *giving themselves away*. The skier pin that the kidnapped girl is wearing when she is abducted represents her not only metonymically but almost literally—it is a stylized, miniature version of her, right down to the

ski hat, the scarf, and the large wistful eyes. Hitchcock within Hitchcock, movies within movies, shootings within shootings, a girl wearing a smaller copy of herself; we see here the beginnings of a mise-
en-abyme, the Quaker Oats box with its picture of a Quaker holding
a box with the picture of a Quaker holding a box. . . .

The levels of the movie (narrative, acting, production; auteur,
character, and audience) are established as a hierarchy, first constructed for us like a staircase only to be collapsed then in front of
our eyes in verbal/visual puns, turns of phrase turning into camera
turns. This twisting and turning itself forms a sort of secondary
Hitchcockian signature system: *The Ring* turning from its locale, the
boxing ring, into a marriage plot, ending with the wedding ring;
Family Plot turning into the family's plotting, turning, graveside,
into the family burial plot; in *Vertigo*, falling in love turning into
loved ones falling — every hierarchy collapsing.

Fragments of the Mirror

Madeleine:	I'm walking down a long corridor that once was mir-rored and fragments of the mirror still hang there. And when I come to the end there is nothing but darkness, and I know when I come to the end I'll die . . . I never come to the end. I always come back.
Scottie:	But the small scenes, fragments of the mirror — do you remember those?

Metonymy becoming identity, the elements of film construction
displaced into plot: in *Vertigo*, Hitchcock's most sustained and most
brilliant exploration of self-reference, film itself is like a fragmented
mirror. Each piece, each of the "small scenes," is itself a mirror, at
once partial and complete. Metonymy dizzyingly becomes mise-en-
abyme, the mirrored corridor reflecting mirrors within mirrors. All
the elements of the film reflect one other: narrative, visuals, dialogue, music, settings, camera shots (from the pans to the famous
"vertigo" trick shot), even the graphics that accompany the opening
credit sequence.

The film begins with the close-up of lips and an eye; they will reappear later, reflected in the mirror of the beauty salon, as one identity
gives way to another, Judy to Madeleine. Out of the eye come first

the letters that spell out V-e-r-t-i-g-o, then a succession of endlessly rotating, spiraling patterns in constant metamorphosis, each growing larger and larger until it fills up the screen and begins to dissolve while within it, from out of its center, comes the next, slightly different, slightly smaller pattern. A geometric representation of the experience of vertigo, of levels turning within levels, these designs function as a grammar of the visual, verbal, and spatial patterns, dizzying and self-engulfing, that we will encounter in the movie that follows.

Midge:	Where do you go?
Scottie:	Oh, just wandering.
Midge:	Oh, where?
Scottie:	Round about.

Indeed Scottie's path, as he turns corner after corner, following Madeleine around and across San Francisco, often describes semi-circles or spirals, whether he circles around Madeleine in the graveyard at the Mission Dolores or walks behind the bench she is seated on in the Legion of Honor picture gallery. The most intricate and lengthy path he travels in pursuit of her leads him back to where he (and she) started from. On the night he rescues her from drowning, she flees his apartment and drives home. In the next scene, the next morning, he too leaves his apartment, drives to her apartment building and follows her as she drives in a series of circles around the city, ending up finally at his apartment, which she later claims she has been "looking for" the whole time. (And all the time that Scottie is following Madeleine he is himself being pursued by Midge, sometimes literally followed, sometimes only metaphorically "chased.")

This spiral figure that Madeleine, and Scottie after her, travel repeatedly, is echoed in one of Madeleine's most distinctive features: in imitation of Carlotta's portrait, her blonde hair is coiled into a spiral at the back of her head. And the posy she carries to match the one in the painting contains — if geometrically reduced as in Scottie's dream late in the film — a number of identical shapes within a larger version of the same shape, like the spiral a self-repeating, self-enclosing figure. The spiral is suggested too by the camera work in the scene near the end of the movie in which Scottie and Judy finally embrace; as they kiss, both the camera and the room revolve completely around them.

Scottie becomes obsessed with the reincarnation (Judy) of a woman (Madeleine) "obsessed" with the past to the extent that she appears to reincarnate her own grandmother. What at first appears a linear plot soon proves as circular as the redwood cross-section that Madeleine uses to mark out the eternal returns of her life, as spiraling as the staircase Scottie must dizzily climb. The actress really falls in love with the audience she is pretending to love; the act and the real become increasingly entangled, imitating each other. If Madeleine is faking and is not really a reincarnation of Carlotta, of the past in the present, then Judy, pretending not to know Scottie, also acts a part to him: she is and is not Madeleine; she is both a reincarnation of the past and a real person whose past (growing up in a small town in Kansas; being picked up by men and losing her "innocence" at age seventeen; plotting to kill Elster's wife), though strangely like Carlotta's story, has little to do with Madeleine's dreamy visions.

In the Palace of the Legion of Honor, we watch Scottie watching Madeleine watch Carlotta in the painting, Carlotta in the picture frame, Madeleine framed by the doorway of the room, Scottie "framed" not only by Elster's plot but also by the edges of the screen. The scene epitomizes the technique of the film, mirroring, matching itself again and again, level after level. For even the film's plot repeats itself almost completely within the time of the movie: after an hour and a half, the whole story begins again. Madeleine and Scottie drive north of San Francisco, south of San Francisco, back and forth; Scottie — first looking for Madeleine, then together with Judy — revisits everywhere he has been with Madeleine. If at the beginning of the film we had the impression that the characters drove all over, even took many long and pointless detours, by the end they can do nothing but repeat old journeys, then repeat the repetition. Many bits of dialogue, too, spoken casually at the beginning of the film, are by the end being reverently repeated, re-cited, recombined.

The Entanglement of the Viewer

As the plot doubles back on itself (the wrought-iron motif by Scottie's apartment door is, ironically, the Chinese symbol for "double happiness"), much of what is originally said about Madeleine comes to refer to Scottie. And Scottie, who is acted upon, made to act as the plotters want, in turn manipulates someone else (who is, only by coincidence and unknown to him, the one who initially manipulated him), trying to make her act as and be what he wishes. He who has taken the fiction to be a reality tries to make Judy over as Madeleine, to make a real person into a fictional one. "You were the counterfeit, you were the copy," Scottie accuses Judy in the last minutes of the film. Yet how meaningful has the distinction between original and imitation remained for us? When Judy falls from the roof, Madeleine dies again with her; the original and the copy break together (and by the end, it is hard to tell which is which, if Madeleine is a copy of Judy or Judy of Madeleine). Indeed, how are we able, by the end of the film, to make any of our usual distinctions? All the levels of the movie have done the same thing, mirrored each other so perfectly we have difficulty seeing them as distinct. Even the camera's representation of vertigo — and the most famous technical feat of the movie — is achieved through a loss of perspective, a denial of dimensionality: the middle distance vanishes, the depth of focus collapses, the uppermost bend in the staircase and the ground far below suddenly look equally far away. The distinctions between levels of vision collapse in *Vertigo* along with all our other distinctions, our accustomed hierarchy of actor and audience, fiction and reality; as we lose our illusions, we simultaneously lose our bearings, our depth perception, our ability to tell apart the two-dimensional and the three.

We have projected ourselves into the movie projected for us; we have become the outermost layer of the spiral: when Madeleine sits looking at the picture of Carlotta, and Scottie stands to one side watching her, we are watching, too, at one further remove. Scottie realizes with shock at the end of the movie that Judy really was Madeleine, and so Madeleine wasn't — anything at all, except the dead body of a woman neither we nor Scottie knew, and a grey suit and a way of speaking and moving. It was a shock to us when we learned the truth fifteen minutes before he did. But we should have known all along: although we may have forgotten it, we have known since the beginning of the movie that "Judy/Madeleine" too is an act, is really Kim Novak, just as "Madeleine" is really Judy.

In concocting his plot, Elster estimates quite rightly that Scottie, who does not and cannot fall in love with the real, down-to-earth Midge, will be allured by his representation of the mysterious Madeleine, and that he would rather desire a fiction (the unobtainable woman represented to him in art) than have a real woman to sleep with. This phenomenon is reproduced in everyday life, as the movie itself demonstrates quite convincingly. The sales clerks and the hairdresser seem not at all surprised that Scottie wants to dress and coif Judy according to a preconceived notion of beauty that has nothing to do with her own wishes and tastes; they act, in fact, as if they see this a hundred times a day.

Scottie's obsession, Scottie's problem, is indeed quite like our own. If until the last minute of the movie he continues to talk of and to desire Madeleine as if she is a real person, we too fall in love with the characters we see on-screen, talk about them as if they are real, returning to the movie theater to see the same actors or those like them, hoping (like Scottie searching San Francisco for his lost love) to find again the fictions that obsess us. Madeleine herself functions throughout the movie as a sort of haunted screen, on which the figures of the past are played out alongside the projections of the present. The reincarnation of Carlotta and of San Francisco's past, Madeleine is like the Proustian "madeleine" of which she is the namesake, making the past present again, joining memory and desire. She becomes thereby a figure for the movies themselves, which, as Cavell and Metz remind us, derive their mystery and their magic from an uncanny ability to transform the already-happened into the being-lived, reexperienced anew at every viewing.[6]

Hitchcock's movie, however, unmasks the movies even as it reveals "Madeleine" to be nothing but a pious fraud, a makeup job, an act. Both Scottie and the moviegoers are forced to watch as their romantic illusions prove little more than neurotic projection, a compulsion to repeat. At the beginning of the movie, we watch a suspenseful nighttime chase across the roofs, the whole sparkling city spread out romantically below us. Two long hours later, the exhilarating suspense has vanished, to be replaced by an anguished identification with both Judy and Scottie, a troubling foreknowledge of what is to come; we pass along a road we have traveled once before, hearing yet again snatches of dialogue we've heard at least once already. In between we have seen too much bumpy driving, in city traffic, up and down hills, around in circles. Secondary characters like Midge and Elster have silently faded away, along with the issue of the murder, until we are left at the end, trapped in the car with

Judy and Scottie, dizzied by the back-projected movies moving past the windows, then dragged up a steep tower toward a certain end. Hitchcock has managed to induce in us, lovers of the movies, a kind of motion sickness.

Never Coming to the End, Always Coming Back

Madeleine: I had a dream, the dream came back again.
Scottie: It was a dream, you're awake again. . . . It's all there —
it was no dream, you've been there before, you've seen
it. When you see what you saw before . . . it'll finish your
dream, destroy it.

On first viewing, the ending of *Vertigo* seems to solve the plot, resolve the movie's ambiguities. Whether or not "Madeleine" can be said ever to have existed, Judy is dead, the murderer's accomplice really dying the death she once pretended to. If at the beginning of the movie he was responsible for the policeman's death by falling, Scottie was, it turns out, not really responsible for Madeleine's death, and Judy dies without his having to push her, her death by falling luckily an unlucky accident. The vertigo which Scottie discovers in himself in the first sequence of the movie disappears again in the last; he is able, finally, to look down.

"There's no losing it, the acrophobia. Only another emotional shock would undo it." But if Scottie needed a second shock, a second fall after the death of the policeman to cure him, why wasn't his vertigo cured at Madeleine's death? Why doesn't the movie end there? "One doesn't often get a second chance. You're my second chance." Judy is, in fact, simultaneously Scottie's second chance and his third one; can her death simultaneously "solve," even out, the deaths of both Madeleine and the policeman? Is Judy's death a "getting even" for Scottie or only the next stage in his "going odd," a cycle of obsession more tormented than the last? If Scottie has lost his fear of falling, will he now fall in love with a real woman, a Midge? Or is he still obsessed with Madeleine, in fact freed by Judy's death from all intrusions of an unwanted reality? The movie's ending is appropriately ambiguous, solving everything, solving nothing, closing the narrative to open a new level of questioning, suggesting that Scottie's drama may repeat itself infinitely; he will "never come to the end" of the mirrored corridor, he will always "come back." When the lights go up we too awake from *Vertigo* haunted, dizzied, entangled, as if we too have come from among the dead, *d'entre les morts.*

The Question Hitchcock

The cracked mirror, with its potential for endless self-repetition, has proved in *Vertigo* a portent of disaster, distorting the usual relationship between seer and seen, twisting the hierarchy of creator and created. In the broken mirror of its recursive plot it has in fact managed to entrap not only characters and viewers but, in a final turn of the screw, the film reviewers themselves. Laurence Schaffer entitles his suggestive article on Hitchcock's film "Obsessed with *Vertigo*";[7] indeed the film has long been the object of unusually obsessive, self-involved, often autobiographical commentary.[8] Donald Spoto, for instance, in an otherwise factual account of Hitchcock's oeuvre, details the circumstances under which he first saw this one film, counts up the twenty-six times he has since seen it, and describes his pilgrimages to all the film's locations,[9] while Brian De Palma literally takes up Scottie's mandate, making *Vertigo* over, reenacting its story of refashioning, his title suggesting circular return, his motivation: Obsession.

Such reception, to borrow Metz's words, "extends the object . . . it *idealizes* instead of turning back on to it, a mirror reduplicating the film's own ideological inspiration, already based on the mirror identification of the spectator with the camera (or secondarily with the characters)."[10] Feminist film theorists like Laura Mulvey[11] and Teresa de Lauretis,[12] on the other hand, in their investigations of the gendering of the gaze, have taken *Vertigo* to epitomize patriarchal logic, a film which (without fully intending to) exposes itself, gives itself away. This essay has taken a third position; it has attempted, to borrow Metz's words on engagement and critical distance, "to have broken with it . . . not in order to move on to something else, but in order to return to it, at the next bend in the spiral."[13] It has tried both to recreate *Vertigo's* fascination and to analyze its manipulative logic, just as the film itself knowingly destroys romantic illusion in its very recreation of illusion's mechanism. *Vertigo's* spiral construction invites the viewer to enter the movie and to become a (male) character, only then to throw him from the tower, collapse the world of the movie on top of him, bury him in its debris.

Recent film theory has argued that both gender and the cinema are auto-reproducing and mutually engendering machines.[14] The question of self-reference, then, far from signifying hermeticism, aestheticism, refuge taken in formalism, can in fact contribute to such debates, engaging crucially the self-perpetuation or self-destruction of institutions, of social systems, of cinematic apparatuses. *Vertigo*'s mise-en-abyme, levels reproducing levels, might serve as a figure of the Althusserean model of subject formation, the self-reproduction, the mutual constitution of socializing ideology and socialized subjects.[15] Yet the film's twisting of levels and its ultimate self-consuming collapse suggest simultaneously the fragility of such constructions: the moment of self-replication is the moment at which the system at once demonstrates its power most confidently and exposes itself to the greatest risks.

Vertigo should be seen as a "limit text," of the status claimed by Stephen Heath (in his essay, "The Question Oshima") for Oshima's *In the Realm of the Senses*[16] and by Teresa de Lauretis in her essay "Now and Nowhere" for Roeg's *Bad Timing*:[17] it is, like them, a movie that at once participates in exploitative desire and unmasks it. The Question Hitchcock, whether the film perpetuates or undoes patriarchy, is rendered undecidable by *Vertigo* itself. And if we look beyond it to the overt misogyny and sadism of a *Psycho* or a *Frenzy*, then the closing shot of *Vertigo*, of Scottie looking down from the ledge, comes in retrospect to seem like a final and precarious moment of balance.

Notes

1. See Jane Feuer, "The Self-Reflective Musical and the Myth of Entertainment," in Rick Altman, *Genre: The Musical* (London: Routledge and Kegan Paul, 1981), 159–74.
2. Sandy Flitterman, "Woman, Desire and the Look: Feminism and the Enunciative Apparatus in Cinema," in John Caughie, *Theories of Authorship* (London: Routledge and Kegan Paul, 1981), 242–50.
3. Raymond Bellour, "Hitchcock the Enunciator," *Camera Obscura*, no. 2 (Fall 1977), 66–91.
4. Flitterman, 247–48.

5. Christian Metz, *The Imaginary Signifier: Psychoanalysis and the Cinema* (Bloomington: University of Indiana Press, 1982), 194.

6. Christian Metz, "On the Impression of Reality in the Cinema" and "Notes Towards a Phenomenology of Narrative," in *Film Language: A Semiotics of the Cinema* (New York: Oxford University Press, 1974); and Stanley Cavell, *The World Viewed: Reflections on the Ontology of Film* (New York: Viking, 1971).

7. Lawrence Schaffer, "Obsessed with *Vertigo*," *The Massachusetts Review* 25, no. 3 (Autumn 1984), 383–97.

8. The film is also the subject of an excellent meta-commentary and reception history. See Virginia Wright Wexman, "The Critic as Consumer: Film Study in the University, *Vertigo*, and the Film Canon," *Film Quarterly* 39, no. 3 (Spring 1986), 32–41.

9. Donald Spoto, *The Art of Alfred Hitchcock: Fifty Years of His Motion Pictures* (New York: Hopkinson and Blake, 1976). Indeed at Stanford (the place where this essay was begun), located as it is in the heart of *Vertigo* country, it has become something of a running joke that virtually all visiting European male academics between the ages of thirty-five and fifty-five will at some point during their stay express a furtive but burning wish to be taken to see either San Juan Bautista or the Mission Dolores. The proximity of these pilgrimage sites, it always turns out, was a primary reason for their interest in Stanford. . . .

10. Metz, *The Imaginary Signifier*, 14.

11. Laura Mulvey, "Visual Pleasure and Narrative Cinema," in Gerald Mast and Marshall Cohen, *Film Theory and Criticism*, 3rd rev. ed. (New York: Oxford University Press, 1985), 803–16.

12. Teresa de Lauretis, "Desire in Narrative," in *Alice Doesn't: Feminism, Semiotics, Cinema* (Bloomington: Indiana University Press, 1984), 106–57.

13. Metz, *The Imaginary Signifier,* 15.

14. See, for example, Metz's *Imaginary Signifier*; Stephen Heath's *Questions of Cinema* (Bloomington: Indiana University Press, 1981); and essays by Jean-Louis Comolli, Jacqueline Rose, and others in Stephen Heath and Teresa de Lauretis, *The Cinematic Apparatus* (London: St. Martin's Press, 1980).

15. Louis Althusser, "Ideology and Ideological State Apparatuses (Notes Towards an Investigation)," in *Lenin and Philosophy* (New York: Monthly Review Press, 1971). See also Michel Foucault's work in books such as *Discipline and Punish: The Birth of the Prison* (New York: Vintage Books, 1979); and for an application of a very different kind, Frederic Jameson's "Reification and Utopia in Mass Culture," *Social Text I* (1979), 130–48.

16. Stephen Heath, "The Question Oshima," in *Questions of Cinema*, 145–64.

17. Teresa de Lauretis, "Now and Nowhere: Roeg's *Bad Timing*," in *Re-vision: Essays in Feminist Film Criticism*, ed. Mary Ann Doane, Patricia Mellencamp, and Linda Williams (Washington, D.C.: American Film Institute, 1984), 150–69, reprinted in *Alice Doesn't*.

III
GENDER AND FAMILY
REVISITED AND REMADE:
THE MAN WHO KNEW TOO MUCH (1956)

In interviews Hitchcock stressed the superiority of the second *Man Who Knew Too Much* (1956) to the 1934 film on the grounds of narrative clarity and technical competence, but the more obvious changes involve enhanced attention in the screenplay to the complex interaction of global politics and sexual politics. In this sense the "MacGuffin" has a more ironic function in the second *Man* than is usual in Hitchcock's films: what Ben McKenna knows about the assassination attempt is indeed too much, but what he knows about the emotional needs of his own wife is apparently insufficient. And what he knows and doesn't know in the film is always related to his need as a male to dominate.

The remake has received new critical attention because of the recent debate inspired by feminism about male and female roles in Hitchcock's films: does the director always subscribe to classical cinema's inscription of female desire *within* the dominant male's definition of personal and sexual identity? The 1956 film certainly focuses on the marital roles of the central couple more so than did the original; the nuances of a relatively stable yet evidently troubled relationship are at times foregrounded in the second film, such as the scene in which the doctor husband sedates his anguished wife before telling her the truth about their kidnapped son. The family unit is restored at the close of the film, yet are the dynamics between the husband and wife altered or unchanged?

Robin Wood, in "The Men Who Knew Too Much (and the women who knew much better)," examines the remake from the recent feminist perspectives of spectatorship and ideology. Rather than concluding that the film asserts the usual male domination and female submission, Wood argues that it is actually a work that reveals how women are abused by male politics of aggression, but how they ul-

191

Doris Day and James Stewart in *The Man Who Knew Too Much* **(1956).**
(Photo courtesy of Photofest, New York.)

timately circumvent and rise above such politics. He identifies the
politics of this film with sexual politics, demonstrating how male
power politics is related to the need to dominate women. In turn,
the film explores the "irrational" intuition of women, which is emotional and liberating. The screams of Jo McKenna and Mrs. Drayton
prevent deaths planned by male power politics — they are the "women
who knew much better." Even the assumption by feminist theorists
that Hitchcock's films adopt the male perspective, literally and figuratively, is undercut by Wood's reading of *The Man Who Knew Too
Much* (1956) as well as of *Notorious* and *Vertigo*: in Wood's view the
director subtly redirects audience identification toward the woman in
each film, encouraging us to support her resistance to male domination.

Wood's reading of *The Man Who Knew Too Much* (1956) is coun-
tered here by that of Ina Rae Hark, who claims in "Revalidating
Patriarchy: Why Hitchcock Remade *The Man Who Knew Too Much*"
that Hitchcock remade the film in order to remove the threat to patriarchy implied in the assertive wife/mother figure of the 1934 version.
In Hark's view Hitchcock's motivation was to reassert the familial
and cultural authority of the father figure. While Hark recognizes

Hitchcock's uneasiness with the excesses of patriarchal repressiveness and power, she does not believe he subverts them, as Wood maintains, by glorifying female emotion and intuition. Hark argues that the woman who does threaten to revolt in Hitchcock's films is portrayed as psychically unhealthy and destructive. For Hark, then, the 1934 version provides fuller scope for female assertiveness and power.

THE MEN WHO KNEW TOO MUCH
(and the women who knew much better)

Robin Wood

Andrew Sarris has described my recent work on Hitchcock, with cautious disapproval, as "revisionist"; it is true that I no longer view the films with the naive and frequently uncritical enthusiasm that characterized the original *Hitchcock's Films*. Yet my estimate of Hitchcock's importance has if anything risen over the past few years, since I have at last (I think) begun to understand his work. Unless one is a great original thinker one's work is inevitably limited by the theoretical and ideological context within which one operates, and the context that determined the nature of *Hitchcock's Films* was severely circumscribed. The description of me (by one of the editorial board of *Screen* magazine) as an "unreconstructed humanist" was largely correct (I now aspire to be a reconstructed humanist): as a good (if troubled) bourgeois I habitually mistook ideology for truth and was unable to perceive the real issues — the conflicts — of our culture, conflicts that our films inevitably dramatize in a wide variety of ways whether their auteurs are conscious of them or not. Hence the emphasis in my early work on coherence rather than on contradiction, and the failure to perceive Hitchcock's work as the site of an ideological battleground.

Neither version of *The Man Who Knew Too Much* receives more than a passing mention in *Hitchcock's Films,* so I begin with the

194

question of evaluation: where do they stand in the Hitchcock canon? I cannot do much here to make amends for the ludicrous dismissal in the book of the entire British period: the 1934 version seems to me a pleasant minor entertainment, one of the least interesting of the films of Hitchcock's first (British) maturity. The lingering belief that it is superior to the American version is incomprehensible outside the most flagrant chauvinism. Yet I cannot place the 1956 version quite in the front rank of Hitchcock's movies: the material does not permit the radical critique of patriarchal structures that Hitchcock undertook (whether he knew it or not) in, for example, *Notorious, Rear Window* and *Vertigo*, which is what gives those films their profundity, their sense of being at once both profoundly disturbed and profoundly disturbing. They resist all attempts at containment within the ideological status quo; *The Man Who Knew Too Much* does not. Its project is epitomized in the contrast between its opening and final images: first shot, the couple (James Stewart, Doris Day) separated by their child; last shot, the couple united by their child. In between, Mr. Drayton's sermon (delivered hypocritically, but God can put the truth into the mouth of the devil) tells us that adversities make us better people. But we should not allow recognition of the film's overall project to blind us to the tensions that continuously threaten it.

I wish to approach the film obliquely, through a number of different channels, most of which reflect current critical/theoretical preoccupations: Hitchcock and politics; Hitchcock and mothers; the complex question of identification in his films, especially as it affects the spectator's relationships to male/female relations within them; the question of genre; Hitchcock's use (in his American period) of established stars and star images. These will lead to a brief comparison of the film to its British original. I hope these various forays from different angles will gradually define the nature of the film's achievement and justify a high evaluation: in general, it has been seriously underestimated.

Hitchcock and Politics

We don't go to Hitchcock (or to Hollywood cinema in general) for helpful or enlightened statements about the practical realities of international politics: as F. R. Leavis once remarked, we don't go to D. H. Lawrence to learn whom we should vote for. The surface level is inevitably dominated by conventional Hollywood (read: popular American) attitudes, evasive, banal or both: bad Nazis, good Americans, the free world vs. duplicitous and torturing Communists, etc. Hitchcock developed intermittent strategies for qualifying these (in *Topaz*, all the energy is attributed to the Cubans), but he couldn't effectively undermine them (even supposing that he had wanted to). In the British version of *The Man Who Knew Too Much,* we learn that the assassination, explicitly compared to that at Sarajevo, could start a world war; in the American version even this elementary political statement is suppressed, and the assassination becomes a matter of internal politics and personal ambition.

Below this surface, however, the treatment of politics becomes really interesting (and truly Hitchcockian) — in that area where politics and sexual politics converge and interact. For Hitchcock, politics is a male-dominated — indeed, exclusively male — world within which women, insofar as they are allowed admittance at all, are pawns to be manipulated, used, exploited, and often destroyed. It is on this level that the bad Nazis/good Americans (etc.) dichotomy becomes thoroughly subverted: the nominal commitment to America, democracy, the free world, demanded by Hollywood, is revealed as a mere facade for a far more sweeping denunciation of masculinist politics in general. Two examples will suffice: (a) *Notorious*: the recurrent round-table discussions of the all-male American authorities which result in the cynical exploitation and eventual near-death of Alicia/Ingrid Bergman are exactly mirrored by the Nazis' after-dinner round-table discussion (again all-male — even that dedicated Nazi Mrs. Sebastian is excluded) that results in the death of Emil Hrupka. It is scarcely coincidental that Cary Grant and Claude Rains are competing for control both of Ingrid Bergman and of the materials with which to build atomic bombs. (b) *Topaz*: Juanita/Karin Dor is actually executed (in the film's most emotionally agonizing scene) by her Cuban lover, but the murder is directly precipitated by her French lover (working for the Americans) and the use he makes of her. We should also note the corollary of this motif of the masculinist exploitation of women: in the two Cary Grant espionage films (*Notorious* and *North by Northwest*), the hero fully redeems himself only when he directly violates the orders of his American superiors thereby expressing his rejection of masculinist politics altogether in favor of identifying himself with a woman and rescuing her from victimization and death.

Domination — power/importance as two sides of the same coin — is clearly the central concern (one might say the driving obsession) of Hitchcock's work on all levels, methodological, stylistic, thematic; the distinction of that work — its importance for us today — lies in the ways in which that obsession is pursued to the point where its mechanisms, its motivations, its monstrousness, are thoroughly exposed. The political level of the films — superficially so trite and uninteresting — in fact represents a logical extension of the films' obsessive sexual concerns (the drive of men to dominate women) into the structures of power politics that men have constructed. The two great liberating screams of *The Man Who Knew Too Much* (Doris Day's in the Albert Hall, Brenda de Banzie's "answering" scream in the embassy) must be read on one level as the protests of women against masculinist politics and the cruelty and violence that issue from it. Allowing for the differences between popular entertainment and "serious" art-works — the differences between what they can explicitly say — we might compare those screams to Liv Ullmann's cowering from the televised Vietnam newsreel and the Warsaw Ghetto photograph in Bergman's *Persona*. They are also, of course, the screams of mothers: real mother, surrogate mother.

Hitchcock and Mothers

It is something of an understatement to say that, in Hitchcock's American films, mothers are generally not presented in a very favorable light. There are three mothers of psychopathic killers (Mrs. Anthony, Mrs. Bates, Mrs. Rusk); the possessive mother of *The Birds*; the love-withholding, guilt-ridden mother of *Marnie*. Other mothers are presented somewhat more sympathetically: the nervous, pathetic, well-meaning Emma of *Shadow of a Doubt*, the caustic and skeptical mother of Cary Grant in *North by Northwest*; but the former may be partly responsible for her younger brother's psychopathic condition by "mothering" him too much when he was young, and the latter obstructs rather than assists her son's efforts to avoid getting

killed. This preoccupation with the darker side of motherhood may
be a consequence of Hitchcock's experience of America rather than
of personal psychology (there are surprisingly few mothers in the British
films, and not a single monstrous one). What is clear is that the one
unambiguously and actively positive mother in Hitchcock's American
work is Jo McKenna — or rather, and importantly, Jo Conway. I mean
that shift to her stage (maiden?) name to signify the essential difference between Jo and Hitchcock's other American mothers: the rest
are *just* mothers, in a culture that has (disastrously) effected a division of labor which makes nurturing almost exclusively the mother's
responsibility: the whole meaning of their lives has been bound up
with their children, and the suggestion of the films is that motherhood can turn sour and twisted when it becomes an exclusive vocation. Jo, along with her male name (a point underlined in the film —
Louis Bernard at first assumes that "Jo" is the name of her son),
possesses traits that our culture commonly defines as "masculine":
she is assertive, active, dynamic, she makes autonomous decisions
and takes independent action. She has also had — and wishes she still
had — a career, and with it a degree of personal autonomy: she is a
good mother because, emotionally at least, she is not *just* a mother.
In this she complements rather than contradicts Hitchcock's character-
izations of mothers elsewhere: if she is the exception to the rule, she
is also its proof.

Identification and Gender

Questions of spectatorship, identification and gender difference
have become a major preoccupation of much contemporary theoretical writing on film, and Hitchcock has often been used as a central
focus for this. It can be argued (because it *has* been) that Hitchcock's
films imply a male spectatorship, and that the only position they offer
women is that of accepting the subordination of female desire to male
desire (construction of the "good object") or that of a more overtly
masochistic complicity in guilt and punishment. Raymond Bellour,
very influentially, has attempted to demonstrate this quasi-scientifically
in his extraordinarily detailed and meticulously accurate analyses of
narrative movement and the technical apparatus of point of view.

Personally, I am at best only half convinced—I think such analyses reveal only one side of a much more complex story. There seem to be two problems here. One is that such approaches tend to ignore the existence of innate bisexuality (however repressed), hence the possibilities of transsexual identification; the other is that, like so many attempts to approach art "scientifically," they privilege what can be proven and ignore or at least play down factors that are less tangible, less amenable to scientific demonstration, yet nonetheless palpably there, such as the ways in which stars function in movies or the ways in which our sympathy for a character's position in the narrative may cut against the technical apparatus of identification (POV shots, etc.) to produce fruitful tensions and disturbances.

What I am suggesting is that films can—and Hitchcock's often do—play on a tension between technically constructed identification and emotional identification. I offer two examples:

a. *Vertigo*, arguably the locus classicus of this strategy. Throughout the first part, Hitchcock uses the technical apparatus of point-of-view shooting/editing systematically to enforce identification with the male viewpoint. The very first sequence after the credits employs this more emphatically than any other Hitchcock opening; thereafter, we see through Scottie's eyes and we are prevented from seeing virtually everything that is beyond his consciousness. Hitchcock's revelation of the truth via Judy's flashback and letter (to neither of which Scottie has access) shatters this identification beyond possible repair—we now know the crucial facts that Scottie doesn't, and the entire intrigue is transformed; it is no longer the romantic drama we have been sharing with him. Yet Hitchcock continues to shoot the film essentially from Scottie's viewpoint, even though he is fully aware that our emotional identification must now be with Judy. The effect is ruthlessly to expose the entire apparatus of male domination and the anxiety that motivates it.

b. The role of *Notorious* provides another sustained example. A highly distinguished article by Michael Renov published in *Wide Angle* provides a useful starting-point: "From Identification to Ideology: The Male System of *Notorious*." Renov (explicitly citing Bellour as influence) makes a convincing case that there is a "male system" operating within the film. Identification with the male gaze is established at the outset (the reporters' flashbulbs and cameras of

199

the first sequence replaced by the back view of Cary Grant's head in the second as males attempt to dominate the "notorious" female of the title); Alicia/Bergman is systematically punished for her notoriety (promiscuity, alcoholism, etc.) by both Grant and Claude Rains; finally, the film, by inviting us to identify with both men, negotiates a double image of Bergman that reconciles two seemingly opposed cultural myths of "woman"—by subordinating herself to Grant she can be reconstructed as the "good object," but by simultaneously betraying Rains she confirms her identity as the "bad woman."[1] The argument is quite brilliantly presented, but what one wishes to ask Renov is, what about the film's female system? It seems to me indisputable that our primary identification throughout the film, whether we are men or women, is with Bergman—partly because she *is* Bergman, and is consistently privileged over Grant as the film's real star, partly because Alicia is a victim and, as Hitchcock is very clearly aware, we always identify with people in peril. (One might also point out a "scientific" fact that Renov neglects, that the overwhelming majority of POV shots in the film are Bergman's, not the men's). Our identification with the film's "female system" turns the male system on its head: it becomes a characteristic Hitchcockian study in male anxiety, in which both men, knowing well that Alicia is no virgin, are absolutely terrified that they may not measure up (so to speak) to the competition, and therefore feel driven to torment, punish and destroy the woman who produces in them such terrible feelings of insecurity. Central to Hitchcock's work (especially the American films, though it's already fully there in, e.g., *Blackmail*) is the culture's investment in masculinity, potency, the phallus, and the dread that actual men may not be able to fulfill the demands that masculinist ideology makes on them. Also central is the corollary to this: the effect of this anxiety on heterosexual relations, the revenge of men on women for arousing these fears, and the monstrous irrationality of that revenge. The methodological strategy—the identification that is enforced on one level is contradicted on another—seems to me crucial to the effect of much of Hitchcock's finest work: it accounts for that extraordinary fusion of fascination and disturbance, with its resultant tension and anguish, the ultimate manifestation of "suspense," that is the dominant factor in most people's experience of the films.

The Man Who Knew Too Much (1956) appears initially to offer us two identification figures of equal status, a married couple, then swiftly problematizes identification by developing tensions between them. The tension is resolved by making our primary identification figure the woman, then doubling her with another woman, Mrs. Drayton: both have husbands who attempt to dominate them, and our identification with the female position exposes the domination drive's very mechanisms.

Genre

I have argued elsewhere that the Hollywood genres represent different ways of resolving — or seeming to resolve — basically similar ideological tensions/contradictions, and that films that cross genres, or are generically impure, are often of particular interest in the way the contradictions become foregrounded.[2] The British version of *The Man Who Knew Too Much* is generically quite unproblematic. To raise the issue of genre is to suggest one of the ways in which the American version is so enriched: the simple action thriller is complicated by the intrusion of a genre that in the 50's reached one of its peaks of significance and expressiveness, the domestic melodrama. *The Man Who Knew Too Much* belongs (and not merely in terms of chronology) to the ten years that produced *The Reckless Moment; Madame Bovary* and *Home from the Hill; There's Always Tomorrow, Written on the Wind* and *Imitation of Life; Rebel Without a Cause* and *Bigger Than Life*. It takes up certain of the domestic melodrama's characteristic concerns — the oppression of women within the family, marriage vs. career, motherhood — and with them its disturbance about gender roles and social positions. No such disturbance is present in the British version.

Stars

Cary Grant and James Stewart appear in four Hitchcock films each; I want to comment briefly on how they function within their respective texts, because I think they are used quite differently. For Hitchcock, Stewart became the epitome of the masculine power/impotence syndrome that both structures and disturbs so many of his films. If invited to picture Stewart in a Hitchcock film, doesn't one (unless one thinks of *Rear Window*!) see him shot from a low angle, towering over someone (usually a woman), looking at once dominating and helpless, out of control, near hysteria? *Vertigo* offers of course the supreme instances: Kim Novak seated, Stewart standing over her, as in the scenes where Stewart forces Judy to dress as Madeleine. But the entire protracted sequence in *The Man Who Knew Too Much* in which Stewart sedates Doris Day unknown to her and against her assumed wishes (when she realizes what is happening, she violently repudiates the action) is in its way equally striking. Cary Grant is never used by Hitchcock in quite this way: he may lie to and manipulate women (*Suspicion*) but he doesn't try directly to dominate them. When he is given something like the Stewart domination image, Hitchcock plays the effect for comedy, as in the celebrated inverted shot near the beginning of *Notorious* where he is seen from Ingrid Bergman's point of veiw as she lies in bed. As Andrew Britton has suggested in his marvelous monograph on Grant, the image typically carries connotations of gender-role ambiguity (so that he becomes, among other things, the perfect medium for Hawks's play on sexual role-reversal).[3] The Hitchcock films with Grant move towards an equalized male/female relationship (a reading that stressed star persona over directorial authorship might go some way towards justifying the "happy ending" of *Suspicion*). Stewart, on the other hand, embodies for Hitchcock the desperate and hopeless drive to dominate — to assert an ideologically constructed "masculinity" that always sits uneasily on the Stewart persona and, in *Vertigo*, provokes the film's catastrophe. *Rear Window*, of course, is built entirely on Stewart's physical inability to assume the position of domination, and his desperate drive to compensate for this via the potency of the "look."

The Two Versions

The most obvious difference between the British and American versions is their respective lengths, the American remake being half as long again as the original. This follows a general pattern of directors remaking their own early films late in life: Ozu (*Story of*

Floating Weeds/Floating Weeds) and McCarey (*Love Affair/An Affair to Remember*) provide striking parallels. There is doubtless some correlation between a director's age and his desire, through the adoption of a more leisurely style, to elaborate. The basic narrative structure of the two versions is very similar. Its main features:

a. Family abroad (Switzerland, Morocco): exposition.
b. Police investigation.
c. Father goes to investigate (dentist, taxidermist).
d. Chapel sequence (the closest to a direct remake—some of the original dialogue is repeated).
e. Albert Hall sequence.
f. Final climax and resolution (Siege of Sydney Street, embassy).

Yet this structure is very differently realized in the two films, the difference relating to far more than the auteurist notion that an individual artist called Alfred Hitchcock had developed, deepened and matured (though I do not wish to discount that as one factor). Cultural difference, the difference in period, greater generic complexity, the Hollywood star system, all make their contributions.

I think the crux of difference is the relative stability of sexual ideology, as between Britain in 1934 and America in 1956. From our present perspective we can see that the structure of the patriarchal nuclear family, and the supposedly monogamous marriage (in effect, monogamous for the woman) that guarantees it, has always been an institution for the subordination of women (whatever else). The hegemony that upholds it, however, has been subject to a whole series of fluctuations and challenges in different times and different places. In middle-class Britain in 1934 (which represents the audience towards which the original version was primarily directed, Hitchcock not being, at that stage, internationally celebrated), the hegemony was very strong (I know—I grew up in that time and class, and was three years old when the film came out). This does not mean of course that British middle-class families in the 30's were any happier than American ones in the 50's—simply that they had less incentive to question whether they were happy or not; all the members of my own family were variously miserable, but none of us every explicitly doubted that we were the ideal happy family. Between 1934 and the remake, two

203

changes occur, the change of place and the change of time. The notion of the "career woman" seems strongly American: it's already there as an established theme in much pre-World War II American cinema, far more than in British, which has no real equivalents for *Stage Door, Christopher Strong, The Miracle Woman*. The Second World War saw the release of women from the home and the subsequent efforts to force them back into it. These factors provide a context in which the differences between the two versions begin to make sense. What follows is an attempt to deal with the major ones systematically.

1. Switzerland/Marrakech. The British version shows us a conventional holiday resort where the family seem quite at ease, as untroubled by external pressures as by internal tensions, with no sense of alienation. The American version gives us a family in a world whose alienness is stressed at every point (see, for example, the elaborate comic detail of the restaurant scene). One feature of the world receives special emphasis in that it provides the starting-point for the entire action: the position of Moslem women, epitomized in the compulsory wearing of the veil which Hank accidentally tears off, thereby giving Louis Bernard the pretext he needs for questioning the McKennas. The Moslem veil is clearly a signifier of the husband's total possession of his wife: no other man must even see her face, "possessing" her via the look. Jo, we recall, has had a triumphant stage career, gazed at by thousands; she has now been compelled by circumstances (in effect by her husband) to give up that career and be gazed at only by Ben. The climax of the film comes when he permits her to return to the public gaze, temporarily at least suspending his sole ownership of her. (We don't know of course what will happen after the film's closure, but we are at liberty to speculate that the internal tensions of the marriage, far from being resolved, may prove to have been exacerbated by Jo's re-experience of recognition as an autonomous person outside the confines of the marriage.) As a footnote, one may add that the point about Moslem women and the look is underlined by Hitchcock in the unobtrusive little visual joke of the woman at the market wearing glasses over her veil.

2. The expositions. Much of the extra running time of the American version is accounted for by its enormously more elaborate exposition. Up to the return to England, the British version contains, by my reckoning, six sequences, 109 shots, and lasts about 15 minutes;

the American version contains 11 sequences, 351 shots, and lasts 46 minutes. This is scarcely necessitated by any greater complexity in the espionage plot; it seems necessitated almost exclusively by the critical concern with marriage, family, and the position of women that simply isn't there in the British version. Related to this of course is the development of the Draytons as a kind of childless mirror to the McKennas (the equivalent couple in the British version offers no substantial parallel to this).

3. The stability of the marriage in the British version and its instability in the American can be pinpointed in one detail: Mrs. Lawrence's teasing of her husband by humorously flirting with Louis Bernard. This testifies to the absolutely solid base of the Lawrences' marriage; contrariwise, the fact that we absolutely cannot imagine Jo Conway behaving in that way testifies, perhaps paradoxically, to the precariousness of the Conways' marital arrangements: the marriage patently could not sustain such a flirtation, and it wouldn't be funny. Similarly, Jill is able to joke about not wanting children, referring to Betty as "it" in her daughter's presence (and to her enjoyment)—the strength of family ideology could scarcely be more eloquently confirmed. The thinness of the British version, in fact, is the result of its not being about anything very much beyond its MacGuffin.

4. Superficially, because it is regarded as a "masculine" activity, one might see the woman's sharpshooting as more "positive"—i.e. dynamic, aggressive, "possessing the phallus"—than singing "Che sera, sera." But what is far more decisive here is the distinction between a hobby and a career: Jill has a hobby, which her marriage can easily accommodate; Jo had a career, and her marriage has depended upon its renunciation.

5. One may consider briefly here the most obvious change between the two versions: Why does Betty change sex to become Hank? Tentatively, I think we may invoke Freud's theory that the woman who is denied the phallus sees her child as substitute/compensation, and that this is especially the case when the child is male. The narrative, one might suggest, provides Jo with a son as compensation for renouncing her career, her autonomy, her power outside the home; Jill, presented as totally contented with her position, has apparently renounced nothing. We should also note that since she relinquished her career Jo has been taking too many pills, has become nervous,

and now wants another child: the compensation has not worked very successfully.

6. The American version's privileging of Jo over Ben is strongly underlined by the one step in the basic structure I outlined in (c) above from which she is absent: the substitution for Bob's visit to the dentist of Ben's visit to the taxidermist. In the remake, the tracking of Ambrose Chappell to his taxidermy studio represents the husband's one solo undertaking. The visit to Barbor the dentist in the British version is a necessary link in the proairetic/hermeneutic chain; it also underlines Bob's phlegmatic, very-British heroism. He discovers important facts, he is endangered, he gets the upper hand. Ben's visit to the wrong Ambrose Cha(p)pe(l)l, on the other hand, is a complete fiasco: he learns nothing (except that he was wrong), he loses all control of the situation, and he is reduced to humiliating buffoonery.

7. In fact, despite her famous Albert Hall scream and her sharp-shooting expertise, Jill's function in the British version is far more restricted than Jo's in the American. (It is striking that in the British version Bob is accompanied to the Chapel by a male friend, not by his wife.) It is true that as the American male Ben plays the more obviously active role (that he prefers his wife to be passive is the point of the sedation scene): he fights, rings bells, bursts in on assassins, and finally rescues Hank. But the recurring motif of the film is that it is Jo who has the right instincts and perceptions and who makes the right decisions: it is she who becomes suspicious of Louis Bernard's questions, she who realizes that Ambrose Chapel is a place not a person; her scream saves the prime minister, her song saves Hank (and redeems Mrs. Drayton).

The film raises very strikingly one of the major features of gender-division in our culture, the notion that men are rational while women are emotional/intuitive. Men have laid claim to rationality as justification for their power, patronizingly granting women "female intuition" as compensation. The film suggests that it is men who are the more impoverished by this division. It is Ben's rationality that leads him to sedate Jo before telling her what has happened, subjugating her emotional response to the kidnapping of her son; the film is quite unambiguous, I think, as to the monstrousness of this, and it colors our reading of the character throughout. One might suggest that the "rational" is what the conscious mind works out for itself without assistance, while the "intuitive" is what the conscious mind comes to realize when it allows itself close contact with the subconscious. It is a structuring motif of the film, established in its first sequences, that Jo knows better than Ben. Her insights and decisions—suspicion of Louis Bernard, sense that the police should be told what has happened, realization that Ambrose Chapel is a place, her scream in the Albert Hall—can all be justified rationally, but they are reached "intuitively." Ben, limited to the purely rational, understands very little, though he can ring bells and burst open doors when required.

Most seem agreed that the ending of the British version is an anticlimax after the Albert Hall sequence, so I want to conclude by celebrating the real climax of the American version, Jo's song in the embassy. Middle-aged academics are not supposed to admit that they burst into tears every time Doris Day begins "Che sera, sera," but in my case it is a fact. What makes that moment so moving is its magical resolution of apparent oppositions. Eric Rohmer (in the book on Hitchcock he co-authored with Claude Chabrol)[4] grandly implies that it resolves the eternal theological quandary of predestination vs. free will: "Che sera, sera," but "the Lord helps those who help themselves." Less metaphysically, I see it as resolving the more practical and prosaic opposition of motherhood vs. career: it represents Jo's triumph simultaneously as mother and performer (and we can admire the power of her voice even if the embassy audience are a trifle taken aback). The shots of Doris Day's voice travelling up the stairs (so to speak) are among the most moving in the whole of Hitchcock. They lead to Hank's whistling and to Mrs. Drayton's scream, which, as I suggested earlier, answers Jo's scream in the Albert Hall: the screams of women who know better. Mr. Drayton's rationality, which reflects Ben's as its darker shadow, tells him that Hank must be murdered; his wife's emotional/intuitive understanding knows that Hank must be saved. Her scream is directly produced by the sound of approaching footsteps which she believes to be her husband's but are in fact Ben's: the parallel between the two couples, introduced in the exposition, is sustained right to the denouement.

Within the safe framework of the reconstruction of an American family, *The Man Who Knew Too Much* has some very important things to tell us about our culture.

Notes

1. Michael Renov, "From Identification to Ideology: The Male System of *Notorious*," *Wide Angle* 4, no. 1 (1980).
2. Robin Wood, "Ideology, Genre, Auteur," *Film Comment* 13, no. 1 (January/February, 1977).
3. Andrew Britton, "Cary Grant: Comedy and Male Desire," *Cine Action!* 7 (December 1986).
4. Eric Rohmer and Claude Chabrol, *Hitchcock: The First Forty-Four Films*, trans. Stanley Hochman (New York: Ungar, 1979).

REVALIDATING PATRIARCHY

Why Hitchcock Remade
The Man Who Knew Too Much

Ina Rae Hark

The 1934 *The Man Who Knew Too Much* was the first film in the Hitchcockian subgenre of the espionage thriller. Yet it was left to its immediate successor, *The Thirty-Nine Steps*, to set the pattern for Hitchcock's subsequent spy thrillers by combining the pursuit of the enemy agents with the culmination of a romance between the male and female protagonists. *The Man Who Knew Too Much*, by contrast, is the only one of Hitchcock's spy stories to feature a male and female protagonist who are already married to each other and are parents of a child when the film begins. *The Man Who Knew Too Much* is also the only film Hitchcock ever directly remade (without even a title change); he seems to have felt that he had not gotten the film "right" the first time. Donald Spoto reports that *The Man Who Knew Too Much* "was a film the director had for a long time wanted to refine and remake"; projected scenarios had been in the works from at least 1941.[1] Hitchcock agreed with Truffaut that "the second version was better" and called the 1934 film "the work of a talented amateur."[2]

Another of Hitchcock's remarks to Truffaut, however, indicates that he perceived in the earlier version, in addition to an overall lack of filmmaking polish, a specific patriarchal deficiency: "Incidentally, there is an important difference between the two versions of *The Man Who Knew Too Much*. In the British version the husband remains locked up, so that the wife carries the action by herself in Albert Hall and till the end of the picture."[3]

Given the cultural construction of upper-class husband- and father-hood in 1934 Great Britain, the patriarchal authority of the film's male protagonist, Bob Lawrence, ought to be unquestioned. Yet it is clear at the beginning of the film that he has either lost or abdicated it. The circumstances surrounding his daughter's kidnapping provide the impetus for enabling him to reassume that authority. Yet since he is locked up midway through the film, his wife, Jill, must take his place, without the film offering her any alternative to or strong condemnation of her usurpation of patriarchal power, represented by that reliable phallic signifier, the gun. William Rothman comments that "the weaknesses of [the 1934] *Man Who Knew Too Much* can be summed up by saying that it has no male figure who is Jill's equal and does not acknowledge the implications of this imbalance."[4] But if the film does not acknowledge the implications of this imbalance, those implications apparently bothered Hitchcock sufficiently for him to eliminate the imbalance in the 1956 remake.

Patriarchy is problematic throughout Hitchcock's films. His distrust of the social institutions like law and government that validate patriarchy in the symbolic order is well known. The narrative impulse in many of the spy films drives the complacent male protagonist to assume patriarchal authority in the face of its misuse or nonuse by these institutional powers. The antagonist is frequently a sort of patriarchal imposter, who, often a generation older than the protagonist, occupies a position of authority but bears the marks of the Other: disfigurement, slight stature, a foreign accent; Peter Lorre's character, Abbott, in *The Man Who Knew Too Much* has all three. Hitchcock's men all too readily surrender their authority to such bogus authority figures, whether our side or theirs is hardly an issue, and the events of Hitchcock's plots propel them, almost against their wills, to accomplish the supplanting of the inauthentic father.

The male hero's saving his country by defeating the false patriarch and marrying the heroine, usually after both country and heroine have doubted his worth, forms the customary double plot of all the spy films modeled on *The Thirty-Nine Steps*. This plot easily adapts itself to the pattern of the Oedipal process, seen most blatantly through the presence of Roger Thornhill's mother in *North by Northwest*.[5] And for Hitchcock films generally the second half of this process, the escape from woman as mother and the subordination of her as wife, is vested with far greater urgency than the overthrow of the father. When women actively seek to deny patriarchal authority to the male, they become monsters, as the portrayals of Mrs. Sebastian in *Notorious* and Mrs. Danvers (and behind her, Rebecca) confirm; when women simply resist submitting themselves to the man's authority, they often find themselves at some point totally dependent on the man, in extreme cases reduced to a semiconscious state like Ingrid Bergman in *Notorious* or Tippi Hedren in *The Birds* and *Marnie*. Although I would agree with Tania Modleski's argument, in *The Women Who Knew Too Much*, that Hitchcock is "*neither* . . . utterly misogynistic nor . . . largely sympathetic to women and their plight in patriarchy, but . . . his work is characterized by a thoroughgoing ambivalence about femininity," I would argue that he is not ambivalent about the dangers he perceives arising from men ceding their patriarchal roles to women.[6]

If the spy film provides the best paradigm for the protagonist's achievement of patriarchal authority, then the plot of another Hitchcockian subgenre, the psychotic-killer-of-women film, often illustrates the grave perils of leaving fatherhood to the Other and authority to mother. Hitchcock's lady-killers tend to inhabit a world devoid of strong patriarchal images (think of Henry Travers and Hume Cronyn as versions of male authority in *Shadow of a Doubt*), and are either dominated or smothered by maternal attention (*Strangers on a Train, Frenzy*). Unable to achieve socially sanctioned dominion over women by marrying them, they resort to killing them instead. The culmination of these warnings comes, of course, in *Psycho*, where the incompletely Oedipalized protagonist cannot escape his mother's domination even though he has murdered and stuffed her.

Turning back to *The Man Who Knew Too Much*, we can see the anomaly that must have nagged at Hitchcock as much as letting the bomb explode on the bus in *Sabotage*. As a document of male incompetence, it might have given pause to filmmakers far more inclined to feminism than Hitchcock was. Every significant male character in the film who tries to act in the name of authority finds himself incapacitated in attempting to exercise that authority. Abbott, Louis Bernard, and Ramon are killed; Bob and Ropa are wounded; Clive is hypnotized and then jailed; the dentist, Barbor, is anesthetized. Gibson, of the Foreign Office, and the police inspector are not physically wounded, but their occupations guarantee de facto impotence in the Hitchcockian scheme of things. At the end, it is only the sharp-shooting mother, Jill Lawrence, whose daughter had earlier caused her to miss her target, who can shoot well enough to save that daughter from the assassin's clutches.

As the film opens, traditional gender roles in the Lawrence family appear to be reversed. Jill is the performer, Bob the spectator who is supervising the child. Bob is very paternal, but not patriarchal. The later scene in which he tries to comfort the hysterical Betty after they are reunited at the spies' hideout is genuinely moving, because of the deep love between father and child that the performances of Leslie Banks and Nova Philbeam convey, but at the same time amusing because Bob has just previously assured Abbott in his best stiff-upper-lip manner that "I'm afraid if you expect a scene from me you'll be disappointed." At San Moritz we see him engaging in none of the many sporting activities going on. Only Louis Bernard, the handsome skier (and undercover British agent), not Bob, is shown dancing with Jill. She, for her part, only half-jokingly denies her role as mother with several dismissive comments: "Your child's going to cost me the match . . . if I lose I'll disown it forever"; "Let that be a lesson to you, never have children"; and "You can keep your brat." She pretends a passion for Louis, the man who wears masculine authority so well. "Come on Louis, perform," is her suggestive lead-in to a staged conversation about Bob's faults as a husband which the two enact on the dance floor as part of an ongoing charade about her leaving Bob and Betty for the dashing Frenchman. Rothman uses such evidence to assert that Jill's foiling of the assassination plot exorcises "her wish to avenge herself on the child she blames for binding her to her husband."[7]

The San Moritz scenes also set up the doubling, not only of protagonist and antagonist in the familiar pattern first articulated by Rohmer and Chabrol, but of their extended families as well. Each of the foreign agents represents a dark travesty of his or her British-allied counterpart. Like Jill, Abbott's female companion (called Nurse Agnes in the credits) appears in public to control her male partner and supplant him in the role of active performer; it is Agnes, not Abbott, who speaks from the dais during the sun worshippers' service. (Moreover, aside from the spies, the entire congregation at the tabernacle is comprised of women.) Agnes's gaunt figure and austere features prefigure Mrs. Danvers's. When she hypnotizes Bob's childishly bumbling friend, Clive, she appears to his distorted perceptions as a monstrous female face refracted through a prism — Hitchcock's female usurper of male authority in all her malignity, and perhaps a cautionary image of what trespassing into patriarchal territory could make of Jill.

Ramon, the marksman (and assassin), is Louis Bernard's double in that he is a suave Continental, charming to the ladies, who poses a threat to the authority of the nominal patriarch, Abbott, as Louis does to Bob's authority in Jill's fantasy. Ramon complains about his rough Channel crossing and swears that he will never again let himself be smuggled into England. Abbott must reassert his authority with the rebuke, "You will be smuggled my friend when, where, and how it pleases me for you to be smuggled." Later, words are not enough to keep Ramon in line. During the siege at the spies' hideout, he refuses to obey Abbott to the extent that Agnes has to pull a gun on him.

Abbott, the paterfamilias of the group of spies, mocks Bob's strong paternal emotions as he expresses affection for Betty with comments like, "one of the sweetest children I ever met" at the same time as he threatens her life. Abbott's endearments are given an additional edge of irony because Lorre had just played the psychopathic child murderer in *M*. Nevertheless, an insert close-up of a distraught Abbott listening to Betty's screams as she is separated from her father suggests that beneath Abbott's cruel travesty of paternal affections may lie real regret over the fate he will have to decree for her. As is the case with Bob, Abbott's demonstrations of paternal feelings are more convincing than his exercise of patriarchal power.

Thus, although Abbott and Bob spend considerable time engaging in witty repartee and puffing cigarettes at each other in an apparent battle for patriarchal ascendancy, both in fact find their authority challenged by other men and women. The organist wants to subordinate Abbott's authority to that of her husband, who will be angry if she stays late at the tabernacle and fails to have dinner on the table at the expected time. During the siege, which had begun when a policeman approaching the door was picked off by one of his henchmen, Abbott complains, "I never ordered the first policeman to be shot." That the spies' enterprise is to assassinate an elder statesman, the bearded, patriarchal-appearing Ropa, shows further that male authority figures are at bay on almost every level of the film's plot.

The immediate consequences of Louis's murder and Betty's kidnapping make this double catastrophe appear to be some kind of retribution for the legitimate patriarchal authorities, both governments and fathers, having let their powers deteriorate to such an extent. (The film further hints at a precarious state of masculine authority in England in the comic interchange between Bob and the German-speaking guard, when confusion over the words *here* and *herr* make it appear that Bob is asking whether the British consul is a man.) Although it is Jill who hears Louis's last words, they direct her to give his room key to Bob so that he can obtain the shaving brush with its coded message. This transfer of masculine symbols to Bob signals a charge to him to start exercising the Law of the Father. The kidnapping blocks him from seeking help from the patriarchal institutions of police and government and so leaves him no choice but to act personally as patriarchy's representative in the effort to thwart the spies' designs.

At the same time, Jill begins acting more like the stereotypical wife and mother. Shown the kidnappers' note, she faints. Back home in London, she remains upstairs while Bob handles the questions from the British authorities. After speaking to her captive daughter on the telephone, she collapses in tears. As Clive and Bob dash off to look for G. Barbor in Wapping, she is told to sit tight by the phone and treated like a petulant child when she objects to the danger of their undertaking. Meanwhile, her husband is cleverly overpowering and impersonating a traitorous dentist, brandishing a pistol, and fending off a gang of spies by throwing chairs at them. So it looks as if the Lawrence family is well on its way to revalidating patriarchy and establishing Hitchcock's espionage thriller archetype. Then, suddenly, Bob and Clive are both locked up, having just been able to pass the knowledge of the Albert Hall assassination plot along to Jill. Told "you're to stop it," she is for a second time the woman who knows too much, and now there are no men available to whom she can surrender her burden of knowledge.

In keeping with her newfound deference to male authority, Jill does make a move toward the police as she enters the Albert Hall, but Ramon intercepts her, handing her Betty's brooch to ensure her silence. This brooch is featured in insert close-up several times throughout *The Man Who Knew Too Much*, and it images the film's contradictory presentation of woman's gender role: a little girl skier holding an upright pair of skis. During the Albert Hall sequence, the brooch not only reminds Jill of her daughter's plight but mirrors her dilemma as woman. She must decide whether paternal responsibility supersedes duty to country, just as she had asserted to Gibson, "Our child comes first; she must come first." She must decide whether woman's role is to suffer and be still or take potentially catastrophic action. The outrageously phallic shots of Ramon's gun protruding from his curtained box and the editing of these shots within the sequence as a whole imply visually that Ramon can only kill Ropa by violating Jill. Jill must decide whether the greater good of husband and child is worth her sacrifice of selfhood by submitting. Her solution, however, is ambiguous. By screaming, she does not passively consent to her rape, but screaming as danger nears is still well within the parameters of female behavior as envisioned by patriarchy. Ramon blames his failure to wound Ropa fatally on "that damned woman screaming."

After the assassination attempt Jill is freed to go to the police and lead them to the spies' hideout. The ensuing gun battle, which Hitchcock based on the Sidney Street siege, damages the film's dramatic rhythm but provides additional evidence of the patriarchal deficiencies of the English law. When an unarmed bobby is sent to knock on the door, the spies promptly shoot him. Others charge, and many are mowed down. The police revolvers are useless in the shoot-out, so a lorry has to be sent for rifles from a neighboring gunsmith. A rifleman preoccupied with ogling a slip-clad young woman accidentally upsets a window blind, drawing gunfire that kills him. When the police finally do break into the tabernacle, they find access to the upper story blocked by a locked metal door that they are powerless to penetrate; the inspector simply shrugs his shoulders and says, "That's done us."

Bob finally manages to free himself and Betty from their rooms and make for the roof, but Ramon wounds Bob and pursues Betty. With the whole world watching, relatively speaking, the police are challenged to eliminate the enemy of legitimate patriarchal authority; their sharpshooter replies, "I daren't sir, I might hit the kiddie." So, let down by men on all sides, Jill once more takes up the rifle and dispatches Ramon herself. Her shot is clearly portrayed as a consummation. It releases the pent up energy of the crowd, which breaks through the police lines to rush the building. The impenetrable door has now mysteriously ceased to be an obstacle. We next see the inspector and his men searching through the upper rooms.

When the police lead Betty in from the roof to the waiting arms of her parents, she at first hesitates to reenter the scene of her ordeal at all, but when she does, she goes first to Bob. As Jill reaches out to her, she momentarily recoils, a look of horror on her face. Although the moment quickly passes, so that the film ends with the reconstituted family locked in a triple embrace, that horror at the prospect of woman wielding patriarchal authority might well be Hitchcock's. Perhaps realizing that he had made a film about so complete a failure of men to exercise their authority properly that at last it compelled the woman to take matters into her own hands, the director redefined his spy film archetype in *The Thirty-Nine Steps*. In this film the gun-wielding woman, Annabella Smith, is killed (and symbolically raped) early on, and the single, uncommitted Richard Hannay is forced to complete her mission while simultaneously developing his patriarchal authority sufficiently to retain Pamela's trust and companionship without benefit of handcuffs.

Still, however, the message of the previous film remained, and as noted above, it didn't take long for Hitchcock to consider a revised version. Eventually the attitudes about women and family current in middle-class mid-fifties America, combined with the availability of James Stewart as icon of the American male and Doris Day as icon of femininity, would provide the ideal opprotunity for a new *Man Who Knew Too Much* that "redresses the imbalance between husband and wife"[8] by restoring familial authority to the father and making it clear that motherhood is a woman's best hobby or profession.

In addition to having the husband, Dr. Ben McKenna, locked up in the chapel for a very brief period of time so that he can join his wife Jo at the Albert Hall before the assassination attempt, the film restores to men all the positions of patriarchal authority that the earlier version ceded to women and attaches patriarchal significance to events devoid of such overtones in the previous version. Rather than simply being on holiday as the Lawrences were, the McKennas are traveling specifically because of Ben's interests. He has attended a medical convention in Paris and makes the side trip to Morocco because he served in North Africa during the war.[9] Louis Bernard, unacquainted with the McKennas when the film begins, sets up his initial encounter with them on the bus (presided over by Hitchcock's cameo appearance) by having a Muslim accomplice angrily berate their son for accidentally uncovering his wife's veiled face. Louis then steps in to mediate this breach of patriarchal law. Rather than Jill's flirtatiousness with Louis, Jo shows only suspicion toward him. Later it is the husband, not the wife, that he searches out when dying, and to whom he directly communicates his knowledge about the assassination attempt. Indeed, Jo has to beg Ben to share this knowledge with her. And Drayton, the character who corresponds to Abbott, takes the pulpit at the chapel and does not leave the preaching to his female companion. Even the focal point of attention, the kidnapped child, has moved from female to male, from Betty to Hank.

At the same time, the two central female characters have been rewritten to stress their womanliness and the power of motherhood to overcome their usual deference to male authority. The female spy is now the matronly, nonsinister wife to Drayton; she eventually lets her maternal feelings toward Hank overpower her devotion to their cause. Like Mrs. Lawrence, Mrs. McKenna is also a performer, in fact the world-famous professional singer "Jo Conway," but she has abandoned her career to accommodate her husband's. The climactic moment in which the mother's talent brings about the return of her child is changed from her shooting the kidnapper to her singing "Che sera, sera, whatever will be, will be," a song whose lyrics delineate how various authorities inculcate a fatalistic passivity in women that they in turn pass on to their children. Her singing is, moreover, a more generally acknowledged female skill than sharpshooting.

Hitchcock does not abandon the 1934 film's concern with a troubled marriage being reborn through the kidnapping ordeal, but this time the trouble is caused by the husband's patriarchal assumptions, not his lack of them. Instead of compromising by moving his medical practice to New York so that Jo can resume her singing career,

Ben insists on remaining in Indianapolis. Whenever events frustrate him, he becomes aggressive: "Once you get worked up, you start a fight," Jo cautions him. He is always trying to deny Jo opportunities to speak, discounting her subsequently validated intuitions about Louis's ulterior motives, and hiding the fact of Hank's abduction until he can sedate her.

Nor is there any hint, as in the earlier version, that the mother resents her child. Indeed, directly before the kidnapping, Jo asks Ben when they are going to have another baby. Her interactions with Hank are never other than those of a devoted mother. And since her last reported London performances were "four years ago," when Hank would have been about four or five, it is clear that her career could have proceeded with the child. It is her husband who has ended it.

The other Hitchcock films starring James Stewart which are the subject of this collection explore the misuse of patriarchal authority, linking it to the gaze, to voyeurism, and to the oppression of women. Ironically, so does the 1956 *Man Who Knew Too Much*. Once Hitchcock has revised the film so that men and woman do not stray from their assigned roles in patriarchy, he begins to cast a cold eye on the patriarchal system's operations. Many commentators have noted Ben's almost brutal drugging and forcible restraint of Jo as he tells her about the kidnapping. (Bob simply handed Jill the kidnappers' note.) Yet Ben's macho posturing as the typical fifties American father aside, he seems rather at sea beyond the familiar confines of Indianapolis. To Jo's sophisticated London theatrical friends, he is Mr. *Conway*, the mere husband of a famous wife. Ben's awkwardness in dealing with the seating and eating customs at the Arab restaurant is just a preview of his blundering encounter with the taxidermist Chappell, his inability to gain access to the ambassador's box at the Albert Hall, his confrontation with the assassin only after the assassination attempt that causes him to fall to his death, thus eliminating a possible source of information as to Hank's whereabouts. So, despite Ben's insistence on taking the lead in dealing with all situations, he, as much as Drayton, deserves the traitorous ambassador's charge that "you've muddled everything from the start." Jo, on the other hand, has all the right instincts about Louis's being a spy and about Ambrose Chapel being a place, not a person.

Nevertheless, Ben finally is the one to rescue Hank by disarming

Drayton and sending him tumbling down the stairs to his death. It is a reversal of the earlier film's conclusion. There Jill dispatched the spy holding her child hostage after Bob had freed the child to come into her sights; here Ben can only locate his child because of the combined motherly talents of Jo and Mrs. Drayton, but he can only end Hank's peril himself. And with the patriarchal mechanism thus restored to working order, this version of *The Man Who Knew Too Much* can end, not with the intense and ambivalent emotions of the original but with a dismissive joke: returning after midnight to their hotel room and the friends they left waiting there in the early afternoon, the McKennas apologize, "I'm sorry we were gone so long, but we had to go over and pick up Hank."

In the 1956 film, then, Hitchcock ridicules the behavior of men under patriarchy yet assures women that if they will pursue their own assigned roles vigorously enough, their men will blunder through to success in the end. One could argue equally that Jo's character is constructed so as to represent a privileging of women's ways of "knowing" over men's, or to validate sexist stereotypes about motherhood and women's intuition. As Modleski observes, "When one is reading criticism defending or attacking Hitchcock's treatment of women, one continually experiences a feeling of 'yes, but. . . . ' "[10]

The most we can therefore conclude from the lesson of the two versions of *The Man Who Knew Too Much* is that Hitchcock feared women's taking over men's roles in patriarchy more than he deplored men's abuses and failings within the patriarchal system. Hitchcockian films may very well call all the various cultural, ideologial, and psychological constructions that authorize patriarchy into question; as long as those constructions retain power, however, the films consistently present the woman who usurps the male position within them as monstrous. Furthermore, scrutinizing the way men use their power is not the same as showing them incapable of using it. To criticize the tyranny of a repressively ineffectual autocrat over his subjects and urge more capable and benevolent rule is not the same as to suggest that an impotent ruling class has so failed in its responsibilities that it must submit to the de facto rule of its subjects. The original *Man Who Knew Too Much* implies just such a radical realignment of male and female authority. And that, I believe, is one reason why Hitchcock, troubled by but not prepared to overthrow patriarchy, remade it.

Notes

1. Donald Spoto, *The Dark Side of Genius: The Life of Alfred Hitchcock* (Boston: Little, Brown, 1983), 359.
2. François Truffaut, *Hitchcock* (New York: Simon and Schuster, 1967), 64, 65.
3. Truffaut, 64.
4. William Rothman, *Hitchcock: The Murderous Gaze* (Cambridge, Mass.: Harvard University Press, 1982), 111.
5. See Raymond Bellour's celebrated study of *North by Northwest*, "Le blocage symbolique," *Communications*, no. 23 (1975), 235–350. Of course Bellour finds American films in general to be overwhelmingly concerned with the process of Oedipalization.
6. Tania Modleski, *The Women Who Knew Too Much* (New York: Methuen, 1988), 3. Despite the title of her book, Modleski does not discuss either version of *The Man Who Knew Too Much*.
7. Rothman, 111.
8. Rothman, 112.
9. The class differences between the two versions of the family also may have contributed to this change. The upper-class Lawrences, neither of whom seems to depend on a job for money, are more likely to take off for St. Moritz for a holiday than would a general practitioner from Indianapolis jet off to Marrakech without having a specific reason.
10. Modleski, 3.

IV
HITCHCOCK'S AMBIGUOUS MORALITY
PLAY: *ROPE* (1948)

Rope is a film adaptation of a 1929 stage play by Patrick Hamilton, loosely based on the Leopold and Loeb case, about two homosexual lovers who murder a college friend for no other reason than pure enjoyment and the satisfaction of a Nietzschean will to power. Hitchcock's first color film is thus a study of moral depravity exercised for its own sake, and *Rope* is clearly intended to be a condemnation of both theorizing about the relativity of moral codes — the two killers were inspired by their college tutor's arrogant intellectualizing about "supermen" — and the inevitable use of such ideas for justification of murder and even genocide (the film clearly addresses the Nazi atrocities by implication). Since the two killers idolize their former teacher and seek his approval for their action, *Rope* also uncovers some of the psychosexual underpinnings of their motivations.

Yet the "themes" of *Rope* have attracted less critical attention than its techniques: a reliance on camera movement rather than cuts and the use of a single set, a Manhattan penthouse. Hitchcock, as evidenced by *Lifeboat* and *Rear Window*, as well as *Rope*, relished the challenge of such self-imposed restrictions, and here he indulges in "ten-minute takes" and a remarkably fluid camera that travels incessantly around the limited space. The form of *Rope* thus expresses its director's dominant control of each frame even more obviously than the usual Hitchcock film, and many of the theoretical discussions of the film focus on *Rope* as a technical exercise, as an "experiment," more than as a serious analysis of amoral ideology.

Thomas M. Bauso's "*Rope*: Hitchcock's Unkindest Cut" argues that the director's structuring of the narrative around continuous camera takes and the barest of editing entraps the audience and makes it complicit in the murder committed at the outset of the film. According to Bauso, the camera's perspective and the placement of

Farley Granger, James Stewart, and John Dall in *Rope.* **(Photo courtesy of Photofest, New York.)**

the film's ten editing cuts unite the audience first with the two young murderers, and then with Rupert, their ambivalent older mentor. *Rope* becomes for Bauso an exercise in humor perpetrated upon a manipulated audience left increasingly uncomfortable about where its sympathies lie. This narrative process implicates us in the crime and the whole film becomes a "disquieting cosmic jest" which disturbs our moral sense of ourselves.

Readings grounded in Lacanian theory uncover subtexts that often contradict a film's surface cultural ideology. Robert G. Goulet, in his essay, "Life With(out) Father: The Ideological Masculine in *Rope* and Other Hitchcock Films," draws upon Lacan and the structural Marxism of Louis Althusser. He insists that Hitchcock undermines the ideological masculine world in the very films that apparently sanction it: *Notorious* (1946), *Rope* (1948), and *Strangers on a Train* (1951), each of which contains beguiling "homosexual villains" who subvert the film's ostensible support of patriarchy's heterosexual hegemony. He sees *Rope*, in particular, as a study of the ambiguous nature of patriarchy's symbolic world of language and law. In Goulet's view patriarchal justice, represented by Rupert Cadell, is undercut by Cadell's own responsibility for inspiring the murderous fantasies and actions of Brandon and Philip, "sons" of Cadell who have taken their master's playful amorality as justification for their crime. Cadell, the representative of masculine reason, unconsciously reveals his own guilt at the very moment in the film when he reveals the culpability of others. Thus, although Cadell reasserts the dominant heterosexual and patriarchal ideology at the film's end, *Rope*'s ambivalence toward the "law of the father" is never fully resolved.

The "experimental" nature of *Rope* has also attracted the attention of critics grounded in the theory of deconstruction, with its concern with inconsistencies in a text's system of "meaning." Thomas Hemmeter's "Twisted Writing: *Rope* as an Experimental Film" sees Hitchcock's film as "reveling" in such inconsistency and undercutting its ostensible support of logic and value. He cites as examples contradictory uses of language in the film which undermine surface meanings. In Hemmeter's view, Rupert Cadell, apparently representing the moral center at the film's resolution, is unaware of the futile nature of his attempt to control language and, therefore, meaning. *Rope* is thus an "experiment" in the sense that it deconstructs its own serious intents; it is film as "play." Hemmeter wants us to see that the main characters are indeed trapped, but within a prison of language.

ROPE: HITCHCOCK'S UNKINDEST CUT

Thomas M. Bauso

Just after Christmas Day of 1956, a man who was popularly known in the New York press of that time as "The Mad Bomber" planted one of his explosive devices in the theater showing Alfred Hitchcock's *The Wrong Man*. Luckily, this act of urban terrorism was thwarted, but it did succeed in eliciting from Hitchcock a characterization of George Metesky as "a man with a diabolical sense of humor."[1] One can't help imagining that Hitchcock's response to the incident was ambivalent. After all, he must have delighted in his own role as "a man with a diabolical sense of humor," and Metesky had cleverly appropriated one of Hitchcock's favorite dramatic situations, a hidden bomb, for his little joke on that New York audience. But no—Metesky's style of humor really wasn't Hitchcock's: too much surprise, not enough suspense, in The Mad Bomber's modus operandi. This was simply no way to treat a film audience. Hitchcock could not, finally, have admired this failed artist whose methods were so abrupt.

But I would like to argue in this paper that a form of diabolical wit extends throughout Hitchcock's planning and execution of his 1948 film *Rope*, that Raymond Durgnat is basically correct when he says that "Hitchcock is like a God playing as many practical jokes on human beings as he can."[2] The interesting difference in

Rope, it seems to me, is that Hitchcock has included himself, as well as his actors and technicians, in this elaborate exercise in cinematic perversity. The primary joke, not unexpectedly, is on the audience, which is made to feel various kinds of psychological discomfort while viewing the film, but Hitchcock has also arranged for himself the role of "victim" of his own experimental style. This unfamiliar role must have given him some pleasure—Hitchcock obviously enjoyed, for instance, the technical challenge posed by *Rope*'s lengthy takes—but it is one which at the same time he strenuously resisted, in part through his manipulation of the audience's emotions. Since a key stylistic element in this strategy of audience manipulation is the editorial cut, it might be useful to begin with a consideration of how Hitchcock both loses and gains power through his shaping of the film's style.

Hitchcock's faith in "the importance of cutting and montage for the visual narration of a story"[3] needs no rehearsal here. So when John Russell Taylor, in a reference to *Rope*, wonders about his "curious denying himself of cutting, the very resource which had always meant most to him in the cinema,"[4] one is struck by the self-consciousness such an artistic decision must have entailed. In his 1937 essay "Direction," Hitchcock talks about his willingness to use a "long uninterrupted shot," but he notes, too, that "if I have to shoot a long scene continuously I always feel I am losing grip on it, from a cinematic point of view."[5] Later in the essay he specifically links this self-abandonment with losing "power over the audience."[6] With its lengthy takes, *Rope* embodies Hitchcock's apparent release of control, yet it may be that he has in fact devised an unparalleled way to fulfill his artistic intentions while also teasing to distraction his audience and his actors.

In playing his novel game, Hitchcock planned to commit the cinematic equivalent of a mortal sin, then redeemed himself ironically through the malicious tricks he practices upon others. In his interview with Hitchcock, Truffaut actually phrases his own romantic defense of *Rope* in the language of spiritual transgression. He imagines Hitchcock as "a director . . . tempted by the dream of linking all of a film's components into a single, continuous action." Hitchcock elaborates on Truffaut's image of sin by replying that "as an experiment, *Rope* may be forgiven."[7] Indeed, repeatedly in the Truffaut interview Hitchcock seeks to dismiss the entire project.

227

Rope, he asserts, was a "stunt . . . I really don't know how I came to indulge in it . . . I got this crazy idea . . . I realize that it was quite nonsensical."[8] My sense is that Hitchcock protests too much, and that from its inception *Rope* was a project that he designed to be, as William Rothman puts it, "disquieting."[9]

Viewed in this way, Hitchcock's statements about the film fit into a carefully contrived pattern of misrepresentation, aimed at making the experience of *Rope* as disorienting as possible and creating for the film an aura of personal dissatisfaction, imbalance, and failure. In a 1968 essay, he says of *Rope* that "I tried to give it a flowing camera movement and I didn't put any cuts in at all."[10] Since this kind of remark can't simply be attributed to faulty memory, one may reasonably posit a deliberate intention to obscure, or perhaps reimagine, the world of the film.

One measure of Hitchcock's success at inventing and perpetuating a mythology of the film is the degree to which its commentators, from the earliest reviewers on, have misread *Rope*. Hitchcock's allegation about its lack of cuts, for instance, was not without precedent. *Time* magazine had claimed that "in photographing the action, Director Hitchcock brought off a tour de force. There is not a single cut in the film."[11] One critic refers to "John Dall's calm piano-playing"[12] — so calm, it isn't even there; another states that "each shot lasts ten minutes,"[13] when in fact only two of the film's eleven takes are that long. At times Hitchcock's flair for publicity seems to motivate his distortions. In a 1948 essay for *Popular Photography* magazine called "My Most Exciting Picture," he boasts of his "magical . . . cyclorama — an exact miniature reproduction of nearly 35 miles of New York skyline lighted by 8000 incandescent bulbs and 200 neon signs."[14] Impressive as the background for *Rope* may be, one must still wonder where it conceals thirty-five miles of New York skyline.

Even James Stewart unwittingly enters the game of reconstructing *Rope*. Hitchcock's account of the direct sound track that was made possible by the elaborate set, with walls swinging on "silent rails" and "furniture . . . mounted on rollers"[15] is contradicted, at least in part, by Stewart's recollection that "the noise of the moving walls was a problem, and so we had to do the whole thing over again for sound, with just microphones, like a radio play. The dialogue track was then added later."[16]

Despite the recurring sense of vertigo that commentaries on *Rope* might induce in the reader, it seems clear that Hitchcock's penchant for anxiety informed his making of a film requiring actors and actresses to master lines, cues, placement, and movement extending over several minutes of uninterrupted action. Such a demanding procedure must at some level have been designed to provoke distress in creator, cast, and crew, and must also have succeeded. Allowing for a degree of self-dramatization, one may still credit Hitchcock's image of his emotional state when production began: "I was so scared that something would go wrong that I couldn't even look during the first take."[17] This hardly jibes with the legend of Hitchcock's immense boredom on the set while his elaborately precut dramas were being enacted, but it plausibly represents what must have been, in Donald Spoto's words, the "unalloyed horror" of filming *Rope*.[18] Hitchcock typically renders his own discomfort in an elegant little narrative that climaxes in a comic reversal. That first take proceeded for eight minutes without a hitch, he explains, until the camera perversely panned to "an electrician standing by the window."[19]

Self-mockery and irony can thus be seen to be a pertinent mode of self-presentation for Hitchcock, nicely complementing his evident delight in upsetting others. He enjoys reporting James Stewart's nocturnal traumas during production, which in Hitchcock's account bear a curious resemblance to the troubled sleep of Stewart's Scottie Ferguson in *Vertigo* ten years later: "'[Stewart] couldn't sleep nights because of the picture,' Hitchcock remarked [about the making of *Rope*]. 'It was the bewildering technique that made him worry.'"[20] And John Russell Taylor extends the melodrama to "the most seasoned professional of them all, Constance Collier, [who] was absolutely terrified to go to the studio when they were actually shooting."[21] Collier, who plays Mrs. Atwater, certainly had reason to be concerned. Take, for instance, that moment in the film when Brandon (John Dall) is narrating his story of Philip's (Farley Granger) wringing chickens' necks on an idyllic Sunday morning in the country. In order to provide the comic counterpoint in the scene, Collier must time her mouthful of chicken so that Brandon's gruesome detail of animal slaughter coincides precisely with her attempt to place the food in her mouth. Appalled, she aborts her gesture and exclaims "Oh, dear!" instead. Almost as nerve-racking from an actor's point of view must have been John Dall's task of dropping the rope into the kitchen drawer at exactly the moment that the door swings open to capture its descent. The film is full of such technically difficult moments whose execution demands not only skill but also a measure of luck.

But these are instances, too, of how Hitchcock's self-teasing is barely distinguishable from a sophisticated game of self-torture. It is one thing for him to insert in the scenario a joke about how difficult it is to remember the title of one of his recent films (*Notorious*), or to have Janet Walker (Joan Chandler) ecstatically "take" Cary Grant and allude to Ingrid Bergman's loveliness. (Hitchcock, we know, would himself have taken Grant for the Rupert Cadell role had he been available from RKO.)[22] These ironic self-references are simply verbal equivalents of Hitchcock's popular cameo appearances in his films. It is quite another thing, however, for him to contrive a "visual technique that had everyone anxious,"[23] for such risk-taking threatens both the creative and financial success of his art.

Andre Bazin's 1954 interview with Hitchcock will help to clarify what was at stake in *Rope*. Hitchcock explains that his artistic aim in his work has been to achieve a "discordant relationship" between drama and comedy, an aim fully realized to that point in his career only in the "adult" humor of his British films. If *Rope* is therefore read as an American experiment in fusing the dissonant elements of terror and humor, then Hitchcock must have perceived that his experiment was doomed, for (in Bazin's words) "Americans have much too positive a spirit to accept humor." The pragmatic American spirit would also resist the kind of morbid fantasy that a film such as *Rope* enacts. For instance, Bazin notes that Hitchcock "could never have made *The Lady Vanishes* in Hollywood; a simple reading of the scenario and the producer would have pointed out how unrealistic it would be to send a message with an old woman by train when it would be quicker and surer to send a telegram."[24] Indeed, this is exactly the style of criticism that Robert Hatch, writing in *The New Republic* in 1948, invokes in his review of *Rope*. It is unrealistic, in Hatch's view, for Brandon and Philip to have overlooked David's hat in the closet, thereby providing Rupert with an important clue, and it violates the probability of New York zoning laws to place a garish neon sign in such close proximity to an elegant penthouse apartment.[25] Furthermore, Bazin claims that Hollywood films are tailored to the sentimental tastes of the women who constitute the majority of the audience, so *Rope*'s aggressive form and "warped sense of humor" (to quote Janet on the subject of Brandon's jokes) flirt with financial disaster. (Typically enough, it is difficult to determine whether it *did* fail in this sense; those directly connected to it, such as Hume Cronyn and Hitchcock himself, speak of its success, whereas later commentators see its profits as "modest."[26]) Durgnat speculates that "*Rope* might be meant for people who . . . irresponsibly play with moral ideas,"[27] but surely it would be folly to expect such a constituency in the American film-going public. In this sense, *Rope* willfully—though playfully—alienates its audience, and forsakes the commercial benefits that were so important to Hitchcock, who told Bazin that "his 'weakness' . . . [was] . . . being conscious of his responsibility for all this money."[28]

Yet *Rope* nevertheless insists on its right to construct, in its own way, what Bazin calls the "essential instability of image"[29] characteristic of Hitchcock's mise-en-scène. Critics who don't dismiss the film out of hand are usually sensitive to the ways in which this instability is rendered, paradoxically, by the precise and suspenseful movements of the camera. One contemporary reviewer said that "Hitchcock's brilliant use of a fluid camera maintains unflagging suspense from the moment the chest is closed until its lid is lifted again";[30] another linked the suspense to "the prying insidious eye of his continuously moving camera."[31] William Rothman remarks that "the deliberateness of every move that the camera makes creates a state of perpetual tension."[32] The anxiety that this photographic style elicits can be seen as Hitchcock's way of restoring his power over the film through an assault on the sensibilities of his audience.

This aggressive manipulating of his audience's emotions is an ironic analogue to the physical and psychological manipulations that Philip and Brandon exert on their victims in the film. Referring to Brandon, Janet at one point exclaims in exasperation, "Why can't he keep his hands off people?" Indeed, the film plainly proposes that Brandon metaphorically enacts the Hitchcockian role of director in his dominance of Philip, who has the artistic talent that Brandon can only imagine and who is commanded by Brandon to execute the crime (a symbolic rape) that he has meticulously arranged. That Brandon is Hitchcock's surrogate is also demonstrated by their common delight in perverse wit and in the unremitting pursuit of technical challenges that will finally enhance their works of "art." Thus Brandon insists on "making [their] work of art a masterpiece" by serving food from the chest containing the murdered David, inviting their victim's family and friends to the "sacrificial feast," and tying Mr. Kentley's first editions with the instrument of his son's death. Viewed in this ironic light, Brandon plays not only "God," as Rupert Cadell suggests at the film's climax, but also Cupid, for it is he who engineers the reunion of the former lovers Kenneth and Janet. This directorial action is particularly unsettling, from a moral perspective, since Janet unwittingly implies, in her half-hearted response to Kenneth's question about whether or not she loves David, that Brandon has performed a socially useful act in eliminating David and in subsequently "maneuvering the other two points of the triangle" into amorous proximity.

That Hitchcock has successfully complicated the moral question of murder is demonstrated by such an ironic twist as Brandon's felicitous matchmaking, but his central achievement in viewer disorientation is his simultaneous provoking of his audience to regard the crime with horror and his implicating of that audience in the performance of the crime. More than anything else, this complex process accounts for the unpleasant sensations that *Rope* seems to produce in many of its viewers. The process, in fact, was underway from the earliest reviews of the film, and can be measured, for instance, by the consistency with which contemporary reviewers reconstructed Brandon and Philip's act of carefully placing David's body into the antique chest. Although the chest is obviously roomy enough to contain David, the reviews almost always state that the murderers "dump" him in, or "stuff" him in, or "cram" him in. What's happening here seems clear. The writers' psychological distress over the film is being unconsciously registered by their colorful but inaccurate diction; evaluative terms that capture their moral revulsion replace descriptive language (say, "put" him in) that would bespeak a degree of objective disengagement from the act itself. The key to such an entrapment of the audience lies in so fundamental a concept as Hitchcock's theory of suspense. In an essay on *Rear Window*, he argues that "the delineation of suspense covers a very, very wide field. Basically it is providing the audience with information that the characters do not have."[33] Note how this works in *Rope*: the audience, which has never seen David Kentley alive and is therefore not encouraged to identify with him, is propelled into the scene of his murder and so knows, from the very beginning of the film, a crucial fact that no one besides the killers themselves knows. A pervasive dramatic irony is thus insinuated into the film. Our mere knowledge establishes our complicity in the crime, and more importantly, it sets us up as an appreciative audience for the continuous flow of double entendres and "malicious" witticisms that swirl around the fact of David's death. What Hitchcock has arranged for, in short, is our laughter, and it is that which troubles us. We may be appalled at Brandon's "warped sense of humor," but since we can't help getting the morbid jokes, we are compelled to laugh at them, and our laughter implicates us in the act of murder. We are thus continuously being forced to identify with the killers, an identification that is, as Durgnat says, "paradoxical and tension-charged."[34] Brandon's wordplay, as well as the unwitting puns of the other characters, is a recurrent comic ploy throughout the film. One of his most sardonic innuendos comes when Rupert asks Brandon if he or Philip were at the club that day, and Brandon replies, "Hardly. We had our hands full, getting ready for the party." As emotionally tentative as he is about their crime, Philip can also play with it verbally. To Kenneth's pleasantry, "Been up to much lately?" Philip replies, "Nothing to speak of." And even Mr. Kentley can be heard in the background referring to Brandon: "What a charming young man. I [wish that] David saw more of him."

Once he has involved his audience in the crime, Hitchcock is then free to explore a range of provocative strategies; in effect, his power over the audience's emotions, like his control over the film text, is absolute. So he can, for instance, have Brandon taunt the film's post–World War II audience with the sarcasm of his remark that "good Americans usually die young on the battlefield, don't they?" Or consider the arrogance of Brandon's approval of Rupert: "Do you know [he says] that [Rupert] selects his books on the assumption that people not only can read but actually can think?"

Yet perhaps Hitchcock's cleverest joke on his audience involves his selection of James Stewart, an actor whose persona is imbued with the values of decency and right-thinking, to play the role of Rupert Cadell. A couple of assumptions seem to be operating here. First, Stewart as an apologist for murder, and a cigarette-smoking one at that, is bound to grate on the audience's sensibilities. One biographer of Stewart suggests that the cigarette smoking is included "so that he can use a missing cigarette case as an excuse to return after the other guests have gone."[35] But if that were the only motivation for Cadell's smoking, Hitchcock could more plausibly have arranged for him to be wearing glasses, which would have fit the bookish stereotype familiar to his audience, and to have left his glasses case behind. In fact, the cigarette smoking is part of the larger agenda of disorientation, but the brilliance of Hitchcock's recreation of the Stewart persona lies in the tact that Hitchcock exercises here. He is cunning enough to blunt the malice implied by Cadell's theory of superior and inferior beings, not out of solicitude for his audience, but rather to set the stage for the trap that ensnares both Cadell and the audience at the climax of the film.

To advance this strategy, Hitchcock makes certain that Cadell's bitterness is always withdrawn before it is allowed to go too far. For example, Cadell will embarrass his former pupil Kenneth but will then hasten to allay Kenneth's discomfort. When he propounds his theory of the art of murder, his language betrays an essential lack of seriousness about his "ideas," a lack that Mr. Kentley is quick to detect. Cadell's entire monologue is thus reduced to a comic performance enacted for the benefit of his appreciative audience, particularly Mrs. Atwater, who laughs delightedly at his trivializing of the subject, just as his cynicism was a pose designed to entertain Brandon and the other boys at prep school. It is important for the audience to perceive that Rupert is *not* Brandon. Rather than constituting a moderation of Hitchcock's strategy of audience alienation, however, this role-playing of Rupert Cadell serves instead to promote Hitchcock's ironic purpose. For the audience can more easily be teased into identifying with this character and thus can be entrapped by that identification at the end of the film, when the deadly conquences of Cadell's cavalier toying with ideas are fully brought ome to him, and the space between his play-acting and his pupils' acting-out of his fantasy is dramatically closed.

The mood of inevitability that prepares for the stunning disclosure — and closure — of *Rope* can be attributed to both the gradual unfolding of the motivation which controls behavior and to the film's distinctive alternation of straight and masked cuts. The motivation and behavior may be thus summarized: Brandon's desire throughout the film is to be exposed by Rupert, his yearning to be admired only superficially delayed by his protests and by the circumstances of the evening's "fun." Just as he is fatefully moving the plot toward its completion in the fulfillment of his romantic wish, so too is he being made the ironic victim of his fatal miscalculation. Not knowing Rupert so well as he thinks he does, he assumes that Rupert will conceal the crime. Philip, for his part, has been so intense on the subject of chickens and strangling throughout the evening that he seems destined to break down and reveal the crime. That he does so just this side of high comedy at the end is dramatized by his hilarious shouting to Brandon that "[Rupert's] caught on . . . He knows!" while Rupert is presumably listening in on the other end of the phone line, and by his incensed responses to Rupert upon his returning to the apartment. Referring to Brandon's offer of a drink, Phillip screams, "He said you could have it!" Hitchcock has slyly made his comic treatment of Philip dramatically plausible by inserting several references in the dialogue to his inebriation, which would presumably account for his exaggerated manner here. As for Rupert, his suspicions about his former pupils' behavior and their stated motives for the party have been aroused virtually from the moment of his arrival. Indeed, Hitchcock's camera underlines the inevitable linking of David and Rupert by taking Janet's cue when she says to Mr. Kentley that David will "probably be here in a minute" and tracking out to reveal the food-laden chest, then panning left to capture the "star entrance"[36] of Rupert Cadell. Rupert is thus wed visually not simply to the eventual revelation of the murder but to the very fact of the crime.

The alternating rhythm of straight and masked cuts contributes decisively to Hitchcock's strategy of audience entrapment in *Rope*. The editorial transitions in the film clearly come at dramatically appropriate moments, for of the eleven continuous sequences, only two are extended to the ten-minute limit. Indeed, some takes are as "short" as four or five minutes, with most falling within the seven- to eight-minute range. The basic principle governing both the timing and the mode of the cuts is this: since an audience will quite naturally identify with the character or characters in jeopardy of exposure or of death, Hitchcock has arranged his cuts in a sequence that unites his audience first to the killers and finally to Rupert, who arguably is the "real" killer in the murder plot. Although there is clear progression, it is from one form of discomfort to another — from one troubling identification figure to another — so in a sense the audience, never released from the cycle of guilt, gets nowhere in the course of the plot's unfolding.

The spiral is initiated by that first cut, following the credits, that propels the viewer, startlingly, into the act of murder. Poised between shock at the horror of the moment and a paradoxical kinship with the killers, one is set up for the dramatic irony that attends the second cut, masked by Brandon's dark-blue suit. In the moment immediately preceding this cut, the audience has been shown the telltale rope, still unnoticed by the murderers. Anxiety is thus aroused, for one's natural instinct is to fear the exposure that the rope signifies. The masked cut then sustains the mood of suspense predicated on the audience's iden-tification with Brandon and Philip. Indeed, throughout the film Philip's unintentionally comic expressions of nervousness can be viewed as Hitchcock's parody of the audience's own fear of disclosure. The third cut follows Brandon's ironic remark to Kenneth that he has "the oddest feeling anyway that your chances with the young lady are much better than you think," and it takes the audience from Kenneth to Janet emerging from the intersecting backs of Brandon and Philip. Brandon's sinister joke is designed to startle the viewer, who has al-ready been made to feel involved in his crime, so the effect of the abrupt cut here is to reintroduce a feeling of guilt over the involve-ment, as well as to reflect the social awkwardness that Kenneth is feeling just then and that Janet is about to feel.

Hitchcock, in other words, is simultaneously linking and distanc-ing his audience and his murderers. The following cut, a masked one, is placed in a verbal context parallel to the third — Brandon has just joked about David — but this time the masking of the cut both sustains one's shock at the joke and encourages a feeling of complacency about its moral implications. In the light of this complacency, the abrupt-ness of cut number 5, which transports the viewer to an intrigued Ru-pert when Philip exclaims that Brandon's chicken-strangling story is "a lie," serves to reinvoke the audience's sense of complicity in the crime, for the transition emphasizes Rupert's deepening percep-tion of disorder and thus prompts the disturbing feeling that Philip is about to reveal that disorder. The sixth cut, a masked one, is a repetition of cut number 4. Sustaining the disquieting possibility that Rupert is about to find "us" out, it also, paradoxically, placates our guilty conscience.

The final important shift in audience involvement comes at the ninth cut, for it is here that Hitchcock's camera repositions from a close-up of Brandon's jacket pocket (his hand on the gun inside) to a medium close-up of Rupert as he considers where he would put

236

David's corpse. By panning toward and then away from the chest at this point in Rupert's description, Hitchcock's camera has just teasingly implied that Cadell will say "in the chest." So the dramatic effect of the cut is to startle the audience, which assumes that the completion of Rupert's imaginary murder narrative will incite Brandon to shoot him. Brandon has already attempted to pacify Philip by saying that Rupert will be gotten out of the apartment in five minutes, "one way or the other."

Subtly but decisively, I think, the audience is made to fear for Rupert's life here, and, by inviting identification with Rupert, Hitchcock has contrived his most diabolical joke on the audience. First, he places the audience and Rupert in analogous positions of physical jeopardy by having the gun point directly at the camera as Rupert is struggling with Philip. Then, in the film's final cut — the one which is masked by the top of the chest — he tilts his camera up to a close-up of Rupert's pained expression as he discloses the body of David. No moment in the film more clearly invites the audience's compassion for Rupert's tragic insight, but the supreme irony of this sympathy resides in the parallel between the audience's identification with Rupert and its own implication in his crime. For he is inarguably, though indirectly, guilty of David's murder, and so his shallow speech of self-justification at the end goes beyond simple hypocrisy or obtuseness and enters a transcendent realm of the absurd. To laugh at Rupert's ludicrous rationalizing is, for the audience, to laugh at itself. And to observe Rupert as he somberly assumes his attentive position in the chair next to David's chest, facing the literal murderers with his back to the camera and the audience, as if he were a mere spectator of this tragedy, is to taste the sour cream of Hitchcock's cosmic jest.

This Hitchcockian style of humor may help to explain why viewers often find *Rope* such a disquieting film. But one can also find consolation — and even pleasure — in being manipulated by such a diabolical genius as Hitchcock. Consider, for instance, what he can do with a simple candle in a candelabrum. Brandon is preparing his dining-room table for the evening's "fun" when the camera captures a single crooked candlestick. It can mean nothing; it can reveal nothing. And yet, out of a natural instinct for neatness and order, we *want* that candlestick straight. And then we realize that our wish masks a hidden, impure desire: we want the crime kept a secret; we want the killers to get away with it. Brandon casually straightens the candle, we breathe a sigh of relief, and so we are trapped. In *Rope*, as in the other master-pieces of his American period, Hitchcock played his audience like a "giant organ,"[37] making it helpless and therefore utterly responsive in the hands of this devilish trickster who was intent on pulling out all the stops.

Notes

1. Donald Spoto, *The Dark Side of Genius: The Life of Alfred Hitchcock* (Boston: Little, Brown, 1983), 384.
2. Raymond Durgnat, "The Strange Case of Alfred Hitchcock, Part Three," in *Focus on Hitchcock*, ed. Albert J. LaValley (Englewood Cliffs, N.J.: Prentice-Hall, 1972), 93.
3. François Truffaut, *Hitchcock*, rev. ed. (New York: Simon and Schuster, 1984), 180.
4. John Russell Taylor, *Hitch: The Life and Times of Alfred Hitchcock* (New York: Pantheon, 1978), 208.
5. Alfred Hitchcock, "Direction (1937)," in *Focus on Hitchcock*, 34.
6. Hitchcock, "Direction (1937)," 35.
7. Truffaut, 184.
8. Truffaut, 179–80.
9. William Rothman, *Hitchcock: The Murderous Gaze* (Cambridge, Mass.: Harvard University Press, 1982), 247.
10. Alfred Hitchcock, "*Rear Window*," in *Focus on Hitchcock*, 41.
11. "The New Pictures: *Rope*," *Time*, 13 September 1948, 105.
12. Raymond Durgnat, *The Strange Case of Alfred Hitchcock* (Cambridge, Mass.: MIT Press, 1974), 207.
13. Donald Spoto, *The Art of Alfred Hitchcock: Fifty Years of His Motion Pictures* (New York: Hopkinson and Blake, 1976), 186.
14. Spoto, *The Dark Side of Genius*, 306.
15. Truffaut, 183.
16. Spoto, *The Dark Side of Genius*, 306.
17. Truffaut, 184.
18. Spoto, *The Dark Side of Genius*, 305.
19. Truffaut, 184.
20. Spoto, *The Dark Side of Genius*, 306.
21. Taylor, 207.
22. Spoto, *The Dark Side of Genius*, 305.
23. Spoto, *The Dark Side of Genius*, 306.
24. Andre Bazin, "Hitchcock versus Hitchcock," in *Focus on Hitchcock*, 65.
25. Robert Hatch, "Movies: Murder for Profit," *The New Republic*, 13 September 1948, 29–30.
26. Taylor, 208.
27. Durgnat, "The Strange Case of Alfred Hitchcock, Part Three," 93.
28. Bazin, 65.

29. Bazin, 69.
30. "Movies: Super Hitchcock," *Newsweek*, 9 August 1948, 68.
31. "Movie of the Week: *Rope*," *Life*, 26 July 1948, 57.
32. Rothman, 247.
33. Hitchcock, *"Rear Window,"* 45.
34. Durgnat, *The Strange Case of Alfred Hitchcock*, 207.
35. Allen Eyles, *James Stewart* (New York: Stein and Day, 1984), 88.
36. Eyles, 88.
37. Spoto, *The Dark Side of Genius*, 406.

LIFE WITH(OUT) FATHER

The Ideological Masculine in *Rope* and Other Hitchcock Films

Robert G. Goulet

Hitchcock's crime thrillers of the forties and fifties, like the domestic melodramas of the same period, often record the repressed and possibly disruptive elements of bourgeois life at the same time that they validate images of heterosexual monogamy and familial hierarchy.[1] In *Rope* (1948) and in several other films, this contradiction is dramatized in the struggles of sons to reject or accept the demands of the figures who represent patriarchal ideals and institutions. These recalcitrant characters resist or misinterpret bonds[2] and obligations that derive their authority from the age-old emphasis on patrilinear succession, the passing of power from father to son, and from the recent repressive and ideological apparatuses that sustain capitalism, in effect the "Law of Culture" defined by Louis Althusser in his essays "Ideology and Ideological Apparatuses" and "Freud and Lacan." In the latter, Althusser elaborates on the psychological basis of the law by associating the individual's entry into the realm of socially sanctioned myths and images — ideology — with the recognition of limitations implied by the Oedipus complex: father's prohibition of further involvement with mother.[3] According to

Jacques Lacan's treatment of the Oedipal crisis, the child's experience of the father's interdiction of incest coincides with access to language and the assumption of the "Name of the Father," hence entry into the order of the symbolic.[4] The individual subject thus inherits a system of combined and related signs and symbols that establishes the primacy of the masculine and defines the feminine as simply nonmale.[5]

Cultural practices and institutions compel adherence to the law by perpetuating idealized images of patriarchy, including that of the ideological masculine.[6] This set of illusory rules and roles, defined and maintained by various institutions, including the cinema, circumscribes the patterns of appearance and behavior appropriate to the social function of upholding and perpetuating the Name of the Father. Hence, the law mandates identification with the heterosexual.[7] Even a veiled suggestion of homosexual orientation and activity in a "mainstream" ideological construct, such as a Hollywood film, is tantamount to challenging or at least inviting a critical examination of the ideological masculine and of the clichés of armchair psychologizing related to it, including the notions of the "dominant" mother and the "weak" or "absent" father. And attempts of the text either to deny or recuperate the "abnormal" only call greater attention to the tension between the text's ideological project and its inassimilable material. Indeed, in *Rope, Notorious* (1946), and *Strangers on a Train* (1951), the élan or the pathos of the homosexual villains threatens to eclipse the virtue of the "normal" patriarchal figure, who is allied with a state apparatus: either repressive, such as espionage organizations or the police, or ideological, such as the government.[8]

In *Notorious* the leading male characters, Devlin, the American agent, and Alex Sebastian, the Nazi entrepreneur, both turn to parental figures at times of crisis. Though identitified only by the name of his natural but absent father, Devlin, the efficient spy without a past, serves the Law of the Father as an operative within the repressive state apparatus. Early in the film he reminds Alicia of her own ideologically correct loyalty to the United States as a means of persuading her to undo the wrong done by *her* father, who clearly abused his natural rights by pressing his daughter to adopt a contrary ideology. But Devlin falls in love with Alicia, and thereby experiences a conflict of loyalties. In keeping with his ideological role, however, Devlin always consults Prescott, his local representative of the Law of the Father. And when he suspects that Alicia may be in danger, he disregards the older man's callous advice to "lie low" and, as a result of his admirable ingenuity, discipline, and compassion, Devlin gains both the information required by the state he serves and the love of the woman he doubted. His action in this case does not contravene the law but rather attests to its transcendence of specific father figures. In the last sequence, as he embraces Alicia, he says, "I couldn't see straight or think straight. I was a fat-headed guy, full of pain. It tore me up not having you." Now Devlin is truly "straight," convinced of the woman's fidelity and hence assured of an appropriate heterosexual union. In addition, he triumphs over her effete, possessive husband, both professionally and sexually. But it must be remembered that the last shot of the film does belong to that husband and one of the villains of the piece, Alex Sebastian.

The fatherless Alex's sexual insecurity takes the form of an obsessive jealousy regarding Alicia, who has become the *object* of his affections, and, though she informs Devlin early on that Alex has become one of her "playmates," her sexual relationship with the older man is represented not with tracking shots of long kisses as in an earlier "domestic" scene with Devlin but with quick cuts of decorous embraces and admiring glances. Jealousy, the vice of the acquisitive, is Alex's passion, which he occasionally — and suggestively — expresses by commenting on the handsomeness of possible rivals. And, by contrast with Devlin's taciturn, clean-cut, "virile" manner, Alex's cultured tone and lavish living arrangements suggest the "decadence" associated with similar types in such film noirs as *Laura* and *The Dark Corner.*[9] These hints of deviance from the norm of the ideological masculine are supported by the twin clichés of the "absent father" and the "dominant mother." In addition, Alex always comes up short — literally, in his physical stature, and, psychologically, in his self-esteem. While maintaining his relationships with all these taller mother-women and present/absent patriarchal men, he is ever engaged in the Oedipal struggle, ever involved in a reenactment of his only partially successful entry into the symbolic order.

The "dominant mother" is the possessive companion who resents the son's attempts at finding an object of desire outside the home and thus forgetting the maternal plenitude of the pre-Oedipal phase. Madame Sebastian does not hesitate to express her disapproval of

Alicia, and, whenever she does so, the shots are so framed as to emphasize her power, especially in regard to Alex. Indeed, it is Mother's help that Alex seeks when he discovers that his wife has betrayed him. In his somewhat circular route from the bedroom he shares with his spouse to the wine cellar where he discovers signs of her treachery, and ultimately to his mother's bedroom, Alex has returned to a presymbolic identification with a more competent other, which could be either Mother or another (mirror) self. In fact, the mise-en-scène reinforces such an interpretation, as we see Alex, hunched in a chair across from his mother's bed, flanked by a framed photograph of himself in a confident pose and a reflection of his present condition in a cheval glass. Even the name "Alicia," of course, represents another taunting mirror of "Alex." In Madame Sebastian, however, he has found not only a maternal protector but also a parodic representative of the symbolic order. Cigarette in hand, Mother plans the removal of the female intruder.

In the last scene of the film, she eventually persuades Alex to participate in Devlin's little drama of rushing Alicia to the hospital, especially since his cold Nazi colleague, Erich, is carefully observing the proceedings. The shift from hallucinatory bravado to fear of another parodic father crosses his face, and Alex's psychic drama commands our attention. The last shot of Alex moving alone toward interrogation and possible execution by Erich and company tempers the irony of the moment with a peculiar sympathy.

At the end of *Rope*, the triumph of patriarchal justice is also portrayed ambiguously, with the implicit acknowledgment of paternal failure. That is, the cultural order may be reasserted through the detection and apprehension of murderers, but not without calling into question the role that the detective — the individual representative of the Law of the Father — played in the commission of the crime. It is doubtful whether Brandon Shaw, the clever and attractive young murderer, and his confused homosexual mate, Philip, ever fully realize their misrecognition of the law, that is, as they conceived of it in the notions of Rupert Cadell, their former housemaster and surrogate father. And Rupert's fierce last-minute defense of logic and compassion, the rhetoric of the law, barely offsets the power of Brandon's malicious wit in the emotional economy of the film.

In the underpopulated world of this melodramatic narrative, there are no references to the natural fathers of Brandon and Philip. Bran-

243

don does have a last name and a mother "in the country," but Philip apparently has no one but Brandon and various substitute parents — Mrs. Shaw, Brandon's housekeeper Mrs. Wilson, and Rupert. Of the two partners, Brandon represents the more seductive aspect of evil, the one that is more likely to counterpoise the moral force of the Law of the Father.

Shortly after the murder Philip suggests that Brandon frightens him, but admits that this quality may be "part of [his] charm," after all. Brandon is the witty creator of this crime melodrama, embellished with ironic rhetoric and ceremonial stage properties arranged on the lid of the chest containing the corpse, but his words and his actions betray deep contradictions in his personality. First, he projects his own insecurity on Philip by suggesting, "It's the darkness that's got you down. Nobody ever really feels safe in the dark. Nobody who's ever a child, that is." As we note the grammatical slip by the usually careful Brandon ("*is* ever" rather than "*was* ever"), the bravado then reemerges: "Pity we couldn't have done it with the curtains open, in the bright sunlight. [Pause] But we can't have everything, can we?" The first lesson of entry into the symbolic order involves recognizing just such a limitation on desire, but, as I have suggested, Brandon's grasp on adult responsibility seems questionable. Finally, he holds up the victim's whiskey glass as a "museum piece" to commemorate the intellectual daring of the deed, and he removes himself from the company of the law-abiding by remarking that "good Americans usually die young, on the battlefield." Murder has become an art, the power to kill parallels the power to create, and the party for the murder victim's family and friends functions as the "signature of the artist." The "artist" in this case has never enjoyed the rewards of creative achievement and has had to satisfy his yearnings in that direction by collecting the works of contemporary painters, overseeing the development of Philip's career as a pianist, and theorizing about the art of murder. To Brandon the only crime is "making a mistake," which is the equivalent of "being weak," the same as "being ordinary."

This belief in the license of superior intelligence can be traced to quasi-philosophical discussions with the housemaster Cadell (the master of the house, the substitute father) when Brandon, Philip, David (the murder victim), and their friend Kenneth were schoolboys in Rupert's house. While he considers Rupert "too fastidious" to participate in such a crime, Brandon is clearly eager to show off his handiwork to his former mentor, however oblique the demonstration, and thus illuminates the dangers attendant on a misrecognition of the law. Rupert's playfully amoral exercises in logic have been translated as "the word," the Name of the Father, by a childlike Brandon still gripped by a fantasy of autonomy.

Meanwhile, Philip's panic suggests an even more profound form of insecurity, since he seems incapable of choosing between the two versions of the law, or, more accurately, feels threatened both by the word of Rupert according to Brandon and by the word of civil law and its representative in the repressive state apparatus. Philip lacks his partner's theatrical sangfroid, his wit and his pleasure in manipulating others. While Philip characterizes mistakes as "human," Brandon deplores their "ordinariness." These young men are truly complementary but without the possibility of ever constituting a mutually productive unit. While one channels feeling into art by playing the piano, the other gives shape to thought with a macabre two-act play. Philip's medium consists of sound and gesture, while Brandon's consists of words. It is ironically appropriate that Brandon should restrain the victim while Philip executes the crime with his strong, expressive hands. Later, in a moment of crisis, Philip breaks a glass in one of those hands, and Brandon stammers. In both cases, the process of symbolization, the very basis of the patriarchal order, fails them, thus predicting disaster through self-incrimination. The only characters who consistently question the behavior of the male couple form a couple themselves, albeit a parodic one—Mrs. Wilson and Rupert Cadell.

The bustle and complaint of the housekeeper's entrance and her scolding, proprietary tone lend her a momentary importance within the menage, but we are soon reminded that she is practically on loan from "Mr. Cadell," the hero who "got a bad leg in the war" and who once invited her to have a drink with him. Therefore, on one level, she is the officious servant of classical comedy, and, on another, the mother temporarily shared with the favored children by an indulgent father, but with the understanding, of course, that she is always his. At one point, Rupert even jests, "Wonderful Mrs. Wilson! I may marry her," obviously aware that for gender and class reasons he will always control the flirtatious byplay. Mrs. Wilson is the spirited but docile mother, one moment complaining that *her* lovely table has been disturbed and the next urging Philip to eat more, especially the pâté "Mr. Cadell likes so much."

Mrs. Wilson's double role provides further access to the homosocial intentions of the film. Her command of practical skills and her straightforward tone contrast with the frivolity and imprecision of the other female characters — the fumbling astrologer, Mrs. Atwater, who cannot remember names and titles, and the sentimental fashion writer, Janet Walker, whose attempts at witty repartee invariably fail. Whatever her accomplishments, however, Mrs. Wilson is never granted the power of a worthy adversary or accomplice for the chief male figures. Her docility marks an acceptance, shared by the other characters and by the film, of the limitations imposed by social class and station.

Her partner in suspicion of the odd behavior of her young employer and his friend, and the principal voice for homosocial values in the text, Rupert proves himself the master of the house once more, even in the presence of a natural father, the earnest but dim Mr. Kentley. Though his entrance is quiet, Rupert takes command shortly thereafter; assured, precise, perceptive, satiric, he is a confident dispenser of the word. When his jolly talk of justifiable homicide upsets Mr. Kentley, he relents, but Brandon continues the line of specious reasoning, thereby reenacting his own problematic entry into the domain of the symbolic.

Later, when Rupert discovers the crime, Brandon appeals to his former housemaster: "I knew you'd understand because you have to. You have to!" After all, a "man should stand by his words." Note the emphasis on the form, if not the substance, of patriarchally approved behavior. Knowledge for Brandon is based not on examination of evidence but on faith in "the intellectual superior," the need to have his interpretation of Rupert's words represent the only Name of the Father; in this case, then, Brandon's claim to knowledge is hallucinatory, not symbolic. Even the pretext for the party, providing Mr. Kentley with the opportunity to examine some first editions, suggests a misuse of the word. By treating books as attractive commodities rather than depositories of partriarchal wisdom, Brandon displays the sort of tasteful decadence that is associated with film noir homosexuals even as he engages in the acceptable capitalist practice of transforming art into an object of exchange.

Rupert's response to Brandon's boast takes the form of a defense of democratic privilege and responsibility, the "right to live and work and think as individuals but with an obligation to the society we live in." Rupert fulfills his ideological role with a particularly vindictive rhetorical style: "Did you think you were God, Brandon?" His invoking the deity implicitly prescribes the full measure of respect due to the estate of fatherhood. "It's not what I'm going to do, Brandon, it's what society's going to do." His words remind us of Althusser's thesis that "all ideology has the function (which defines it) of 'constituting' concrete individuals as subjects." Thus the person is both "subject-ive and "subject-ed" to the subject (God, State, Family, etc.).[10] And, lest Brandon's transgression be interpreted as a negative reflection on any system — social, economic, or otherwise — Rupert defines the crime as an individual aberration with psychological roots. His last line resounds with the power granted the Father both in the Oedipal crisis and in the formation of ideology. He cries at the transgressors, "You're going to die!" Then he fires the gun, which he has apprehended from the other irresponsible son, Philip, and draws the attention of the "ordinary" people in the street.

The composition of the last shot partially redresses the enunciative imbalance created by Rupert's tirade. During his hypothetical recreation of the crime and his interrogation of the murderers, Rupert's point of view dominates the mise-en-scène, not without some irony. His skillful analysis of the order of events suggests that his complicity in the crime is more than philosophical; he can think and plan the way Brandon does. At the end, the camera dollies slowly backward from the family group. Father sits next to the coffin of the dispatched sibling, with his back to the camera and his wounded hand hanging limp, another sign of his partial culpability. Some toppled books rest against the back of the chest, perhaps suggesting the disruption of the symbolic that has occurred. One son, Philip, begins to play the piano. The other, Brandon, pours himself a drink.

The ambiguous balance of beleaguered rectitude and morbid wit in *Rope* is paralleled in the relationship of Guy Haines and Bruno Anthony, the title characters of *Strangers on a Train*. In that text Guy, another dutiful "son," seeks the advice and protection of Senator Morton, his fiancée's father. The older man is grooming Guy for a career in politics, and so alike are they in their unimaginative submission to the Law of the Father that Morton's advice that Guy "be guided by [his] experience" hardly seems necessary. (Still one must ask why Guy feels it is appropriate to wipe Ann's lipstick from his mouth before greeting her father!) Aside from a few stale jokes about the senator's Eastern WASP snobbery, his presence in the film serves as a perfunctory acknowledgment of his ideological purpose, cautioning Guy to be discreet and, more importantly, to abide by the law.

Later Guy seeks another father; in one of his rare moments of daring, he attempts to warn Mr. Anthony of his son Bruno's treacherous design on his life. There, in the father's place, in his room and his bed, he finds Bruno; this witty usurpation may be temporary, but it also reminds the audience of the unresolved Oedipal struggle that marks Bruno's family life. Mother has performed her prescribed duty by representing the interdictive demands of the father to the son, but she has also indulged the son and protected him from the threats both of father and of the outside world. This triangular relationship is portrayed strikingly in a shot of the hall and the living room of the family mansion with a medium close-up of Bruno at the telephone on the right side of the image while Mr. and Mrs. Anthony, framed by an archway on the left, discuss their son's condition in the distant background. Later, when Ann Morton visits Mrs. Anthony, we realize that the older woman's dottiness is as much willed as it is "natural."

As a result of these tensions, Bruno manifests the psychotic's distorted view of the symbolic order. He has been given a name. Indeed, Mother's present of the tie clip identifies him as "Bruno," but he has not accepted the Name of the Father, the subjectivity that comes with recognizing the limitations set by patriarchal edict. He has mastered the skills of social intercourse (casual acquaintances attest to his charm), but he also dwells in a hallucinatory realm, lacking the means to decode his unconscious desires and finding only violent outlets for his frustration. Even Mrs. Anthony does admit to Ann that Bruno "sometimes goes a little too far." His cunning and his purposiveness, then, reflect not the compromises dictated by the symbolic order, subjection to the Name of the Father, but the need to realize emotional goals whose symbolic meaning he foreclosed long ago.[11]

This diagnostic description, however, fails to account for Bruno's subversively appealing presence within the film. He recalls Brandon Shaw in his flair for creating and sustaining dramatic situations. After he proudly reports that he has murdered Guy's wife, Miriam, he shrugs off the husband's alarm by suggesting that they are both fatigued. He rolls his eyes and, with a mock sigh, he says, "I've had such a strenuous evening." He later follows Guy obsessively to remind him that the imagined bargain of exchanging murders must be fulfilled. Guy sees him in the distance, at various monumentally scaled, pillared public buildings which, ironically, also represent the place of the Father. And, of course, at the tennis match, Bruno's gaze is steadily focused on Guy while the other spectators follow the trajectory of the tennis ball in the match. Even in his hallucinatory moments — at the Mortons' party, for example — Bruno can move from a bizarre conversation with Senator Morton about "harness[ing] the life force" to a penetrating question about capital punishment directed at a complacent judge. He also retains this histrionic sense when he becomes angry and disillusioned with Guy, as in the bedroom scene; "Guy" becomes "Mr. Haines," the friend becomes a stranger who welshed on a bargain.

As with Alex Sebastian, Bruno's life of wealth and privilege has provided him with a cosmopolitan charm, but he also evokes a sympathy which we find it difficult to extend to the "good" son, particularly at the end, when, like Brandon, Bruno retains his characteristic, amusingly perverse style. As he dies, he resists Guy's appeal to redeem both of them by telling the truth: "They got you at last, eh, Guy?" A bitter joke, since he also realizes that "they," representing the Law of Culture, have "got" him too. At the conclusion of their struggle, Guy's disparaging assessment of Bruno as "a very clever fellow" seems not so much a verbal irony to serve the interests of the Production Code as a dramatic one to point up the shallowness of Guy's own moral sense. And the audience is left to mourn the departure of yet another of Hitchcock's beguiling villains.

In the representation of urbane and mad miscreants, one can locate the tension between the vision of patriarchally sanctioned family and heterosexuality that is the primary project of classic Hollywood cinema and the glimpse of "decadent" skepticism that threatens such an ideological construct. By dividing its villain and its representative of the law into complementary halves, *Rope* epitomizes the characteristic textual rupture in these films. Brandon combines the fastidious good taste of Alex Sebastian with the dark humor of Bruno Anthony, while Philip expresses Alex's debilitating insecurity and Bruno's dangerous impetuosity. Set against these "deviant" figures

is the inexorable but dull law of Prescott, Kentley, and Morton, supported by the appealing but "guilty" investigator-heroes — Devlin, Cadell, Haines. In exploring these dichotomies, we discover that the generational struggle is as much textual as it is diegetic, with the story of crime and punishment framed by another "story," of a film discourse in uneasy servitude to the "universal discourse" of the Father and the limitations of his Name.

Notes

1. The two genres merge in the nightmarish ambiguities of the representation of small-town life and family relationships in Hitchcock's *Shadow of a Doubt* (1943).
2. Eve Kosofsky Sedgwick, *Between Men: English Literature and Male Homosocial Desire* (New York: Columbia University Press, 1985), 3. The younger men must take their place in homosocial structures, defined by Sedgwick as "male-dominated kinship systems" in which "men promot[e] the interests of men," both socially and economically.
3. Louis Althusser, "Freud and Lacan" (1964, 1969), in *Lenin and Philosophy and Other Essays*, trans. Ben Brewster (New York: Monthly Review Press, 1971), 215–16: "The Oidipus complex is the dramatic structure, the 'theatrical machine' imposed by the Law of Culture on every involuntary, conscripted candidate to humanity, a structure containing in itself not only the possibility of, but the necessity for the concrete variants in which it exists, for every individual who reaches its threshold, lives through it and survives it."
4. Jacques Lacan, "The Function and Field of Speech and Language in Psychoanalysis" (1953), in *Écrits*, trans. Alan Sheridan (New York: Norton, 1977), 67: "It is in the name of the father that we must recognize the support of the symbolic function which, from the dawn of history, has identified his person with the figure of the law." In the essay, "Lacan and the Subject of Psychoanalysis" (in *Interpreting Lacan*, ed. Joseph H. Smith and William Kerrigan [New Haven: Yale University Press, 1983], 60), William J. Richardson describes the symbolic as an "order of signifiers . . . an arrangement of relationships that has enough stability and firmness to be called a 'law.' . . . Moreover, the pattern of relationships has been woven into the entire fabric of human history to which the infant now falls heir and becomes 'subject to,' and thereby made a subject of [*assujettissement*], this law. This fabric includes the cultural myths of his race, his ethnic style, his social traditions, the particularity of his ancestral lineage, the personal and social milieu of his immediate family . . . in short, the universal 'discourse' that has preceded him and into which he has been born."
5. Richardson suggests that the subject is "integrated" into "a network that is governed by its own laws," 61. Regarding the economy of gender, Juliet Flower MacCannell says, in *Figuring Lacan* (Lincoln: University of Nebraska Press, 1986),

107: "If men are strong, women are weak; if men like sex, women don't, etc. The couple masculine-feminine does not exist. What we have structurally is simply + masculine / − masculine masquerading as heterosexuality. Lacan was not too polite to name that 'couple' for what it is: homosexual. He said simply that sexual intercourse has never existed, because we do not have, at least not yet, heterosexuality."

6. Ellie Ragland-Sullivan, *Jacques Lacan and the Philosophy of Psychoanalysis* (Urbana: University of Illinois Press, 1987), 285: "Such normalcy does not confer happiness or freedom from conflict but demands blind submission to the social order and eschewal of unconscious truth."

7. Sedgwick, 3: "From the vantage point of our society, at any rate, it has apparently been impossible to imagine a form of patriarchy that was not homophobic." Such homophobia accounts for the clichés of "dominant" mother and "weak" father. See C. A. Tripp, *The Homosexual Matrix* (New York: New American Library, 1976), 73n.–74n.

8. *The Paradine Case* (1947), which immediately precedes *Rope* in the Hitchcock oeuvre, betrays the same tension but without the wit. In that film patriarchy exacts a heavy price—even from beyond the grave—for dereliction of duty. André Latour, the "bodyservant" of the murder victim, commits suicide in self-disgust at having been involved in an affair with the murderous wife. The vertiginous quality of this heterosexual distraction from the fulfillment of his homosocial (and homosexual?) responsibilities is conveyed not only in the tortured Latour's testimony of his loving loyalty to his master at the climactic trial but also in the mise-en-scène, particularly the pair of 200-degree pans (with Anna Paradine at the center) that frame the sequence. The second pan is fragmented by alternating reverse-angle shots (between close-ups of Anna Paradine and full shots of the departing André Latour), but the framing effect is preserved. Mrs. Paradine's attorney, Anthony Keane, loses the requisite distance from the case by falling in love with his client and practically ruins his career in flinty Judge Horfield's courtroom, but finds redemption in the legitimate heterosexual union of his marriage. Thus all ends safely within the domain of the patriarchal.

9. Foster Hirsch, *The Dark Side of the Screen: Film Noir* (New York: Da Capo Press, 1981), 159. Regarding *Laura* and *The Dark Corner*, Hirsch says: "In both parts [Clifton] Webb plays a cosmopolitan dandy whose passion for unattainable women leads him to commit murder. Webb has a civilized, over-refined veneer, which, in Hollywood iconography, is suspicious; in the anti-intellectuality that has always plagued American movies, well-bred aesthetes are usually morally and sexually questionable. . . . The films could acknowledge the decadence of Webb's aestheticism, but could not, in the forties, link it to homosexuality. Webb embodied an old-fashioned idea of what homosexuals were supposed to be: dandified, affected, superficial, addicted to fine living, concerned excessively with fashion and with appearance." Sedgwick comments on "decadence" in the context of the representation of homosexuality: "Decadence is a notably shifty idea, but clearly its allure to the middle-class adolescent lies in its promise of initiatory shortcuts to the secret truths of adulthood. . . . [T]he secrets of class are represented in decadent literature by elements of the bourgeoisie that can dissociate themselves from

the productive modes of their class and, by learning to articulate an outdated version of aristocratic values, can seem to offer some critique of . . . the bourgeois official culture" (90).

10. Althusser, "Ideology and Ideological State Apparatuses (Notes towards an Investigation)" (1969), in *Lenin and Philosophy*, 171.
11. For Lacan's discussion of psychosis as foreclosure, see "On a Question Preliminary to Any Possible Treatment of Psychosis" (1955–56), in *Écrits*, 217.

TWISTED WRITING

Rope as an Experimental Film

Thomas Hemmeter

In 1948 Alfred Hitchcock released a movie filmed as no other has been before or since, in ten-minute takes, the camera continually traveling over a single set to avoid cutting. This film, *Rope*, is generally considered a minor work, a film whose technical experiments confer an inferior status. Hitchcock himself always agreed with this judgment, declaring, "I undertook *Rope* as a stunt; that's the only way I can describe it. I really don't know how I came to indulge it."[1] He explicitly cited the technical experimentation as the site of its inferiority: "As an experiment, *Rope* may be forgiven."[2] Implicitly, then, as a serious and complete work of art it may not be forgiven. Something is missing, and the term "experiment" defines even as it excuses this lack.

One group of critics takes him at his word. Raymond Durgnat dismisses the film (indeed most of Hitchcock's oeuvre) as the work of a bold stylist, a slick entertainer who displays considerable technical virtuosity at the expense of profound seriousness and moral depth.[3] David Thomson faults Hitchcock for his display of bravura technical completeness at the expense of human mystery and doubt, deploring the empty craftsmanship which results from technique severed from meaning, from devices of the medium used without any bearing on theme or content.[4] Thomson's is an established position in Hitchcock criticism, descending from the 1940s British critics like Lawrence Kane, Lindsay Anderson, and John Grierson, a position summed up by Anderson's verdict on *Rope*: the film displays "a preoccupation with technique, to the detriment of the material."[5]

Other critics pick up on the moral tone of the terms Hitchcock uses in dismissing *Rope*—terms such as "indulge" and "forgiven"— and seek ways to salvage the film even as they apologize for its experimentation. They deny that the film's technical virtuosity is mere empty formalism and insist that the elaborate ten-minute takes, an almost constantly moving camera, and the rigid confinement to one location bear a direct relation to the film's themes. Robin Wood asserts that *Rope*'s techniques embody Hitchcock's moral purpose; indeed, the moving camera creates conflicts in audience response which force moral evaluation by revealing a connection between technique and moral sense.[6] Donald Spoto finds that the moving camera technique conveys the complexity of the characters' moral arrest, impotence, and entrapment.[7] Implicit here is a rejection of technique separated from theme and moral purpose: a moralistic condemnation of style for its own sake out of fear of its free play, its irresponsibility, its lack of internal centering.

Though they arrive at opposite conclusions, these two groups of critics rely on a common critical construct: The film is either experimental (technique separated from theme and moral purpose) or nonexperimental (technique integrated with theme and moral purpose). Confined by this dualistic structure of thought, critics see only two ways to approach *Rope*: either to salvage the film as serious, moral art despite its technical experiments, or to savage the film as experimental and therefore without moral purpose or artistic value. Both positions need to invoke the nonexperimental—the morally serious film standing as the polar opposite of a film like *Rope*—to center and guide their judgment. Only the unshakable belief in the notion of films uncontaminated by dangerous experimentation can domesticate *Rope* and keep it safe from its more radical potential.

The critical discourse on *Rope* follows closely the flawed strategy of structuralism described by the deconstructionist Jacques Derrida in "Structure, Sign, and Play in the Discourse of the Human Sciences."[8] A structuralist tries to organize the coherence of a system through a contradictory organizing principle, the structural center. This center does two things: it makes possible the play of elements within the total structure; however, it does so only by denying the possibility of play at this center. In discussing *Rope*, critics perceive Hitchcock's experiments — with color, with the moving camera to replace editing, and with the single set — as permissible only if this technical play does not violate the values at the center of any good film, that is, the union of technique and moral purpose. As long as the technical experimentation does not take over the film and become an end in itself, the film is acceptable; otherwise it becomes a tasteless or even immoral experiment. The notion that cinematic technique (or play) must serve to develop theme or moral meaning is the structural center of the critical thinking on *Rope*.

Derrida argues that it is contradictory to define as the center of a structure that thing in a structure which, while governing the structure, escapes the play which a structure permits. Since all structures are discourse, like the critical language used to analyze *Rope*, a critic should recognize that no conceptual center (such as the integration of technical experiment and moral theme) can escape its own playful language. Yet a structure tries to do precisely this, to close off its center from linguistic play, just as *Rope*'s critics try to close the film off from serious consideration since it allows play with the structural center of thematic and moral seriousness. But the playfulness of language, its puns and metaphors and multiple meanings, threatens the presumed order of any structure. Indeed, a fear of disruptive language is evident in the critical discourse on *Rope*, especially in Robin Wood's explicit concern about the film's clever talk of superior beings and their right to murder — a talk which is lighthearted, free, irresponsible, joking. Wood implies the need for another, moral perspective lest we fall victim to this aesthetically attractive talk.[9] From Wood's perspective, the film should be read as an argument against open-ended talk and experimentation with ideas that threaten human life. A deconstructionist reading of the film reverses Wood's humanistic logic, finding in the film an equally justifiable (if logically incompatible) argument for experiment.

THOMAS HEMMETER

Rope's Fable of Meaning

Rope expresses the structuralist's fear of disrupting language in the struggles of Rupert Cadell, a former teacher, to deny that he seriously meant his words justifying murder by the superior few. Two former students, Brandon and Philip, have taken his playful talk seriously (or have extended the play of talk into action) and, as an "experiment" — a term Brandon explicitly uses to describe the murder — have killed their friend David Kentley. For the two young men the murder is an aesthetic game: after killing David, they hide his body in a chest and invite Rupert, the victim's parents and fiancée, and a few friends to a party. The party (and its immediate aftermath) is the focus of the entire film, which takes place inside the young murderers' apartment with Hitchcock's camera as one more guest. The food is served on a chest containing David's corpse. Before the guests arrive, Brandon says, "Now the fun begins." Rupert shares their frivolous attitude toward murder — but only in the realm of ideas. He joins Brandon in making jokes about the right of superior people to kill inferiors, although he is given a warning by Mr. Kentley, David's father, that such Nietzschean talk leads to the brutality of a Hitler. Though sobered, Rupert continues to play a cat-and-mouse game with Brandon and Philip until he discovers the murder.

Then, at the end of the film, he rigidly excludes the killing of David from the realm of play, delivering a lecture on the sanctity of human life and declaring a clear distinction between playful talk and murderous action. He attempts to recover his earlier words which to Brandon justified the murder of David, denying that he meant what Brandon understood him to mean. He finally declares that "something deep inside" him could never allow him to murder or to sanction murder, and he calls in the authorities to bring the two young men to justice: "You've murdered, and you're gonna die." He prefaces this speech with a statement that ends play: "I don't want to fence anymore." Rupert can be seen as attempting to escape the play of language, withdrawing from words back to the safe ground of principles and concepts (located in some mysterious inner place, the "something deep inside") which keep words under the control of his intended meanings.

Rope thus seems to establish a clear distinction between serious responsibility to life and irresponsible gamesmanship (or experiment). Like Hitchcock, the contrite experimenter, Rupert attempts to separate serious moral concern from his playful words about the right of the privileged few to murder, a maneuver giving him the freedom to experiment with ideas while reserving the foundation of moral seriousness. Rupert's strategy of control—similar to that used by the critics of *Rope*—is to set up a network of differences which revolve around a central duality: experimentation, as the inferior entity, is associated with games (like fencing) and with language (signifiers); in opposition is real meaning, associated with seriousness, with internal moral structures, and with signifieds.[10] The hope is that in verbal discourse meaning places dangerous talk under control; in film discourse theme and moral purpose place dangerous technique under control. Rupert, like *Rope*'s critics, creates a dualistic structure whose balanced opposites demand that form serve content and technique serve moral purpose. But the radical experiment of Brandon and Philip which leads to David's murder, like Hitchcock's unregulated technical experiments in *Rope*, threatens these balanced oppositions, asserting a right to experimental play regardless of moral purpose. As Rupert condemns the murderers, *Rope*'s critics condemn Hitchcock. Both experimenters have violated the rules of the game—the structure—which establish moral and aesthetic order. A close examination of the language of this structure, however, subverts its claims precisely because they are stated in terms which themselves lack stability and veer into playful double meanings.

Rupert Cadell the Structuralist

Both Brandon Shaw and Rupert Cadell are established as verbal pranksters, Brandon in making puns and double entendres and Rupert in questioning the literal meaning of people's statements and in exaggerating the comic possibilities of killing people who irritate the superior few. The film's climax, however, presents Rupert with the need to close off this playful use of language when Brandon confronts him with his own words to justify murdering David.

Brandon: Remember the discussion we had before with Mr. Kentley? Remember we said the lives of inferior beings are unimportant, remember we said—we've always said, you

257

	and I—that moral concepts of good and evil, right and wrong, don't hold for the intellectual superiors? Remember, Rupert?
Rupert:	Yes, I remember.
Brandon:	Well, that's all we've done. That's all Philip and I have done. He and I have lived what you and I had talked. But I knew you would understand because you have to, don't you see, you have to.

To recover his words from Brandon, to deny their use to justify a murder, Rupert delivers a long, self-righteous speech whose chief argument is that he did not mean what he said. In the central portion of his speech, Rupert qualifies the notion that a man should stand by his words.

| Rupert: | You've given my words a meaning that I never dreamed of. And you've tried to twist them into a cold, logical excuse for your ugly murder. Well, they never were that, Brandon, and you can't make them that. There must have been something deep inside you from the very start that let you do this thing. But there's always been something deep inside me that would never let me do it. |

In an attempt to regain control of his language, Rupert retreats to the notion of mysterious origins as a source of his authority—something deep inside you from the very start—making use of the structuralist "arche" or source of meaning as a defense of the structure against the distorting play of signifiers.[11] The symmetry of the balanced sentence structure ("There's something deep inside you"/"there's something deep inside me") reveals Rupert's attempt to make a clear distinction between himself and Brandon, but instead such binary distinctions draw the two more closely together since Brandon uses similar balanced syntax ("Philip and I lived what you and I talked"). Rupert Cadell the structuralist attempts to remove from play internal principles like love and respect for the rights of individuals, but he finds himself caught up in the play of language, which undermines his attempts to make clear distinctions.

The phrase "something deep inside" further undermines Rupert's attempt to use language to escape language, for his previous use of the term *something* suggests quite the opposite of a stable term whose stability might anchor his meanings. In fact, the word *something* seems like an empty nonsense term, a detached signifier. Earlier in the film Rupert mocks the inability of silly Mrs. Atwater (an unexpected guest at the party) to remember the name of a film. As she stumbles around trying to remember the film's title, she muses, "He was thrilling in that new thing of Bergman's . . . what was it called now? . . . the something of the something. No, no, that was the other one. This was just plain something. You know, it was sort of, you know. . . . " She as much as says, "You know what I mean; I don't have to choose a specific word to express a meaning we both share." Rupert, however, denies that he knows what "something" means, parodying her vague speech which assumes common knowledge in her listeners to complete her ideas. He talks about a film whose title is "the something, something. Or was it just plain something. Really, something rather like that." His repetition of the term *something* not only mocks her bad memory but makes obvious how empty a signifier *something* is.

But when Brandon challenges him to acknowledge his words justifying the right of the superior few to murder, Rupert resorts to the same term in the phrase "something deep inside" to bind his words to his meaning and to deny that his words ever meant what Brandon says. Earlier mocked as an empty signifier, *something* now ascends in Rupert's discourse to the status of a transcendental signifier above the play of language — the signifier distinguishing Rupert from Brandon and preserving his words from Brandon's misunderstanding. Of course Rupert has to repress the indeterminate and ungrounded nature of the term *something*, whose very repetition reveals a hidden sameness between its use by Mrs. Atwater and Rupert's use. This term expresses without Rupert's consent the hidden meaning that the faculty deep inside Rupert which keeps him from killing is, like Mrs. Atwater's film title, something unremembered, something so insubstantial that it is now forgotten. Just as in Mrs. Atwater's use, the term *something* in its vagueness signifies the absence of any reason or principle denying the right to murder another.

Despite Rupert's declaration that "something deep inside" stands as the final authority, a structural guarantee of his meaning, the term *something* carries a trace of the opposite meaning: there is precisely nothing to guarantee Rupert's meaning. Repetitions of terms can infect structures like Rupert's, undermining even hidden intentions. This subversive quality of repetition is a motif in the film, frustrating the efforts of characters to pin down meaning, evident in Brandon's stuttering, in repeated adjectives in expressions like "the real, real me," in the film's endlessly repeated camera movements, in the neon letter *S* appearing again and again through a window: over and over, sounds and images without meaning, repeated signifiers with no attached signified.

Twisted Writing: Brandon the Deconstructionist

Rupert has similar problems in controlling the signification of the term *twisted*. In accusing Brandon of twisting his terms to justify murder, he apparently means that Brandon has altered or distorted his words to mean something other than what he intended. In talking about the rights of the privileged few to kill, Rupert seems to want his meaning and the words he spoke to be one unified construct, where the meaning is the assumed agreement between speaker and listener that the words don't count, protected as they are by conventional unanimity of values. Thus when he speaks of the superior individual's right to kill, he means the right to speak about the right, not the right to the action of killing. In referring to Brandon's twisting (distortion) of his words, then, Rupert means merely that Brandon understood the words as most people do, as signifiers with a defined relationship to their signified meaning. For Rupert this is not the meaning of his words. Robin Wood wonders "just how Rupert *did* mean his teaching to be taken."[12] The answer is that he wanted his teaching to be taken as mere words, as signifiers without a signified, certainly unconnected to any referent outside of language.

In accusing Brandon of twisting his words, Rupert uses the term *twist* to denote "division in two" (from the etymological root term *twa*). Brandon has divided Rupert's words from his hidden meaning. But the root term *twa*, itself divided in signification, also confers on Rupert's use of the term *twist* its second, opposite meaning of "combining into one," as in twisting strands of hemp into a rope. Thus Brandon twisted Rupert's words in the sense that he joined them to their conventional signifiers and the sign to the referent in the act of murder. This is precisely the unity Rupert claims to want between signifier and signified, sign and referent, in order to protect his meanings, but he finds he must deny this meaning of *twist* in order to defend his hidden meanings from Brandon's distortions.

Twist is a double-edged word whose condensed articulation expresses Rupert's conflicting assertion: Brandon has connected my words to conventional meanings, and Brandon has divided my words from my real (and also conventional) meanings.[13]

The Play of Experiment

The efforts of *Rope*'s critics to control the film's perversity are similar to those of Rupert to control the perversity of his own speech. Both deny the legitimacy of pure experiment. Since it threatens to make everything playful, the experimental must be separated off, designated as unusual or deformed, and put in a special place (like a laboratory) to keep its destructive potential under control. To make a film like *Rope* safe, commentators try to contain its perverse formal play by placing the film in a special category, the experimental. Here Hitchcock may toy with camera dollies and editing all he wants because such play does not threaten the real "something" outside of film techniques — the values or ideas which make technique meaningful. The critical maneuver is similar to Rupert's, asserting the control of structure in removing the disruptive signifiers (be they language or the techniques of filmmaking) from the center of the structure by putting them into a special category, and setting borders which the play of signifiers may not cross. For critics like Robin Wood, the clear borders between the experimental and nonexperimental allow *Rope* — like Rupert — to play at the margins of the experimental; for critics like Raymond Durgnat these borders allow the condemnation of *Rope* — and Brandon — for crossing the borders. To make these judgments requires a clear concept of the nonexperimental, for if the world were a place where all was experiment, such play and such distinctions would be impossible.

But differences working within this very term *experiment* undermine the notion that *Rope* is a safe text — to be dismissed as superficial or patronized as marginal — because it is an experimental text. The more radical implications of Hitchcock's film can be ignored only by repressing differences in the word *experiment*, which implies both the control of a laboratory method and the absence of control in any trial or attempt (from the root term *experiri*, to try, the same root as the term *experience*). This absence of control is a trace even in the use of the term *experiment* to assert control, that is, to define something as allowable or not allowable because it goes beyond the tried and true methods. Murder as an "experiment" (like films as an experiment) is denied legitimacy because its claim to complete control covers a complete loss of control, just as Brandon and Philip apparently lose control in trying to commit the perfect murder. But in the very denial of the right to experiment is included a desire for the same control as that conferred by the laboratory experiment: in designating *Rope* an inferior experimental film, critics seek a freedom from the chance meanings of playful technique; in designating Brandon's experiment with killing an unlawful act, Rupert seeks to free himself from the randomness of language which can lead to uncontrolled acts like murder.

Thus the need for experimentation is a trace within the desire to escape from it. Linguistic experiment shares this contradictory quality with laboratory experiment. For example, Rupert the structuralist attempts to create a special place where everything he says is under control of "something deep inside," but in so doing he assumes the legitimacy of the experimental play with language which he later seeks to evade. In conceiving this "something deep inside" as a place apart from the disorder of the world and the random play of language, Rupert in effect creates a laboratory to deny the legitimacy of laboratory experiments like Brandon's. In adopting the experimental procedure to claim control, Rupert takes up the illusion of experimenters that they can separate meaning from language. From this perspective, Brandon's desires for the freedom to experiment with Rupert's ideas and words are not different from Rupert's own desires for this same freedom.

In the effort to integrate the experimental techniques of *Rope* with nonexperimental values, the discourse on *Rope* unconsciously follows Hitchcock's lead in privileging pure film (technique) over dialogue, focusing more attention on camera movements and visuals than on verbal langugage. Though in this paper I have reversed the emphasis to privilege the script over the visuals and camera movements, a deconstruction of the film language in *Rope* proceeds much as a deconstruction of the film script. For example, in terms of mise-en-scène *Rope* seems to establish a dual world: the artificial and confining laboratory world of Brandon's apartment and the "real world" outside the curtains which Rupert calls in at film's end with pistol shots. But several devices/tropes undercut this clear division. The film opens outside the apartment with a high-angle shot of a policeman helping children across the street, an artificial image with a pointed reference to a similar shot from the supposedly idyllic Santa Rosa in *Shadow of a Doubt* (1943). Though *Rope* offers only this one image of the "real world" that Brandon's experimental apartment world perverts, this grounding image alludes not to any documentary or representational world but to an earlier film image, itself a parody of the Norman Rockwell image of America. This multiple referentiality of the film's only exterior image suggests that the world outside Brandon's apartment is no more real than the world within.

Also the obvious theatrical metaphor structuring the film seems to establish Brandon's apartment as a stage where dangerous artifice plays out a false scenario while the audience beyond the window curtains — the ordinary, law-abiding people in the "real" world — remains ignorant of the play. *Rope*'s set physically divides these two worlds, associating the apartment with theatrical unreality and death and the world dimly heard from beyond the windows with sober reality, morality, and life. Brandon's murder of David was an act self-consciously performed for this "real" world and its representative, Rupert. Brandon perversely wants them to witness his ritual killing even as he wants to hide his act. In the conventional reading of the film this audience outside the apartment, called in by Rupert's pistol shots, ends Brandon's dramatic experiment, the sirens and shouts expressing its grim applause and a return to reality. What is suppressed is the necessity of this audience for Brandon's dramatic murder. He needs spectators inside the apartment, on his stage, as well as outside. The apparently clear distinction between onstage and offstage, inside the apartment and oustide, does not hold.

Rope also creates a second audience in opening up space behind the camera. The restless camera movements create in the film audience a self-conscious awareness of the film theater as a second offstage space mirroring the space occupied by the theatrical audience outside the apartment. The fourth wall opens to the background and foreground both. The film spectator joins Rupert in denying moral approval of Brandon's theatrical indulgence in murderous play — even in coming to the movie theater to watch precisely this sort of play — and, like Rupert, demands closure. In demanding an end to Brandon's experiment and to the movie, the film spectator joins Rupert onstage, creating through a fascinated disapproval the very conditions making for Brandon's performance. The apparently simple duality of the theater metaphor itself divides, and the "real world" lying beyond the apartment's curtains shares the stage with the characters within the apartment just as the "real" world of the movie theater becomes part of Hitchcock's fiction.

The audience is a necessary part of the staged events. The neon sign blinking a repeated *S* outside Brandon's windows speaks the language of the roped-in audience, a theatrical hiss at Brandon and Rupert which itself is duplicated visually by the camera's slithering glide through the film. *Rope*'s most overt cut, moving the camera from the street outside to the interior of the apartment, is not a technical statement of difference between a safe outside world and a threatening inside world; it is a statement revealing the trace of a camera dolly within the film edit and the vestigial sameness of the two worlds. There is no way out of this film's imprisoning apartment house of language: experiment is all there is. Meaning coils and coils in the twists of *Rope*'s writing.

Notes

1. François Truffaut, *Hitchcock* (New York: Simon and Schuster, 1967), 130.
2. Truffaut, 134.
3. Raymond Durgnat, *The Strange Case of Alfred Hitchcock* (Cambridge, Mass.: MIT Press, 1974), 36–37, 198, 208.
4. David Thomson, *Overexposures: The Crisis in American Filmmaking* (New York: William Morrow, 1981), 191–92, 200.
5. Lindsay Anderson, "Alfred Hitchcock," in *Focus on Hitchcock*, ed. Albert J. LaValley (Englewood Cliffs, N.J.: Prentice-Hall, 1972), 57. See also Lawrence Kane, "The Shadow World of Alfred Hitchcock," *Theatre Arts* 33, no. 4 (May 1949), 33–40; John Grierson, *Grierson on Documentary*, ed. Forsyth Hardy (New York: Harcourt Brace, 1947), 74–76.
6. Robin Wood, *Hitchcock's Films* (New York: Paperback Library, 1965), 36.
7. Donald Spoto, *The Art of Alfred Hitchcock* (New York: Hopkinson and Blake, 1976), 187.
8. Jacques Derrida, "Structure, Sign, and Play in the Discourse of the Human Sciences," in *Writing and Difference*, trans. Alan Bass (Chicago: University of Chicago Press, 1978), 278–93. See also his *Of Grammatology* (Baltimore: Johns Hopkins University Press, 1976), 3–93, passim; and Gayatri Spivak, "Translator's Preface," *Of Grammatology*, xix, lxv, etc.
9. Wood, 37, 39.

10. Derrida, "Structure, Sign, and Play," 279–80.
11. Derrida, "Structure, Sign, and Play." He also discusses the myth of structural origins in *Of Grammatology*, 87–93.
12. Wood, 39.
13. A lucid discussion of the differential nature of language can be found in Barbara Johnson, *The Critical Difference* (Baltimore: Johns Hopkins University Press, 1980).

265

V
HITCHCOCK'S BLACK COMEDY
OF REBIRTH:
THE TROUBLE WITH HARRY (1955)

Set in a remote, pastoral hamlet in Vermont, Hitchcock's only pure comedy of his American period, *The Trouble with Harry*, gives viewers and critics an opportunity to study his art not only in an atypical Hitchcockian setting, but without the formal and narrative elements of the suspense genre. The story of the repeated burials and exhumations of the corpse of an unpopular local figure, the film gives Hitchcock the opportunity to expand on the touches of grotesque humor that enliven all his work, and his sense of the absurd dictates the film's themes and techniques. The result is therefore complex, since the comic tone of the film interacts with its ruminations on death and sexual relationships in ways unique in the Hitchcock canon.

The bucolic environment created by the rural, New England setting bathed in autumnal colors gives the film an aura of myth, especially with the archetypal imagery of corpses, fallen leaves, and unearthed caskets. Although some discussions of the film regard it as the work of a brooding Hitchcock, engulfed in his dark vision of human nature, Lesley Brill finds in the film a mature, psychologically healthy acceptance of death as part of the cycle of nature and erotic love as its primal driving force toward fulfillment. According to Brill a mythic pattern of death and rebirth is central to the comic mode of *The Trouble with Harry*, a pattern which he feels runs implicitly throughout Hitchcock's films. He believes that a spirit of redemption and renewal touches all of the characters in this film and joins them at its end. The film thus becomes a parable of an unfallen world and the purest expression of Hitchcock's preoccupation with two of his favorite themes: lost innocence and redemptive love.

Edmund Gwenn and John Forsythe in *The Trouble with Harry.* **(Photo courtesy of Photofest, New York.)**

"LOVE'S NOT TIME'S FOOL"

The Trouble with Harry (1955)

Lesley Brill

Although Hitchcock occasionally indicated that *The Trouble with Harry* was one of his favorite films (thereby showing unusual fondness for a commercially disappointing venture), most commentators have taken only a slight interest in it. It is generally regarded as a pleasant but insubstantial and, for Hitchcock, rather anomalous performance. My understanding of Hitchcock's career and of *The Trouble with Harry* suggests the opposite. *The Trouble with Harry* stands out among Hitchcock's works chiefly because it insists overtly upon a theme usually more implicit in his films, but almost always central to them: that of descent and return, of death and rebirth. Its unbroken comic mode—though I shall pay it less attention—bears a similar relation to the comedy of other Hitchcock movies: it is atypical only in its insistence and uniformity.

Far from constituting an anomaly in Hitchcock's career, *The Trouble with Harry* sets forth with unequalled bluntness and economy the romantic vision of innocence and immortality which informs the greater part of its director's work. In their triumphant conclusions, the comic romances fulfill that vision; when Hitchcock's films become more ironic, the anxiety that redemption lies beyond possibility in a corrupt world increasingly dominates the faith that it can

271

be achieved. Whether romantic or ironic, however, Hitchcock's other films admit the existence and power of evil. Only *The Trouble with Harry* incorporates from its beginning conditions that all of Hitchcock's movies represent as the highest good fortune. Its world is in essential alignment with the needs of its characters. The tensions and alarming suspense that shape Hitchcock's other works are therefore largely absent. *The Trouble with Harry* is constituted of nearly pure nectar, the Hitchcockian summum bonum unadulterated.

Actions suggestive of rebirth are of crucial importance in most of Hitchcock's movies. They pervade *The Trouble with Harry*. From the opening credits, virtually every detail figures forth the renewal of the natural and human world. Death itself enlists in the creation of life. This thematic basis is embodied so fundamentally that the continuous rejuvenations of the movie occur with little excitement or even emphasis. Re-creation is something to be expected, as basic a fact of nature as gravity or heat. Urgency would be misplaced in this film, for resurrection may be safely assumed. Death passes and life renews without effort or anxiety. The bland tone of *The Trouble with Harry* constitutes more than comic technique; it results from a profound confidence that death lacks the power to destroy and that hope can scarcely help but prosper.

Hitchcock's pastoral comedy takes place in a New England countryside that appears prelapsarian; the knowledge of sin and death are excluded from its latter-day Eden. In their stead reign innocence and optimism. Whether we take the setting as having escaped The Fall or as having somehow recovered from it, the result is the same. The woes that afflict humanity and its corrupted world constitute little more than enlivening comic alarms in Highwater.

Among the inhabitants of the small community, only deputy sheriff Calvin Wiggs is at all tainted by post-Edenic mistrust and disillusionment. His first name, indeed, might playfully allude to the gloomy theology of his famous Protestant forebear. However that may be, his long distance call to the State Police attempts to recruit an agency of rigid law and punishment into the hamlet in which *The Trouble with Harry* takes place. Harry himself is an intruder from outside, a representative of the less pure and sequestered human beings whom Sam Marlowe refers to scornfully as "little people with hats." (The last detail of his description serves also to emphasize their separation from nature.) Calvin Wiggs may bluster, but his power does not extend beyond that required to make a fool of himself. The State Police do not come, and Harry's invasion quickly turns him into a benign corpse.

This ascendancy of the Edenic makes *The Trouble with Harry* unique among Hitchcock's films. All his other works, whether finally dominated by romantic innocence or ironic cynicism, explicitly acknowledge the stained and vulnerable condition of humanity. In films like *Vertigo* and *Psycho*, the inevitable corruption of human life and of the world defeats all attempts to rise above it; in happier works like *The Lady Vanishes* and *Rebecca*, a spirit of redeeming grace acts through love to repel the nightworld, restore the protagonists to innocence, and allow them to achieve full self-realization. But such sources of conflict — whether tragic or comic — scarcely exist in *The Trouble with Harry*.

We do not expect such an absence in any movie, and the unfamiliar, radical fantasy on which Hitchcock's comedy is based has led some commentators to an understanding fundamentally opposite to mine. Despite its tone and the outcome of its plot, Rohmer and Chabrol and Donald Spoto — the latter more equivocally — pronounce it a film of singular misanthropy.[1] Nothing obvious in *The Trouble with Harry* reveals a secret Puritan hatred for sex or obsession with death; but we cannot forget the mixture of sorrow and crime in our own lives, and so we may suspect satire in the portrayal of unalloyed innocence in *The Trouble with Harry*. But its characters are unafflicted by the circumspection that experience has engendered in its audience. The movie itself is innocent of moral double entendre. It is no more or less than it appears to be. And in being so, it could hardly be more surprising.

The primitive drawings accompanying the titles are composed of child-like, mostly natural, images. They are followed by the brilliant colors of the New England fall woods, at their most lively just before winter dormancy. Both the Steinberg sketches and the glorious dying of the forest embody dominant themes of the rest of the film, in which growth and death mix inseparably. Again and again, Harry will be buried and exhumed, die and return, be planted and harvested. Other intimations of regeneration proliferate. Over coffee, Miss Gravely tells The Captain about the demise of her father, "caught in a threshing machine." Calvin Wiggs asks Marlowe if he might have been sketching "somewhere down by Mansfield Meadows," an appropriate place, perhaps, for the inadvertent harvesting of Miss Gravely's parent. (The name of the meadow recalls a Hitchcock film of twenty years earlier, *Young and Innocent,* with its dominant images of woods and fields and its hero's aliases of "Beechtree Manningcroft" and "Beechcroft Manningtree.") The Doctor's last name is "Greenbow"; and Miss Gravely's first name, "Ivy," balances her funereal surname. These associations of human life—and death—with greenery and harvest further connect the characters of *The Trouble with Harry* to the natural process of recurrent growth that infuses the film.

As summer ends with the blaze of fall and the abundance of harvest, so death itself in *The Trouble with Harry* brings a marvelous fecundity. Captain Wiles will be proved as wrong as drought when he urges that the corpse of Harry is "no good to anyone now." The late Harry's first posthumous matchmaking comes when Miss Gravely, stepping over his body, invites The Captain to her home. Shortly thereafter the spinster, full of new life obliquely injected by Harry's corpse, exclaims on the beauty of the day and of Marlowe's painting and singing. The flattered artist, in his turn, supervises her haircut and make-up, the restoration of her neglected youth. Sam promises to recreate "the true Miss Gravely, sensitive, young in feeling, timeless with love and understanding." The Captain takes a similar, if less ethereal, view of his new friend: "Not too late, you know. She's a well-preserved woman . . . yes, very well-preserved. And preserves have to be opened, someday."

The Cupid-like corpse also works its wonders on The Captain. Burying Harry, he pounds the dirt with his shovel: "There's nothing like finding yourself in love! No! It adds zest to your work, zest!" Love and death in the autumnal romance of The Captain and Miss Gravely are reemphasized when the amorous spinster confesses, "I'm grateful to you for burying my body." And, she might add, for resurrecting her body also.

More directly, Harry's death yields a pair of shoes for a passing bum. Much more importantly, it brings Jennifer Rogers and Sam Marlowe together and sets Jennifer free to marry again. The Captain acknowledges Harry's part in the engagement of the central lovers when he apologizes to Sam, "If I grumbled too much at my share of the work in burying Harry, I'm sorry. I can see now it was well worth it." Even Harry benefits. As she's cleaning him up at her house,

Jennifer remarks, "Isn't it odd? After refusing for so long, here I am finally doing Harry's laundry."

The dead rabbit maintains in its small way the same sort of post-mortem fertility as Harry. For Arnie, it produces a pet frog and two blueberry muffins. For The Captain, when he realizes that his third bullet killed the rabbit rather than Harry, it brings release from the misapprehension that he is an inadvertent murderer. "You never know," says Arnie with broader accuracy than he understands, "when a dead rabbit might come in handy." The theme of resurrection works in even so minor and sometimes dissonant a figure as Calvin Wiggs, who restores antique automobiles — brings them back, as it were, to life.

Rebirth and the fecundity of death are ordinary and natural in *The Trouble with Harry* because of the transcendence of time by love, and the flexibility of time itself. Just after one of Harry's disinterments, Doctor Greenbow arrives on the scene, reading aloud from Shakespeare's 116th sonnet. The four lovers overhear fragments: "Love's not time's fool . . . Love alters not with his brief hours and weeks, / But bears it out even to the edge of doom. / If this be error and upon me proved, / I never writ, nor no man ever loved." We may infer the importance of these lines from the fact that they are not quoted in the novel on which the movie is based.

The themes of the redemption of time and love's triumph over death are not realized in the novel either. The film adds them to what is otherwise little more than a zany but inconsequential tale of love and adultery, a sort of outdoor drawing-room farce. In accord with the Edenic environment of Highwater in Hitchcock's movie, several actions of adultery central to the novel are removed entirely from the film.

In his child-wise confusion, Arnie stumbles to an understanding of time which is, in its own way, as sophisticated as Shakespeare's. He asks Sam when tomorrow is, and Sam replies, "day after today."

Arnie: That's yesterday. Today's tomorrow.
Sam: It was.
Arnie: When was tomorrow yesterday, Mr. Marlowe?
Sam: Today.
Arnie: Oh, sure, yesterday.

Yesterday, today, and tomorrow fuse. As the movie ends, Arnie again finds Harry, who has been restored to his first last resting place. Since tomorrow is yesterday for Arnie, he will tell his mother, and presumably deputy sheriff Wiggs, that he found Harry's body today.

Given the productivity of the dead and the fertile fluidity of time, death itself becomes neutral at worst, more often genuinely friendly to human aspirations. Jennifer tells Arnie that Harry is "in a deep sleep. A deep, *wonderful sleep.*" Later she tells Sam that Harry "looked exactly the same when he was alive, except he was vertical." Dr. Greenbow trips repeatedly over Harry without noticing that he is dead. When he does finally examine the corpse, the doctor pronounces that Harry died naturally, of "a seizure" — a diagnosis so vague and exculpating that everyone, including the audience, must take satisfaction in it.

For the rejected Harry, dying turns into homecoming. "A long way from home," pronounces The Captain, but "he died around here, that's what counts now." Discussing a burial place for the body, The Captain almost envies Harry the comfort of being "cozy in winter and cool in the summer." "You're a lucky fellow, Harry Worp," he concludes. When Jennifer says that she'll take the body to her house, the doctor responds with absent-minded, professional sentimentality: "going home for the last time." But the final time, in this asynchronous world, is also the first. Jennifer at last, for the first time, receives her now late husband.

Love, the paradoxical fruit of death in *The Trouble with Harry,* is similarly characterized by homey comfort. As Jennifer and Sam come together, their attraction takes a curious form. "I feel awful comfortable with you, Sam," confesses Jennifer. Sam admits to the same relaxed passion: "you know, I feel the same way too. It's a good feeling — feeling comfortable with someone who feels that way too." The Captain, after Jennifer agrees to marry Marlowe, congratulates him with the mild observation that "marriage is a comfortable way to spend the winter." His own courtship of Miss Gravely has been fueled with the peaceful domestic satisfactions of muffins, coffee, and elderberry wine.

Love and death in *The Trouble with Harry* are treated straightforwardly, without shame, terror, or prurience. Sam's response to Jennifer when he first meets her could hardly be more direct: "You're the most beautiful, wonderful thing I've ever seen. . . . I'd like to paint you nude." "Some other time, Mr. Marlowe," she replies calmly. Within minutes she is telling her visitor of her first marriage to

Robert, her second to his brother Harry, the "certain enthusiasm" she worked up for her second marriage night, and the dismaying fact that Harry "never came in." At lower voltage, the Captain and Miss Gravely pursue their romance with a similar directness and innocence.

A closet door that spontaneously swings open in Jennifer's living room suggests, in addition to Harry's tendency to pop out of his grave, simple harmlessness. The closet is conspicuously empty and the closet door "only a closet door," as Miss Gravely assures the startled Captain. Love, death, and closets are no more than themselves. They harbor no guilt, no fright, no skeletons. We should scarcely wonder that Sam's unfallen world allows him the conviction that "we're all nice. I don't see how anyone could help but like us."

"Blessed are they who expect nothing, for they shall not be disappointed." The Captain's benediction is part of a series of Christian allusions which, quite typically for Hitchcock, forms a subset of the more general pattern of death and rebirth. The opening shot of *The Trouble with Harry* frames a country church, its bells ringing tranquilly. When Arnie brings his mother to see the body he has discovered, she greets it with "Harry, thank Providence, the last of Harry!" The vaguely religious overtones continue as Sam assures The Captain that in accidentally killing Harry he became the instrument of divine will, and that he should be grateful that he was able to do his share "in accomplishing the destiny of a fellow being." The Captain himself nods again toward devoutness when he murmurs that they are burying Harry "with hasty reverence."

Religious motifs are unquestionably present in *The Trouble with Harry*, but they do not signal a central preoccupation. They rather make up one of many iterations — imagistic, aural, allusive, psychological — of the theme of death's fertility and life's indefatigable rebirth. Those who expect nothing are indeed undisappointed. Grace extends its power toward all of them, in the undiscouraged millionaire who returns to buy Sam's paintings, in the abundance of a dead rabbit and a dying season, and, most crucially, in love.

The portrayal of art within the movie repeats the comfortable directness of life in Highwater. The simplicity of the drawings that accompany the opening credits anticipates the same quality in the film and its characters. Sam, the artist within the work of art, has the same casual ingenuousness about his painting that he shows during his courtship of Jennifer Rogers. Sketching the autumn landscape of Mansfield Meadows, he notices Harry's body only when its feet appear unexpectedly in his drawing. Once he does discover the corpse, it becomes grist for his artistic mill, just as it is for Hitchcock's. He crouches by Harry's face, sketching it with a naive absorption rather like Arnie's unalarmed interest when he comes across the body.

On every occasion, Marlowe behaves unselfconsciously and naturally. His wristwatch broken, he tells time by the sun. He is too excited about his restoration of Miss Gravely to bother with the passing rich man who stops to inspect his paintings. Without rudeness, he makes it clear that he could not care less about the opinion of the art critic with whom the millionaire returns. The payment he asks for his paintings is the barter of an affectionate child. He requests what his equally innocent and modest friends want: for Jennifer, strawberries; a chemical set for Arnie; a chrome-plated cash register for Wiggie; for Miss Gravely, a hope chest "full of hope"; a Davey Crockett outfit for the tugboat captain who aspires to be a hunter. For the artist himself, in love and planning to marry, a discreetly whispered request for a double bed.

The art in and of *The Trouble with Harry* is as straightforward as its characters; it constitutes just one more ordinary fact in the harmonious world of man and nature. By the standards of most of Hitchcock's movies, conspicuous cinematic virtuosity and startling twists of the plot are subdued. The camera, in particular, remains unusually transparent in its recording of the action. Its most obtrusive composition, the repeated short focal length shot of the body of Harry with looming feet pointing skyward, has about it the same artless bluntness as Arnie's declarations or the Captain's harmless yarns.

Artistic expression elsewhere in the film retains similar simplicity and naturality. The style of Marlowe's painting is abstract, but the paintings which we see are saturated with the colors and shapes of the New England landscape in which he lives. His themes, at least as he describes them, are as extravagant and basic as his style. One of his paintings is about nothing less than "the creation of the world." Though he tells Calvin Wiggs that his imagination "is peopled with enough faces to cover the earth," Sam lives and creates in pastoral tranquillity away from the fallen city hordes. His art and his life as an artist are ultimately as ingenuous as the movie in which he appears.

"The trouble with Harry is over," reads a superfluous closing title superimposed on the last image of Harry's feet and the fading New

England fall landscape. The sentence recalls in its direct clarity the end of old folk tales and stories for children. Everyone will surely live happily ever after. The closing title also recalls the primitive phase of the cinema itself, the early silent era, with its technical unsophistication and its rudimentary narratives.

The comedy of *The Trouble with Harry*, contrary to what Hitchcock and some critics have asserted, does not originate primarily in verbal wit or incongruous, dead-pan humor. It rather derives from the total exclusion of destruction from the world of the film. No event or person in *The Trouble with Harry* is allowed to cause or suffer real pain. Nor do they seriously threaten to do so. The comic mode of the film finally results from its obsessive repetition of the theme of rebirth; for if time and death have no power to injure, what terrors can remain?

From another point of view, the comedy of *The Trouble with Harry* exists traditionally alongside its romance. It portrays the coming together of a group of strangely separate people whose only social bonds, at the beginning of the movie, seem to be the legal ones enforced by deputy sheriff Wiggs. By the end of the film, they are united in typical New Comic fashion, with the freshly engaged lovers at the center of a reinvigorated and cohesive small society.

For all its superficial eccentricity, *The Trouble with Harry* does not drift anomalously outside the mainstream of Hitchcock's films. Like Sam Marlowe's renderings of New England, it may be seen as a compression of the essential dream that nourishes Hitchcock's work as a whole. That dream, which Hitchcock shares with the greater part of all storytellers, envisions a life in which human beings are complete and fulfilled, justice prevails without the rigidity and inaccuracy of law, and the world and its inhabitants live in harmony retrieved from the corruptions of experience.

Because *The Trouble with Harry* assumes rather than achieves such a world, it is the strangest of Hitchcock's films at the same time that it reveals most clearly what is most typical. The unfallen good which it embodies may even remind us of the glory it lacks. In such romances as *North by Northwest, Saboteur,* or *Spellbound,* that glory springs from harrowing journeys reluctantly undertaken but leading finally to safe harbor, from confrontations with the darkest recesses of society and human nature, and from the transcendence and completion of self that is achieved in love. We may also miss in the undisturbed characters and settings of *The Trouble with Harry* the terrible beauties and artistic magnitude of more dangerous Hitchcock works, from *The Manxman* through *Shadow of a Doubt* and *Notorious,* to the ironic films of the 1950s and 1960s.

The catastrophe of The Fall from Paradise has always been recognized as also being paradoxically fortunate. If *The Trouble with Harry* avoids the misery, neither can it express the stature and complexity of men and women who struggle, albeit sometimes to defeat, against the corruption of the world and of their own natures. Hitchcock needed to make only one *The Trouble with Harry,* only one parable of an unfallen world. Virtue, as diverse thinkers have argued in various ways, has few forms; error has many. The polymorphous fascination of evil puts Hitchcock, along with Milton, Blake, and most artists, at least partly in sympathy with the Devil.

The gorgeous thematic richness of Hitchcock's last film, *Family Plot,* makes an illuminating contrast with the relatively monothematic *The Trouble with Harry.* In the exuberance of its postlapsarian knavery and moral fluidity it creates a world that is at once wicked and forgiving; one in which the wish fulfillments of art, religion, and sheer fraud penetrate and energize ordinary reality. The convolution of its plot has moral and aesthetic ingenuity very different from the simplicity of *The Trouble with Harry.* This is not to say that *The Trouble with Harry* is an inferior, or less interesting, film than *Family Plot.* It is to say that the absurdities of human vanity and foolishness, the sorrows of human frailty, and the terrors of hatred are for Hitchcock, as for other artists, the source of most subject matter.

Forms of death and rebirth not only occur in virtually all of Hitchcock's works, but they usually occupy the thematic center of them. *The Trouble with Harry,* distant as it may appear at first viewing from other Hitchcock films, is in a crucial way entirely characteristic of its director's work. Its relaxed comedy embodies a theme that serves as mainspring to the vast majority of Hitchcock's movies. As we watch his mother's music rescue Hank near the end of the second *The Man Who Knew Too Much,* or the nick-of-time breaking of Jefferies' fall at the end of *Rear Window,* or Judy's plunge and Scottie's anguish in the last sequence of *Vertigo,* we are watching variations on the same theme, that of miraculous escape and resurrection, or of its hope and disappointment. When we watch *The Trouble with Harry,* we see a peculiarly radical, cheery rendition of the same central action. We see the filmmaker's purest realization of uncorrupted identity, innocent love, and restorative time — the quest for all of which in one way or another shaped Hitchcock's movies for more than five decades.

Notes

1. Eric Rohmer and Claude Chabrol, *Hitchcock: The First Forty-Four Films,* trans. Stanley Hochman (New York: Ungar, 1979), 137; and Donald Spoto, *The Art of Alfred Hitchcock* (New York: Doubleday, 1976), 260.

VI
REFLECTIONS ON *VERTIGO*

Vertigo is often singled out as the most important film Alfred Hitchcock ever made; indeed, the 1982 critics' poll in the British journal *Sight and Sound* selected it as one of the ten greatest films of all time, a tribute to both director Hitchcock and screenwriter Samuel Taylor. Perhaps better known as a playwright than a screenwriter, Taylor's stage credits include *Sabrina Fair, The Pleasure of His Company, No Strings,* and *A Touch of Spring.* Raised in San Francisco, where *Vertigo* is set, Taylor came to the production of *Vertigo* after Hitchcock decided that an earlier screenplay written by the late Alec Coppel needed to be redone. The final shooting script is essentially Taylor's, created, as was usual for Hitchcock, in conjunction with the director's ideas about settings and situations. In addition to writing the screenplay for *Vertigo,* Taylor collaborated with Hitchcock on the film *Topaz* (1969) and composed screenplays for several other directors, including Billy Wilder.

In this talk given at the Pace University conference on the rereleased films, the writer reveals the elements he added to the conception and screenplay of *Vertigo.* He discusses the film and its director from the perspectives of both drama and short fiction, but also focuses on what was uniquely cinematic in Hitchcock's work. Having seen the film at the conference for the first time since its release in 1958, Taylor speculates on how he would now revise the film, and during the question and answer session he responds to queries about character and motivation in the film as well as about alternative endings.

James Stewart and Kim Novak in *Vertigo.* **(Photo courtesy of Photofest, New York.)**

A TALK BY SAMUEL TAYLOR, SCREENWRITER OF *VERTIGO*

Today is the first time I have seen *Vertigo* since I first saw it more than twenty-eight years ago. I saw it in Hitchcock's screening room. I probably also saw it in New York. I mean, I probably just bought a ticket and walked in. I was quite surprised at what I saw today. It's a pretty good picture. It needs work, though. It was rather a strange experience because I discovered there were things in the picture that I did not remember at all, and I think the things I do not remember are probably more interesting to you than the things I do remember or the things I like. I do not remember the Saul Bass titles, or the scene of Midge and her portrait. I don't remember writing it. I really don't and I'm not going to accuse Hitchcock of writing it, but I just don't remember writing it. If I would write it now, I'd write it a different way — it's not a subtle scene. I don't remember the nightmare either, which is technical stuff.

Now, I know that you know much more about *Vertigo* than I do, obviously. And you also know much more about Hitchcock as a craftsman and as a filmmaker. I counted up the other day and I have only seen about one half of his films. I saw all the early ones. You know I go back pretty far in movie-going. I had a very indulgent mother and movies were only five cents in my day. I saw the original release of *Shoulder Arms*. And I saw Charles Ray in *Over the Hill to the Poorhouse*.

As for *Vertigo*, I suppose you first want to know what happened to Hitchcock and me when we first came together because it was one of those situations where he was in a slight panic. Jimmy Stewart kept saying that these characters are completely unreal. Hitchcock knew that, but didn't know what to do about it. He had his set pieces in mind — that was always true of Hitchcock. One critic talked of him as being novelistic — he wasn't novelistic at all. He was a short-story writer. He thought in terms of scenes, situations. In *The Thirty-Nine Steps,* for example, he was very proud of a scene in the country built around Peggy Ashcroft. He said that it was a complete short story in itself. That's the way he thought.

In other words, when I came to him for *Vertigo,* the opening scene, the Mission Dolores scene, obviously the tower scenes, and the scenes in Ernie's were already in his mind. Most of the crucial scenes. He just didn't know how to put them together. And after all, you have to differentiate between the plot and story.

The plot is absurd — so farfetched — and the story is honest and true. It's the story of a man who is tricked into something that becomes an obsession. The story has a great deal of depth, even though it's based on Hitchcock's love of playing practical jokes. *Vertigo* is the most horrible practical joke ever played on a man, when you think in terms of the basic plot.

Anyway, when I read the screenplay that had been written, I was quite confused because I couldn't follow it at all. As I said, the set scenes, most of the set scenes, were already there. You must remember that in any screenplay written for Hitchcock, a great part of it was written by Hitchcock: the scenes without dialogue are usually Hitchcock's.

People don't seem to understand that, and certainly the Writer's Guild never admits it. That's why Alec Coppel's name is on the film. All the scripts of *Vertigo* from the very beginning had those wonderful descriptions in them. When I saw Hitchcock after I read the script, I knew what the problem was, I said to him, "It's a matter of finding reality and humanity for these people. You haven't got anybody in this story who is a human being; nobody at all. They're all cut-out cardboard figures." I told him immediately that I would have to invent a character who would bring Scottie into the world, establish for him an ordinary life, make it obvious that he's an ordinary man. So I invented Midge.

I thought of Midge, as she is in the picture now, as an old college pal. They had an affair in college, and then had gone their own ways, and then came back as friends: something that happens in college all the time. You see, there was nothing of that sort in that picture. You saw him saved from falling, you saw the policeman fall to his death, and next he was talking to Gavin Elster. It didn't make much sense. So it wasn't any great job for me to think of Midge and to think of a scene for her that established the reality of the man and also established the reality of his illness. Looking at it today I wondered what it would have been like if instead of Midge, the old love, I'd made the woman his older sister. I thought there would be ironies there and there would be some indecisive comments that could be made that I couldn't make with Midge. Midge is much more an attractive character than, let's say, a Thelma Ritter character would have been. But it's an interesting thought. I don't, however, remember that portrait scene at all.

Having made Midge, the whole thing fell into place, and if you think about the picture, you'll find that it wouldn't work well without her. It wouldn't be believable. All the Midge scenes were mine. I say that because in writing about Hitchcock all writers say they slavishly attended to him and discussed everything with him. I never had that experience. I told him I was going to create a character. He said, "Fine." I went off and I created the character. It was as simple as that. He didn't know anything about Midge until he read the script and liked it.

Somebody asked me about the book-shop scene because, apparently, somebody has written an article about trying to find all the places in San Francisco where the film took place. I was told that people couldn't find the book shop and finally decided that I had put it right in the middle of Union Square. Well, that's pretty close. You see, I grew up in San Francisco, and I wandered an awful lot. The word "wandered" in the picture is certainly my word. There was a book shop, but it wasn't run by a man named Pop Liebl — the Pop Liebl I knew had a candy store on a corner in the Western Addition. But that book shop did exist in the twenties and thirties. I used to hang out there a lot. It was facing Union Square, right on the corner of Stockton Street and Maiden Lane, but it wasn't called the Argosy Book Shop. The Argosy Book Shop is in New York on Fifty-ninth Street. I used the name because "argosy" is a California word.

But the thing that struck me most about the picture, seeing it today after twenty-eight years, was the place where, I think, Hitchcock and I goofed. It is in the second part of the picture. You see, this picture falls into two acts very nicely, and both acts end with the same scene: a fall from the tower. At the end of the first fall from the tower, you could almost go blank on the screen in the plaza and then pan up to the coroner's inquest scene which is the start of the second act.

Incidentally, that coroner's speech is the one thing in the script that I didn't fool with very much. It was already there. I suspect Hitchcock wrote it. I changed some words, I shifted lines, gave it some rhythms, things like that, but I have a hunch Hitchcock wrote it. It isn't anything like the rest of the Coppel script I read, and it sounds like Hitchcock to me. There's a sort of a censoriousness there, a moralistic quality that makes me think Hitchcock wrote it. But I never asked him.

Anyway, we're into the second act and you have the coroner's scene and you have what I call my Mozart scene: Midge talking about Mozart to Scottie at the sanitarium. At that point, I should have said, and Hitchcock should have said: "What about the girl?" I think it's a flaw because even though the audience doesn't know who the girl is and what her function is, we, the authors, do, and it was our obligation to tell the audience what we knew so that the audience would also know. If we had done that we wouldn't have had scenes of a man pathetically wondering around San Francisco looking for a ghost.

Actually, ethos is better than pathos, always. You can call that Taylor's rule. We should have at that point said, "What about the girl?" Because we knew what we had to say to the audience. There was no point in saving the surprise for the end of the film. Surprise is a highly overrated commodity in literature and in birthdays. We did it in a very inept way. That letter scene startled me. How bad it is!

Actually, a scene with an overriding voice is a very inept device in all films. I remember that when I was doing *Sabrina Fair* with Billy Wilder, I said that in order to keep this girl from being a complete nonentity — even though she was played by Audrey Hepburn — there are four scenes from the play that we ought to get in, just to prove that she has a mind. Usually in film there isn't anyplace to put lines of that sort because you're always moving things along. So, finally, Billy said, "All right, we'll have her write a letter and we will just have the lines on the sound track." We did it. But it's a terrible device. It should never be done. It's even worse in the theater because in the theater, you have somebody writing a letter and saying the words out loud.

There's only one letter scene I know of that works, and it's wonderful. That's in Wycherley's *The Country Wife,* which has a magnificent letter scene in which a girl writes a letter and tells you what she's writing. You fall on the floor laughing.

Anyway, here is what we should have done. After the Mozart scene, we should have said, "What about the girl? This is the time to tell the audience what is happening." And we should have gone back to Gavin Elster. We shouldn't have forgotten about him and the girl that cavalierly. Somerset Maugham did the same thing in *The Circle.* There is a very important character in the first ten minutes. She's needed to help the story. Then she says, "I have a terrible headache, I'm going upstairs. You mind if I have my dinner on a tray?" And you never seen her in the play again. But we should have treated Gavin Elster much better. We should have had a scene between him and the girl which could have been a very strong scene. I realized it watching the picture today. It suddenly occurred to me what fools we were not to play that scene because you would know from the scene that she realized she was being ditched and left behind. In other words, the "argument scene" was gone. We played that offstage. But you would get a much stronger feeling about the girl if she had to face Gavin Elster and say, "You're going away, and without me."

Gavin Elster picked up this girl; she was probably a waitress in a waffle shop. He was eating a waffle, looked up and said, "Oh my God! She's the spitting image of my wife." And he got the idea. Now, all that plotting had to go on before the picture started. Since the girl is real, therefore, you ought to know about her, and you have to realize that all the things that she did in the first act were plotted, were planned, that the man trained her.

I knew the problem. After all, in the first half of the picture, I used a kind of language for her deliberately to heighten the feeling of somebody who is trying to be vague, trying to be unearthly, trying to be seized by an otherworldly identification. I kept the language extremely economical because I knew at the same time that you had to know almost immediately that this was a love story—that these two were falling in love. So I created a pattern of language for her. After all I knew the "non-acting" qualities of Kim Novak when I started because I had done a picture with her before. So I knew what I was up against. Therefore, I tried in every way I could to make it seem that this was a waitress from a waffle shop who'd been trained to be a lady from the Brocklebank apartments on Nob Hill.

That was very important and actually I think Kim Novak was awfully right for it just because of that. And if you look at the picture again, you'll see there's a great contrast between the way she talks when she's Madeleine, and the way she talks when she's Judy. When she says, "Go on, beat it. You want to see my driver's license?" That sort of thing. There's quite a difference there, and it's important. It's very important in the picture. But that scene with Gavin Elster should have been written, and should have been shot: a scene in which she says, "What about me?" We should have had Gavin Elster say, "I'm taking off, and if I were you, I would take off, too. You're perfectly safe because Scottie has been put away and the chances of your meeting are slim."

If I were writing the scene now, I would have had her bring all the clothes he'd given her and say, "Here. I don't want these anymore." So that the necklace would have had that much more importance later on. It's the one thing she did hold on to. But the best thing about this kind of scene is that you would have had a much stronger feeling of the humanity of the girl, and then right on top of that, when you would have seen Scottie wandering around San Francisco looking for her, you would have had a much greater sense of apprehension, anxiety, and foreboding just because of what you know, and it would have eliminated the letter-writing scene entirely: it would have made that scene much better. So, I apologize.

Now, I can't think about anything else about this picture that I know that you don't know, but it may be that there are questions in your mind, and they may lead me into more things that I may have thought about. Do you want to ask questions? Where do we start?

Questions and Answers

The original ending, I understand, before it was released, had a scene in which Midge and Scottie heard a report on the radio of Elster

being caught. Could you talk about how that ending changed?
Never heard of it.

*It's also reported that after previews the audience was so con-
fused that at least one or two additional scenes were shot. Is there
any truth to that?*
I can't think what they would be. I honestly can't think what they
would be. Hitchcock never told me that they shot additional scenes.
As I said, I didn't remember Midge's important scene, but I did today remember the other scenes in the picture, and I haven't the faintest
idea. A copy of my screenplay is in storage somewhere in Bangor,
Maine. I really ought to dig it out, but I know of no scenes.

[Andrew Sarris] *I'm very fascinated by your ideas. You know, we
think of all the possibilities. It's interesting you want to go back even
before the letter-writing scene. I agree. That's a very weak scene and
it takes me a long time to sit still while she writes the letter. I agree
with you. But most people criticize Hitchcock for giving the show
away as early as he does in the middle. If the audience knows that
this girl is playing a part and that Stewart is a fool, I think that Hitchcock would have felt that the audience would just have had no respect
for the character.*
No, the whole point is, as I say, that you divide this into two acts.
The whole first act is the deception, but once you get past the death
and actually have destroyed the man, you've got to tell the audience
this was all a plot. It can't be a surprise. You can't go all the way
to the end of the picture.

[Continued] *In other words, that scene with Gavin and the girl
after the fake fall.*
Yes, in other words, just taking it logically, after the scene with Midge
in the mental hospital, you ought to see what we know about the
girl. At that point, instead of waiting another five minutes to come
to the letter scene, that would be the proper way to say to the audience this is what these two people did to that man.

[Continued] *Well, we can't read Hitchcock's mind. We don't know
what he did. I would argue against that for one reason. I think you*

hit on two very strange things. In terms of plot and narrative. First, Gavin disappears and you never see him again. I mean they talk about him, but you never see him again in the film. And Midge disappears after the hospital scene. She walks off. By these two characters disappearing, I think the effect in the film is to intensify Judy and Scottie and the situation. They become the only two people on earth. I think you become much more aware of all the ramifications. The other way it becomes something that leaps out of the plot. I think Hitchcock would have preferred it.

No, I don't think so. I know, I could almost say positively, that when I was writing the screenplay, if I had said to him, "At this point instead of doing that letter scene, let's do it three or four minutes earlier as a scene," I'm sure he would have said yes. I'm sure of it because it's the same dramatic principle, you see? It is basic dramaturgy. If you tell audiences that they have to know something that the principal character does not know, you just have to decide where to do it. With this story, it's absolutely essential that the audience know, because this is a suspense story, not a mystery. But I'm sure that Hitchcock would have said yes because he didn't like the letter-writing scene either. As a matter of fact, you don't miss losing Gavin Elster. But you do give him one more scene which will round out his character and will make the picture have a little bit more body at a point where it needs it badly. But I'm really sorry we lost Midge. Hitchcock said she served no further purpose. Actually, if you look at the whole picture, it's a picture about two people and a bystander. Gavin Elster has nothing to do with it. He's just the MacGuffin.

I just want to say I agree with you completely about your rewrite that you would have done.
Thank you. I'll start on it tomorrow.

[Continued] *One other reason, too. I too felt that was the one weak spot in the film. It would have helped the audience's reaction to and feeling about Stewart. What you feel is that he's excessively silly and romantic instead of a victim. There would have been apprehension and tension the other way.*
Yes, well you're absolutely right because you would be feeling all the time: "When is he going to succeed?" Having set this up, you know

that he is going to, and you would think when, and how, under what circumstances? And you haven't any idea, since it's Hitchcock. It could have been terribly dramatic.

[Continued] *It would also have suggested the possibility that he has some sense that she may not be dead.*
Well, that inner urge, that inner obsession is very important. I think that the thing that made me think of it when I was watching the picture today was that I wanted more body for the girl and that scene that I just thought of would have given her more body and would have helped the picture tremendously. Kim Novak was all right in the picture. But think about the possibility of Ingrid Bergman in the role, and the depth of emotion in this picture would be so tremendous that you would be overpowered by her. It is pretty overpowering anyway.

I think you two are right. I think the picture would be more successful. At the time, I think, the audience would more likely have bought the Stewart character. I think precisely the reason that it failed back in 1958 is why today it seems more profound, because he is mad. I think the other way, he's less mad and we could relate to him more easily and, therefore, the audience would have accepted that plot better at the time. So, I think you're right in terms of the commercial success . . . and Hitchcock might have bought it.
No, you're looking at it from a commercial viewpoint, and that's not what I mean at all. I'm looking at it from an emotional viewpoint. I know that there would be much more emotion in the picture as a whole if you knew what had happened to that girl. You're dealing with two people and there's no question in my mind that when we reached that point Hitchcock and I were both intent on Stewart. We weren't thinking about the girl at all. We said, "The hell with her." We were just thinking, "Let's go with Stewart," and we were mistaken. If it had been Ingrid Bergman instead of Kim Novak, we would never have made the mistake.

I just wanted to say, for me, there's a point in the film, one of my favorite parts, where you first meet Judy Barton walking on the street in the sweater up to the point where she writes the revealing

letter. I didn't know it was Kim Novak. When we see her the first time, she has dark hair. I didn't know this was Kim Novak. I wasn't positive.
The way the picture is now, that's good. Anybody who reacts as you did makes a marvelous audience. Absolutely wonderful! I'm just looking for greater, deeper, and more valid emotion in the overall picture itself. I think that we sloughed off with the girl, and she's important.

I'm curious about this supernatural aspect. We know that Carlotta is suicidal and I noticed that she talks about being afraid of the nuns. In the last scene, when the nun appears, there's no shot of her going off the tower. Now is that a suggestion that, perhaps, there was some truth to the legend of Carlotta and that she jumped? Did you mean to make that ambiguous?
No, No, not really. It was just there. That was Hitchcock. That was a physical thing, the way he set up the shot, really. He worked it out very carefully. Yes?

I have a copy of the script here in front of me that has that ending with Scottie and Midge hearing over the radio about them arresting Gavin Elster. If you'd like to see it again. . . . This is the script and it's got that scene at the end.
What scene?

[Continued] *It's got a scene after the bell tower and it is in Midge's apartment: "(night) — Midge is huddled in a chair listening to the radio and the radio is describing Gavin Elster being captured."*
Oh, really?

[Continued] *Yes, I'll show it to you.*
After all, my memory isn't that good.

[Continued] *Well, maybe someone else stuck it on there.*
No. I don't think that's the final shooting script, though. I would doubt very much if that's the shooting script that I left behind.

[Continued] *This gentleman says the scene was shot and he has seen it.*

*A Finnish friend of mine told me about actually seeing it in Fin-
land long before those rumors about the extra scene—that final scene.*
You cannot, you just cannot cope with that sort of thing because
in every picture there are scenes that somebody else doesn't know
about. I don't remember. I wouldn't remember that. I might easily
have written it. But I doubt it.

[Continued] *There seems a very good reason for it to have been
put on safeguard, because all that time the Motion Picture code was
extremely strong about murderers not getting away.*
You know, now that you talk about it, it's beginning to sound familiar.

*There are two interpretations of the existing ending that we see
now in the present film. Donald Spoto, in his book,* The Art of Alfred Hitchcock, *says that the ending is totally oblique and Scottie
is probably going to jump off and follow her down to death. I believe
Robin Wood, in* Hitchcock's Films, *takes the opposite approach and
says it's a very positive ending because in a way Scottie is cured of
his vertigo. He can stand here and look down like in Greek tragedy
where someone is in a sense cured of what he's gone through. Which
of those two interpretations of the existing ending we've seen do you
feel is right?*
Tell me what the first interpretation was again.

*Oh, it was Donald Spoto who said it was a totally bleak ending.
Scottie undoubtedly jumped off and joined her in death.*
Oh. I've always felt that he probably went completely mad at the end.

*People have pointed out that the space she had to jump off was
too great. There was much more space than was required to fall accidentally as she does.*
Well, I was watching that very carefully today because I couldn't
remember exactly how it happened. I thought that Hitchcock did it
very well—that she saw the figure of the nun, backed away in fear—
and my instinct of it was she stumbled backwards. After all, she
wouldn't remember that the drop was right behind her.

Well, I've always felt that when he puts his hands out like this

297

at the end that the gesture is one of ultimate guilt. I've failed twice.
I've done it twice.

I agree. I was watching that ending very carefully, and I felt that it
was a wonderful gesture on Stewart's part because he projected not
only a feeling of "I have done it again," but the gesture also said,
"The Pity of it — the tragedy of the world." I thought it was a
marvelous gesture.

I feel as far as what happens this is what Hitchcock called "icebox
talk," which tells you how old he was. "Icebox talk" is when you go
home after seeing a movie and you go to the kitchen and open the
icebox and see what there is to eat. You're arguing like mad about
something you saw in the picture. That's "icebox talk" and very good
it is, too, when you have "icebox talk."

Why the nun? We've all been arguing for over twenty years about
the significance of the nun on the top of the tower. Why is that device
used for her to fall off? Is there a symbolic meaning there?
Nothing symbolic about it. It's the only thing Hitchcock could think
of to scare her, that's all. You must remember that Hitchcock by instinct had a fantastically wonderful sense of situation and story and
he used the word "yarn" a lot, which is an old-fashioned English word.
He'd say, "That's a good yarn." Any time you find things of that sort
you don't really have to dig very deep. Because he, by instinct, said,
"Ah, that will do it." But you mustn't, therefore, think that he contrived it. It comes from inside and it was just as important to him
to think that the nun was the perfect device as for Dostoevsky to
imagine a scene in *Crime and Punishment.* Same creative juice.

See, Hitchcock gets sold short an awful lot because he dealt with
inconsequential material, but his artistic juices were wonderful. After
all, I saw the original release of *Shoulder Arm,* so I go pretty far
back. Now, I don't believe that in my movie-going there's anybody
who in purely cinematic terms is Hitchcock's equal. Nobody. I could
ask you, why are you all here? Why are there conferences like this
all over this country to talk about Hitchcock? Why not Howard
Hawks? Why not John Ford? Great men. Great directors. Why not
even Ernst Lubitsch, who was consistent the way that Hitchcock was
consistent? He stayed in his own genre. But you don't have conferences about Lubitsch, and he was a wonderful director. Hitchcock
was unique, I think.

At the end of the novel, the hero deliberately kills the heroine by strangling her in her hotel room in bed. Were you aware of this ending?
No! I had no idea. I never read the novel and Hitchcock and I never discussed the novel. But you can't blame him. As a matter of fact, there's another ending — I'll give you another ending. Suppose Scottie had not discovered the deception after recognizing that necklace? If she hadn't had that necklace, they would have got married and five years later, inadvertently, she would have revealed who she was and he would have killed her.

I'm bothered by Judy; how much does she know about the husband's intention to kill his wife?
We assumed that she was aware of what she was doing and that she was very, very well coached. I'm sure Gavin Elster spent hours and hours coaching her on all the possibilities, on all the scenes she was going to have to play with Scottie, telling her what to say or not to say, to keep her sentences short and so on.

Why was she pulled back when the body was falling, and why does he hold her back and hold her mouth?
Oh, because she started to scream. No matter how involved the girl was in the plot, she would still feel a terrible sense of shock seeing that body thrown over the edge.

The scene earlier in the boardinghouse which once belonged to Carlotta where Madeleine disappears. Did you feel that was a loose end?
We talked about that. I mentioned it to Hitchcock and he said, "That's icebox talk." A lot of people have asked that. They say, "How did she get out of the house without Stewart seeing her"? I could figure out how she could have gotten out of there into her car and away. It's possible. There was a back way. That's good icebox talk. As Hitchcock used to say, "It's only a movie."

RECOMMENDED BOOKS ON
ALFRED HITCHCOCK

Brill, Lesley. *The Hitchcock Romance: Love and Irony in Hitchcock's Films.* Princeton: Princeton University Press, 1988.

Deutelbaum, Marshall, and Poague, Leland, eds. *A Hitchcock Reader.* Ames: Iowa State University Press, 1986.

Durgnat, Raymond. *The Strange Case of Alfred Hitchcock: Or the Plain Man's Hitchcock:* Cambridge, Mass.: MIT Press, 1974.

LaValley, Albert J., ed. *Focus on Hitchcock.* Englewood Cliffs, N.J.: Prentice-Hall, 1972.

Modleski, Tania. *The Women Who Knew Too Much: Hitchcock and Feminist Theory.* New York: Metheun, 1988.

Rohmer, Eric, and Chabrol, Claude. *Hitchcock: The First Forty-Four Films.* Trans. Stanley Hochman. New York: Ungar, 1979.

Rothman, William. *Hitchcock: The Murderous Gaze.* Cambridge, Mass.: Harvard University Press, 1982.

Ryall, Tom. *Alfred Hitchcock and the British Cinema.* Urbana: University of Illinois Press, 1986.

Spoto, Donald. *The Art of Alfred Hitchcock.* New York: Doubleday, 1976.

———. *The Dark Side of Genius: The Life of Alfred Hitchcock.* Boston: Little, Brown, 1983.

Taylor, John Russell. *Hitch: The Life and Times of Alfred Hitchcock.* New York: Pantheon Books, 1978.

Truffaut, François. *Hitchcock*. Rev. ed. New York: Simon and Schuster, 1984.

Weis, Elisabeth. *The Silent Scream: Alfred Hitchcock's Sound Track*. Rutherford, N.J.: Fairleigh Dickinson University Press, 1982.

Wood, Robin. *Hitchcock's Films Revisited*. New York: Columbia University Press, 1989.

Yacowar, Maurice. *Hitchcock's British Films*. Hamden, Conn.: Archon Books, 1977.

BOOKS IN THE CONTEMPORARY FILM AND TELEVISION SERIES